# Skills Development in Higher Education and Employment

SRHE and Open University Press Imprint
General Editor: Heather Eggins

Current titles include:

Catherine Bargh, Peter Scott and David Smith: *Governing Universities*
Catherine Bargh, Jean Bocock, Peter Scott, and David Smith: *University Leadership*
Ronald Barnett: *The Idea of Higher Education*
Ronald Barnett: *The Limits of Competence*
Ronald Barnett: *Higher Education: A Critical Business*
Ronald Barnett: *Realizing the University in an age of supercomplexity*
Neville Bennett, Elisabeth Dunne and Clive Carré: *Skills Development in Higher Education and Employment*
John Biggs: *Teaching for Quality Learning at University*
David Boud *et al.* (eds): *Using Experience for Learning*
Etienne Bourgeois *et al.*: *The Adult University?*
Tom Bourner, Tim Katz and David Watson (eds): *New Directions in Professional Higher Education*
John Brennan and Tarla Shah: *Managing Quality in Higher Education*
John Brennan *et al.* (eds): *What Kind of University?*
Anne Brockbank and Ian McGill: *Facilitating Reflective Learning in Higher Education*
Stephen Brookfield and Stephen Preskill: *Discussion as a Way of Teaching*
Sally Brown and Angela Glasner (eds): *Assessment Matters in Higher Education*
John Cowan: *On Becoming an Innovative University Teacher*
Heather Eggins (ed.): *Women as Leaders and Managers in Higher Education*
David Farnham (ed.): *Managing Academic Staff in Changing University Systems*
Gillian Evans: *Calling Academia to Account*
Harry Gray (ed.): *Universities and the Creation of Wealth*
Sinclair Goodlad: *The Quest for Quality*
Norman Jackson and Helen Lund (eds): *Benchmarking for Higher Education*
Merle Jacob and Tomas Hellström (eds): *The Future of Knowledge Production in the Academy*
Mary Lea and Barry Stierer (eds): *Student Writing in Higher Education*
Elaine Martin: *Changing Academic Work*
David Palfreyman and David Warner (eds): *Higher Education and the Law*
Craig Prichard: *Making Managers in Universities and Colleges*
Michael Prosser and Keith Trigwell: *Understanding Learning and Teaching*
John Richardson: *Researching Student Learning*
Stephen Rowland: *The Enquiring University Teacher*
Yoni Ryan and Ortrun Zuber-Skerritt (eds): *Supervising Postgraduates from Non-English Speaking Backgrounds*
Maggi Savin-Baden: *Problem-based Learning in Higher Education: Untold Stories*
Peter Scott (ed.): *The Globalization of Higher Education*
Peter Scott: *The Meanings of Mass Higher Education*
Anthony Smith and Frank Webster (eds): *The Postmodern University?*
Peter G. Taylor: *Making Sense of Academic Life*
Susan Toohey: *Designing Courses for Higher Education*
Paul R. Trowler: *Academics Responding to Change*
David Warner and Elaine Crosthwaite (eds): *Human Resource Management in Higher and Further Education*
David Warner and David Palfreyman (eds): *Higher Education Management*
Diana Woodward and Karen Ross: *Managing Equal Opportunities in Higher Education*

# Skills Development in Higher Education and Employment

Neville Bennett
Elisabeth Dunne
Clive Carré

The Society for Research into Higher Education
& Open University Press

Published by SRHE and
Open University Press
Celtic Court
22 Ballmoor
Buckingham
MK 18 1XW

email: enquiries@openup.co.uk
world wide web: www.openup.co.uk

and 325 Chestnut Street
Philadelphia, PA 19106, USA

First published 2000

A catalogue record of this book is available from the British Library

ISBN 0 335 20335 3 (pbk)     0 335 20336 1 (hbk)

*Library of Congress Cataloging-in-Publication Data*
Bennett, Neville.
    Skills development in higher education and employment / Neville
Bennett, Elisabeth Dunne, Clive Carré.
      p.  cm.
    Includes bibliographical references and indexes.
    ISBN 0-335-20336-1 (hardbound). — ISBN 0-335-20335-3 (pbk.)
    1. Training—Great Britain.  2. Occupational training—Great
Britain.  3. Education, Higher—Aims and objectives—Great Britain.
4. Professional education—Great Britain.  5. Industry and
education—Great Britain.  I. Dunne, Elisabeth, 1952–  .
II. Carré, Clive.  III. Society for Research into Higher Education.
IV. Title.
LB1027.47.B46  2000
370.11′3′0941—dc21                         99–40907
                                                    CIP

Typeset by Graphicraft Limited, Hong Kong
Printed in Great Britain by St Edmundsbury Press,
Bury St Edmunds, Suffolk

# Contents

# List of Figures and Tables

# Acknowledgements

We are most grateful to the following people, and their organizations, who cooperated so willingly with us in pursuance of the research reported in this volume:

- The 32 teaching staff who gave so freely of their time in order to answer questionnaires, provide interviews and allow themselves to be observed teaching.
- The undergraduate students who enthusiastically contributed in focus groups about their experiences in the teaching and learning of skills.
- The 24 graduates in their first years of their employment, and in particular the 10 who allowed us to follow their experiences over one year.
- The company training and recruitment managers from the following companies, who found time in their busy schedules to be interviewed: Arthur Andersen, Bass, British Airways, British Telecom, Cadbury, Civil Service: Foreign & Commonwealth Office, Commercial Union Assurance, Frenchay Healthcare NHS Trust, Glaxo Wellcome, Halifax Building Society, Hitachi Europe, ICI, Lloyds–TSB Bank, GEC–Marconi Defence Systems, Marks & Spencer, Mott MacDonald Group, Nortel, Rolls Royce Engineering, Rover Group, Royal Marines, Sainsbury's Supermarkets, Thames Water, The Boots Company. We wish to make it clear that the views expressed in the text are our own, and do not necessarily represent the view of any particular company in the sample.
- The trainers and organizers of the BP and Shell schemes, and Shell themselves for providing funding for research on aspects of skills development that were drawn into this study.
- The Economic and Social Research Council who funded the main study under its Learning Society initiative, and to Professor Frank Coffield who so ably coordinated that programme.

Last, but by no means least, we want to record our thanks to our two research students, Moira Fraser and Nick Davis, who helped in the collection and analysis of data on student and graduate employee experiences; to Mary MacMullen for her careful collation and analysis of some of the data sets and to Anita Davidson for her editorial assistance on many aspects of the final manuscript.

# 1

# Generic Skills in the Learning Society

## The contemporary context of higher education

Higher education in the UK has changed profoundly in the last decade. Indeed, Griffin (1997) asserts that higher education is in a state of crisis – of funding, of how to conceive and manage teaching and learning and of the management of academics' time and priorities. Others would add that there is a crisis in the purposes of higher education. Scott (1997), for example, sees the increasing emphasis on what he calls 'personal transferable skills' and 'generic competences' as indicative of this.

The genesis of these various crises appears to lie in the early 1980s, when the traditional autonomy of the university sector was first challenged by both government and employers. Maclure (1987) identifies the drive to control public expenditure, coupled with a concern to obtain value for money in higher education, as the greatest influences on the way in which the framework for policy making was changed; the subsequent cut in funding led to higher education being more directly at the mercy of government policy. At the same time, government was being persuaded by employers that traditional curricula were out of step with their requirements. In some sectors of the labour market there was a 'lessening of concern about what a graduate needs to *know* and increasing interest in what she or he needs to be able to *do*' (Silver and Brennan 1988). Thereafter, a series of changes in the funding, governance and administration of higher education: 'reflected a new order in which instrumental rather than liberal educational objectives were to be given precedence' (Jones 1996a).

The analysis of the UK's poor economic performance relative to its major competitors, contained in the 1987 White Paper *Higher Education: Meeting the Challenge*, exemplified the changed policy context and was a seminal influence in initiating the shape of future provision. The much lower participation rates in further and higher education in the UK were identified as a significant factor in poor competitiveness, and the paper concluded that a larger workforce with more advanced knowledge and skills was the key to greater economic success. Not only should students in higher education receive an academic, professional or vocational education, they should also exit with the competences, skills, attitudes and values that allow them to contribute to the revitalization of the economy. It was against this background that the Enterprise in Higher Education initiative was launched, with the objectives of developing in students the competences and attitudes relevant to enterprise. These were to be acquired, in part, through participation in real economic settings. The subsequent expansion of student numbers, combined with the overt attempt by government to influence the curriculum of higher education, heralded, and in part created, the 'crises' of the following decade.

Since 1988 there has been a massive increase in the rate of participation in higher education. Between 1988 and 1994, when student numbers were again capped, full-time students increased from 600,000 to over a million, and part-time students rose to over half a million. The composition of the student body also changed. Nearly one in six students was mature (over 21 on enrolment to undergraduate courses) and most of these were part-time and in employment. Within this same timescale, the participation of women and students from lower socioeconomic groups also rose (Dearing Report 1997), as did the number of universities, by the removal in 1991 of the binary divide between polytechnics and universities.

The enthusiasm of central government for student expansion was not matched with an equal enthusiasm for maintaining the value of the funding unit. Since 1989 there has been a 36 per cent reduction in the unit of funding per student (CVCP 1996). The provision of housing and appropriate teaching and research facilities for the extra students has also been threatened by severe reductions in capital funding, which was slashed by almost a half between 1995 and 1998. The threat by universities to make up this shortfall by the introduction of student fees, together with an impending general election, led to the setting up of the Committee of Inquiry, which reported in 1997 (Dearing Report 1997). The report confirmed the funding crisis, pointing to the fact that 55 per cent of higher education institutions in England, and 70 per cent of those in Wales, were expected to be in deficit by 1999/2000. Further, it calculated that additional recurrent funding of £100 million was required in 1998/9 and another £270 million in 1999/2000, that there was a shortfall in capital expenditure of £250 million and a £400–500 million shortfall for research infrastructure.

This diminution in the unit of funding – a consequence of both a brake on public spending and the ideological and philosophical commitment of successive governments to make public services more efficient, more responsive to customer needs and more accountable to the taxpayer – has generated yet another crisis – a crisis of quality. The 'massification' of higher education at a time of constant demands for greater efficiency has led to concerns about both the quality of student intake within a competitive higher education market and the quality of teaching and curriculum delivery. There is a fear that quality may be sacrificed for increased efficiency, given that efficiency gains have largely been achieved by changes in approaches to teaching and learning (D. Green 1994). These changes have been far-reaching and include larger classes, fewer tutorials, the development of independent and student-centred approaches to learning, modularization of programmes, a large increase in the proportion of staff on short-term contracts and soaring student–staff ratios. The government's reaction to such fears was the requirement, contained in the 1991 White Paper and subsequent Act of Parliament, that the funding councils establish quality assessment units to inform their funding decisions, thus overturning the assumption that quality was safe in the hands of the universities.

Quality assurance and audit processes have become familiar elements of the higher education landscape since 1991. In considering this landscape, Harvey and Knight (1997) claim that four interrelated themes concerning quality have dominated the mass higher education agenda: (i) accountability and value for money; (ii) maintaining standards; (iii) measuring outputs; and (iv) external quality monitoring. They are sceptical about their purpose however, arguing that the notion of quality has been employed largely as a vehicle to legitimate a policy of a steadily reducing unit of resource and increasing central control. In other words, this definition of quality is rooted in a philosophy that asserts that the economy cannot support the full cost of expansion in higher education while at the same time arguing that higher education is a central element in the future competitiveness of the economy in the world market.

This brief catalogue of financial, ideological and political tensions and crises, especially those relating to the interface of higher education and work, begs further questions. What factors have influenced changing conceptions of higher education? What arguments underpin the inclusion of core or transferable skills in the higher education curriculum? To what extent have they been implemented in practice? How are such skills defined and conceptualized? How valid are the assumptions about their transferability?

## Visions of higher education

What is higher education for? What should characterize the aims, purposes and outcomes of a university education? Such questions have been the subject of debate for centuries. Newman's (1853) idea of a 'university man', independent of the subject studied, included cognitive skills, such as clarity of thought and analysis, communication and interpersonal skills and certain affective qualities. He saw the ends implicit in higher education as both the fulfilment of the individual and the improvement of society, the same ends that underpinned the burgeoning growth of the universities in medieval Europe. One hundred years later the Robbins Report on higher education

(1963) also stressed these dual ends by highlighting those skills suitable 'to play a part in the general division of labour', in recognition that economic progress and the maintenance of a competitive position depended on them. A good general education, the report argued, is frequently less than we need to solve many of our pressing problems. Nevertheless, the report also postulated that what is taught should be taught in such a way as to promote the general powers of the mind.

Twenty years later, the University Grants Committee (UGC) (1984) presented its strategy for higher education in the 1990s and, although it commended the Robbins objectives, it argued that the world had changed and that the focus of higher education had to be broader. Providing instruction in skills and promoting the powers of the mind should remain the main teaching purposes but, in carrying out this role, higher education needed to meet the needs of the economy (for highly skilled manpower) as well as those of the individual. The faster pace of scientific, technological and economic change demanded a shift in the types of skills offered. As such, the report urged that underlying intellectual, scientific and technological principles should be emphasized rather than narrow specialist knowledge, on the grounds that the abilities most valued in industrial, commercial and professional life, as well as in public and social administration, are the transferable intellectual and personal skills. These include the abilities to analyse, identify and solve problems, synthesize disparate elements, use numerical information, cooperate with others and communicate well both orally and in writing. It concluded that a higher education system which provides its students with these skills is serving society well.

Perhaps not surprisingly, given that these reports were instigated by central government, their recommendations were paralleled by government thinking and action. The 1987 White Paper, *Higher Education: Meeting the Challenge*, for example, added to the Robbins definition an emphasis on meeting the needs of the economy by achieving greater commercial and industrial relevance, and shortly afterwards the Enterprise in Higher Education initiative was born (Training Agency 1989). Underpinning this initiative was the view that there was a need for graduates who are in tune with the enterprise culture and aware of the needs of industry and commerce, who know how to learn and have some experience of the world of work. The cornerstone of the initiative was thus a partnership between higher education, employers and practitioners such that students could acquire transferable skills which will allow people to succeed in a wide range of different tasks and jobs. Another initiative, Education for Capability, sponsored by the Royal Society for Arts, shared a similar rationale and prescribed a similar, if somewhat broader, set of skills (Stephenson and Weil 1992).

Employers' organizations provided enthusiastic support for such skills development. P. Slee, then Head of Education Policy at the Confederation of British Industry, wrote:

The common denominator of highly qualified manpower will ... be the ability to think, learn and adapt. Personal transferable skills – problem solving, communication, teamwork – rather than technical skills defined with narrow occupational ranges, will come to form the stabilising characteristic of work. If higher education is to meet the needs of the economy and the individual it must seek actively to develop these generic core competences that will in future define work.

(Slee 1989: 66)

Continuing surveys of employers confirm their desire for graduates with core or transferable skills (Green 1990) but show their continued dissatisfaction with the level of many of their new graduate employees, particularly with regard to communication skills, which embrace graduates' ability to express themselves, make oral presentations and write reports or business letters (QHE 1993, 1994). The latest survey, of 258 managers and recent graduates, found that employers want adaptive, adaptable, transformable people to help them maintain, develop and ultimately transform their organizations in response to, and preferably in anticipation of, change. They concluded that they did not believe that a degree course suitably prepares students for work (Harvey *et al.* 1997).

The latest vision statement for higher education (Dearing Report 1997) reiterates the fact that external factors have affected the development of higher education since the Robbins Report and that these will be even more influential in the next 20 years. The report restates the now familiar economic mantra:

Powerful forces – technological and political – are driving the economies of the world towards greater integration. Competition is increasing from developing economies that have a strong commitment to education and training. The new economic order will place an increasing premium on knowledge which, in turn, makes national economies more dependent on higher education's development of people with high-level skills, knowledge and understanding, and on its contribution to research.

(Dearing Report 1997: 4)

The report advocates the development of what it calls key skills – of communication, both oral and written; of numeracy; of the use of communications and information technology and of learning how to learn. These skills, which are little different from those proposed by the UGC a decade earlier, are seen as necessary outcomes of all higher education programmes, together with knowledge and understanding, subject-specific skills and cognitive skills such as critical analysis.

Significantly, in the light of the above, the Dearing report also argues that over the next 20 years the UK must create a society committed to learning throughout life, and that this should be realized through a new compact involving institutions and their staff, students, government, employers and society in general:

We see the historic boundaries between vocational and academic education breaking down, with increasingly active partnerships between higher education institutions and the worlds of industry, commerce and public service . . . There is a growing interdependence between students, institutions, the economy, employers and the state which needs to be recognised by each party.

(Dearing Report 1997: 1)

This acceptance, indeed advocacy, of the role of the state and employers in the determination of the higher education curriculum is antithetical to some. Barnett (1994), for example, decries the move from what he calls epistemic supremacy, where definitions of knowledge formed by the 'tribes and territories' serve to define the nature of higher education (Becher 1989), to a situation in which society is framing the character of higher education by defining the forms of knowledge it deems valuable. This shift, he argues, is seen vividly in the Enterprise initiatives, where the state identifies the forms of knowing and development it sees as worthwhile. In this situation, academics become state servants, fulfilling the state's agenda. Transferable skills are a means of disenfranchizing discipline-based academics of their expertise. The curriculum is framed and owned by the state, hence higher education becomes part of the ideological state apparatus (Althusser 1996) and the student's pedagogical identity is predetermined to fulfil instrumental ends of economic and state survival.

Barnett's central argument is that an ideology of academic competence is being displaced with another ideology, that of operational competence, reflecting a shift in higher education from what Gibbons *et al.* (1994) call mode 1 to mode 2 knowledge; in essence a shift from contemplative to operational or instrumental knowledge, which equips students with skills and competences that are of value and effective in the workplace. The substantive point about operationalism, he argued, to reassert that a general lurch of this kind *is* taking place, and that the shift is happening under the direction, orchestration and active influence of the state. Barnett further argues that adherents of 'personal transferable skills' raise too few questions about their transferability, too easily accept their appropriateness for higher education and ignore human capacities that are not designed to improve economic competitiveness, such as altruism, generosity and the like.

This analysis is not universally accepted, however. Woollard (1995) believes that the gap between the philosophical approaches of higher education and employers is not as great as Barnett suggests, and argues that employers are key stakeholders in higher education and it is not therefore unreasonable that they should question what graduates know, understand and can do. Assiter (1995) similarly argues that higher education cannot ignore the development of core skills simply because some see it as an initiative that is market driven. Core skill development is not incompatible with development for life.

Notwithstanding this debate, the Committee of Vice-Chancellors and Principals (CVCP) has accepted the role of personal or core skills acquisition in higher education, an acceptance illustrated by the statement of the then Chairman (Edwards 1994: 2) that: 'the world we live in is highly knowledge intensive, and graduates will increasingly require core transferable skills'. This acceptance is also reflected in a joint declaration of intent by CVCP, the Confederation of British Industry and the Council for Industry and Higher Education (1996), which asserted that most British people, most educators and most students now believe that it is one of higher education's purposes to prepare students well for working life, and agreed a joint national effort to see that those in higher education are enabled to develop attributes thought useful for success in employment and future life. These attributes are general personal and intellectual capacities that go beyond those traditionally made explicit within an academic or vocational discipline.

Thus, despite Barnett's concerns, many universities have accepted the implications of the political and economic agenda, at least at the level of policy. The majority now have policies and central directives that assert their commitment to skills development (Drummond *et al.* 1997).

There nevertheless appears to be much scepticism of this view of university education among university tutors, many of whom believe it is not part of their role to provide skills for employment. Many have little sympathy for the newly emerging definitions of quality in higher education and, in the current climate of accountability in British universities, many tutors see teaching for skills as a distraction in the drive for better research ratings (Gubbay 1994). Not surprisingly, therefore, the little research that has been carried out in this area indicates that progress towards teaching transferable or core skills is patchy. Dunne (1995) carried out interviews with, and observations of, staff and students in every department in one university and reported that initiatives and innovative practices were few and far between. Although many claimed that core skills were being taught, there was little evidence of it in course planning and assessment documentation. Of further concern was the finding that the staff lacked a coherent theory of student learning. The provision of skills was often conceived in terms of student 'activity' or 'learning by doing' and skills acquisition was provided by courses that were frequently 'bolt-on'. In these, students were rarely given the opportunity to use the skills in similar or new contexts, and transfer of skills was seldom planned for.

The teaching quality assessments carried out by the Higher Education Funding Council for England (HEFCE) provide a similar picture of patchy development. Within many institutions there are pockets of innovation and evidence of good practice but there are a number where there is little, if any, development. These assessments indicate that there are very few examples of actual practice where programmes for personal transferable skills development correspond closely with a situation defined by established models of good practice. Moreover, this situation persists despite the considerable resources that have been invested in this area of curriculum development through a variety of initiatives at both sectoral and institutional levels.

In a recent study, Drummond *et al.* (1997) identified strategies for effective curriculum change for the teaching of personal transferable skills, largely in architecture departments. The most common situation they found is where a small number of committed individuals are struggling to effect meaningful change but where their potential to achieve it is limited by their frequent marginalization within departments. Of interest, and concern, is the finding that where development has been judged to be effective it has often come about by accident rather than by design.

It is interesting, in the light of the above picture, that during the course of this research study the Department for Education and Employment (DfEE) has been responsible for several initiatives on what it now calls key skills. These include the implementation of a dissemination strategy for key skills in higher education and a development study on embedding key skills within a traditional university (Murphy 1999).

## International perspectives

Changes in conception of the role of higher education in developing skills are not restricted to the UK. For example, a series of reports commissioned by the Australian Business/Higher Education Round Table (1991, 1992, 1993), a body comprising 43 chief executives and 24 vice-chancellors, demonstrates a commitment to joint initiatives that will advance the goals and improve the performance of both business and higher education for the benefit of Australian society. Their extensive surveys highlight a perceived need for the development throughout education of thinking and decision-making skills and the ability to apply knowledge to the workplace.

This same thinking is reflected in considerations at the (Australian) national level of the competences required for employment by the Finn (1991) and Mayer (1992) Committees. The former asserted that there are certain essential things that all young people need to learn in their preparation for employment, which the committee labelled 'employment related key competences'. It recommended that steps be taken to ensure that all young people are able to develop these regardless of the education or training pathway taken. The Mayer Committee followed this by developing seven key competency strands that it considered as essential for effective participation in work and other social settings. These are:

- collecting, analysing and organizing information
- communicating ideas and information
- planning and organizing activities
- working with others in teams
- using mathematical ideas and techniques
- solving problems
- using technology.

This list has obvious, and extensive, overlaps with those produced in the UK and, as in the UK, these competences appear to lack a theoretical rationale: 'a theoretical or empirical base for the establishment of the Key Competences is difficult to ascertain' (Beven and Duggan 1995: 10).

Similar economic rhetoric is also driving educational reform in the US. Stasz *et al.* (1996) begin their review of the economic imperative behind school reform by stating that there is growing consensus that American education needs fundamental reform in order to provide youth with an adequate preparation for the current and future workforce. This belief is based on the view that changes in the workplace will require new and different skills of workers, and that America's competitive edge in the world economy will increasingly depend on the skills of its workers. Stasz also reports that it is common for scholars and policy makers to assert that students are ill-prepared for the future workplace and that they need new kinds of skills. Marshall and Tucker (1992) sum up what they claim is the emerging consensus on the skills needed to power a modern economy. These turn out to be: capacity for abstract thought, to solve real-world problems, to communicate well in oral and written forms and to work well with others. Other reports, such as that from the Secretary's Commission on Achieving Necessary Skills (SCANS 1991) present a broader conception of skills including, in addition to the above, those relating to information, systems and technology.

Scepticism among academics in higher education also appears to pertain in the US, where Zemsky (1997) reports on a meeting of personnel from 130 colleges and universities where most participants are reported to have grown tired of 'the clatter of the market'. Most institutions felt themselves under assault by a society that expects them to accept market demands as their own agenda. Consequently, many faculties have been told to justify their practices by a set of criteria and a language that seem to them foreign and even hostile to the values and professional purposes they profess.

Finally, Otala (1993), arguing from a European perspective, presents the now familiar economic prognosis that the output of education and training systems in terms of both quantity and quality of skills at all levels, is the prime determinant of a country's level of industrial productivity and hence, competitiveness. The main conclusion is equally adamant; that the workplace has a growing need for competence development that can only be filled by institutions of higher education. The shortfall in skilled labour is highlighted by Healy (1996), who presents recent analyses of labour market trends by the Organization for Economic Co-operation and Development (OECD). These show that new employment opportunities requiring higher skill levels are increasing at a rate of 10 per cent of the total labour force each year. However, the inflow of recently qualified young people from the initial education system is typically around 3 per cent of the total labour force in any given year.

It is clear that an international consensus has emerged with regard to the diagnosis of the needs of the future economy, to the prognosis of the skills base necessary to confront it and of the central role of higher education in developing that skills base. Unfortunately, in achieving this agreement, prescription has outrun conceptualization. Little or no thought has been given to the theoretical or empirical base of the skills deemed necessary, to their definition or to their underlying implicit assumptions. Arguably the two most important aspects – the conceptualization of core skills and the issue of transferability – are now considered.

## Conceptualizing core and transferable skills

The conceptualization of core skills is problematic for several reasons. The term has several synonyms, including personal transferable, key, generic, process, common, work- or employment-related and even soft, skills. To add to this semantic confusion, these skills are also referred to as competences (including such variants as generic and meta-competences), capabilities, elements or attributes. Similarly, the various lists of such skills derived from surveys of employers, and those contained in government reports, are diverse in terminology, size and purpose, reflecting differences in definitions and interpretations of their significance. The conceptualization of core skills in higher education also requires an understanding of the history of the use of the term in relation to post-16 and vocational education, as policy in higher education was clearly influenced by these developments.

Hyland (1994) and Tribe (1996) trace the history of competences and core skills back to the Crowther Report on secondary education in the late 1950s, which called for more broad-based general studies in the later stages of schooling, a recommendation also taken up in further education under the banner of liberal studies. This general studies movement was subsequently transformed into a common skills or core knowledge programme, a movement evident in the recommendation of the Further Education Unit (1979) for a core entitlement of knowledge and skills in all further education (FE) programmes and in the various core skills projects funded by the Manpower Services Commission in the early 1980s as part of the New Training Initiative (Lawson 1992). These initiatives were all a response to perceptions by employers and educators that there was an urgent need to improve basic skills, particularly literacy and numeracy, among young people, and that there was a need to broaden and integrate vocational studies and to supply students with the all-purpose transferable skills so highly valued by trainers and employers.

The concept of core skills was reinforced as a key element in reform as a consequence of the CBI report *Towards a Skills Revolution* (1989) and as other bodies such as BTEC, TVEI and CPVE began to require a core of related knowledge, skills, qualities and attitudes in their programmes (Maclure 1991). It was from this base that the then National Curriculum Council supported the idea of a common set of core skills that could be incorporated in both A/AS levels and post-16 curriculum in schools, and in National Vocational Qualifications (NVQs), or as units within the NVQ framework. Hyland thus asserts that the inclusion of core skills in general NVQs (GNVQs) can be seen as a natural development and reassertion of ideas that have been put forward by a wide range of different bodies and agencies over the last 20 years or so.

Unfortunately, not all these agencies were singing from the same core skills song sheet, leading to differences in the terms used to recommend core elements. For some it was common skills, for others, common learning outcomes, general skills or personal transferable skills. This problem of terminology is now endemic, as indicated earlier, a situation that is exacerbated by the remarkably short shelf-life of many of these terms. In the limited life of the study reported in this book, the favoured skill label has shifted from personal transferable, to core, to employability and, most recently, to key – a shift not paralleled by any theoretical or conceptual development or justification. Indeed, the key skills recently advocated by the Dearing Report (1997) not only confuse because of the use of mixed vocabulary, such as key, transferable and generic, but also exemplify the lack of theoretical justification, containing a mixture of technical skills such as IT, interpersonal skills such as communication and cognitive skills such as problem solving.

Confusion over labels is matched by confusion over definitions. Reflective of this are the differences in definition applied to the terms 'personal transferable' and 'core' skills. The Department of Employment (Industry in Education 1995) sees them as identical. There are some skills, it argued, which are by their nature transferable to a variety of settings. They are therefore the core skills, i.e. it is only skills which transfer which are core, all core skills are therefore transferable skills. Jessup (1997), on the other hand, takes a much broader definition, referring to all knowledge, skills and understanding which are potentially transferable. To further confuse matters, the Association of Graduate Recruiters (AGR 1995) and Harvey *et al.* (1997) both use an almost identical definition for attributes.

Also reflective of the semantic and conceptual confusion in the literature is the assumed relationship between the notions of skill and competence, as discussions of core skills has become entangled in debates about generic competences, general competences, process skills and common learning outcomes (Jessup 1991). Psychologists have adopted a definition of skills that includes the notion of practised ability, covering any organized sequence of behaviour that, through practice, becomes fast, accurate and efficient. Their approach to characterizing skills is dynamic in that the focus is on the acquisition of knowledge and the modification of processes as a skill develops (A. Green 1994). Notions of competence, on the other hand, tend to be performance- or outcome-based: 'A competence is a description of something which a person who works in a given occupational area should be able to do. It is a description of an action, a behaviour or outcome which a person should be able to demonstrate' (Training Agency 1988: 5). So, from a psychological perspective, skills encompass competences.

However, this assumption is not always shared by policy makers. For example, the Employment Department (Training Agency 1989) claimed the opposite – that competence is a concept, 'which embodies the ability to transfer skills and knowledge to new situations within the occupational area', a definition that, to add further confusion, has been used for the notion of 'generic' competence (Fletcher 1991; Jessup 1991).

Hyland (1994) presents a thorough analysis of the various meanings, imprecision and muddle surrounding the term competence and concludes that the rich and ever-expanding metaphysical universe of competence is made almost complete with the introduction of 'generic' competences, which are meant to ensure the transferability of occupational skills, and by the identification of 'meta-competence' – competences that work on other competences. He concludes that the debate surrounding the notion of competence is shrouded in conceptual fuzziness and equivocation and that the introduction of new conceptions such as core and generic competences has not helped matters. Despite this, indeed partly because of it, the term has proved very effective as an educational slogan.

There have been few attempts to clarify the fuzziness of skills and competences. Cheetham and Chivers (1996) make one such attempt in developing, what they call, a holistic model of professional competence. This draws on both the British occupational standards model, which they criticize as being largely untested, ignoring personal and behavioural competences, and as representing a static and atomized view of competence, as well as the reflective practitioner model of Schön (1987).

The Cheetham and Chivers model classifies competences into three levels. At the centre are four interlinked 'core components' of professional competence:

1. Functional – the ability to perform a range of work-based tasks effectively to produce specific outcomes.
2. Knowledge/cognitive – the possession of appropriate work-related knowledge and the ability to put this to effective use.
3. Personal/behavioural – the ability to adopt appropriate behaviours in work-related situations.
4. Values/ethical – personal/professional values and ability to make sound judgements.

Each of these components is made up of a number of 'constituents' – subgroups of individual competences – and overarching the core components are a number of meta-competences, defined as generic, overarching, transferable between situations and tasks, and fundamental to effective performance, i.e. core skills. Their list includes communication, self-development, creativity and problem solving, all of which, it is contended, are capable of enhancing or mediating competence in the core components. These meta-competences, the four core components and their various constituents all interact together to produce specific outcomes.

Although Cheetham and Chivers label core skills as meta-competences, they contend, on the basis of their model, that not all skills identified as core are indeed overarching. Information technology and personal communication skills, which appear in many skills lists are, they argue, personal or functional competences. A consideration of the key skills identified by Dearing (1997) from the perspective of this model would indicate that communication, learning how to learn and problem solving qualify as meta-competences but that the remainder are not overarching and thus count only as core components.

This model of professional competences is as yet untested but, however useful it might prove to be in identifying the nature of competences in different professions, it does little or nothing to cut through the conceptual fuzziness of skills and competences. For example, Cheetham and Chivers' definition of knowledge/cognitive competence is almost the same as Jessup's generic competence, which in turn is deemed synonymous with core skill, whereas other skills normally accepted as core are labelled meta-competences. Worse, this group of supposedly overarching competences is clearly not homogenous, as problem solving, for example, is a cognitive skill, whereas communication is normally represented as an interpersonal skill.

There are identical problems with the model developed by Anderson and Marshall (1996), which is very similar to the previous model in terms of both structure and terminology. This too is hierarchical, identifying six skill areas on three levels or stages. The stages are seen as linked, with lower skill acquisition being essential for the development of skills at the subsequent stage:

- At the lowest level, Stage 1 'Underpinning Basics', are the skills essential for employability. These include those identified as 'educational basics' – reading, writing, numeracy and oral communication – and 'personal traits', including honesty and reliability.
- Three types of skill are identified at Stage 2 'Skills, Knowledge and Attitude', which are needed for individual effectiveness on the job. These are 'occupation-specific skills' such as book-keeping and welding; 'generic skills' such as communication, problem solving, application of number and reasoning skills; and 'personal competences' such as motivation and leadership.
- At Stage 3 are the 'Overarching Capabilities', for maximizing organizational performance. This is achieved through skills of 'system thinking', which include teamworking, self-management, business thinking and customer orientation.

Thus, according to this model, core skills are located on all three levels. Numeracy and aspects of oral communication at Stage 1, communication and problem solving at Stage 2 and teamworking and self-management at Stage 3. This model is also untested and does little to clarify the conceptual confusion surrounding the definition and status of the skills and competences identified. It is little wonder that Tribe (1996) concludes that the theoretical justifications for the characterization of skills demonstrate an alarming circularity and lack of depth.

Although the relationship of skills and competences has been highlighted so far, there has been a recent movement of vocabulary towards the use of the term attributes, a movement that has only served to exacerbate the conceptual confusion. The Association of Graduate Recruiters (AGR 1995), for example, set out to identify the attributes – vaguely defined as a mixture of knowledge, skills, understanding and attitudes – which graduates will need in the light of the changes taking place in graduate careers. They concluded that they needed to be self-reliant in career and personal development: 'skills to manage processes rather than functional skills'. The report identifies 12 such attributes and claims that, without self-reliance skills, other skills can be wasted.

The most recent study of managers is also framed in terms of attributes and indicates clearly the extent of employer demands of higher education. Harvey *et al.* (1997) report that employers want people who are going to be effective in a future changing world – intelligent, flexible, adaptable employees who are quick to learn and who can deal with change. They want graduates who can fit rapidly into workplace culture, work in teams, exhibit good interpersonal skills, communicate well, take on responsibility for an area of work and perform efficiently and effectively to add value to the organization – they want adaptive recruits. They want employees who can use their abilities and skills to evolve the organization, who exhibit an ability to learn and add to knowledge and skills, and who have the ability to use their knowledge and skills in the face of change. They want people who have bright ideas, who are able to communicate them to others, develop them in teams and persuade colleagues to attempt new approaches – adaptable people. And they are looking for people who can anticipate and lead change, to help them transform their organizations, who can use high-level skills like analyses, critique, synthesis and multi-layered communication to facilitate innovative teamwork – transformative employees. However, it is unclear from this report whether there is any substance to this rhetoric, or whether it is yet another example of employer 'wish lists'.

There is thus little rationale for the conclusion of the AGR report that the attributes they identified should be developed within the curriculum of every institution, or for the further unjustified prescription that these will improve the quality of learning, enable students to make an informed choice of degree module and provide the techniques needed to manage lifelong learning. As Coffield (1997) argues, the strategic assessment of graduates' future roles turns out on examination to be a highly selective amalgam of untested speculations from focus groups and interested parties. He concludes that fundamental changes to the curriculum of higher education need to be based on more robust evidence than this.

Whether discourse is framed in terms of skills, competences or attributes, recent empirical research on the situational or contextual factors in learning and performance casts doubt on the value of labels such as communication because the nature, demand, content and quality of skills like communication are largely determined by the work setting. For example, Beven (1996) reports, with particular reference to problem-solving skills or strategies, that the degree of applicability of each strategy to each site, and the degree of success achievable with each strategy, varied according to the specific contexts of each site. In this context Bridges (1993) expresses concern that classifications of transferable skills usually lack any accompanying classification of contexts and calls for a theory of domains to make the notion of such skills not only intelligible but also applicable.

A final barrier to a clearer understanding of skills is that of language. Both Barnett (1994) and Holmes (1994) ask whether the voices of the labour market and of academe are expressing similar points of view when they talk of transferable skills. Do they mean the same thing, for example, when they talk of 'communication skills'? In Barnett's (1997) view they do not, or ought not to, arguing that since there are no universal forms of communication, the attempt to identify any such 'transferability' is an imposition of a particularly favoured set of performativities backed by powerful alliances. Holmes (1994), on the other hand, seeks a common language because it is only when this is achieved that any judgement can be made on whether there is indeed a gap between what employers expect from, and what higher education considers valuable and appropriate for, a university qualification.

With regard to another aspect of language, it is apparent that a failure to involve university teachers in this debate has engendered further semantic confusion. Our interviews with such teachers, which are reported in Chapter 3, show that the term core skills for them typically connotes those skills that are central to their discipline, as distinct from personal transferable skills, which they define as cross-disciplinary and generic, such as effective note taking and organizing study time (see also Dunne 1995).

In sum, therefore, core skills is but one of several related terms, each of which has been used to label sets, or lists, of skills or attributes deemed important by employers and government and, like their counterparts in the fashion industry, these skills labels seem prone to rapid and unpredictable change. The lists contain different numbers and combinations of skills, although there does appear to be some agreement about the importance of aspects of communication, numeracy, teamwork, technology and problem solving. What the lists also have in common is that they are theoretically and empirically threadbare and have rarely, if ever, contained the perceptions of those who are expected to deliver these skills in higher education.

The term core skills has a variety of contested meanings and therefore any study of these skills in higher education first necessitates a conceptualization that provides both a clear and justified definition, together with a theoretical model of course provision in terms of the knowledge and skill outcomes planned for and taught. The two models developed on the basis of this analysis for this study are set out in Chapter 2.

## Transfer

A major problem in the conceptualization of core, or transferable, skills has been the assumption that such skills transfer easily, or indeed, automatically, from educational to work contexts. The Department of Employment (1993) emphasized this in stating that the core skills movement is based on beliefs about transfer. It assumes that it is possible to identify generic skills that are transferable across education and work contexts and that the acquisition of such skills will enhance learner flexibility, adaptability and autonomy. However, consideration of the research literature on transfer fails to support such an assumption.

Transfer of learning occurs when a person applies knowledge or skills acquired in one context in a new context (Perkins and Salomon 1994). This may be as prosaic as applying mathematical skills acquired in school in the supermarket or as esoteric as the utilization of chess skills to underpin strategic thinking in politics or business. Schooling is predicated on such transfer taking place, as it is assumed that the knowledge, skills and understanding acquired in school will be useful and applicable to a range of contexts outside of school. Unfortunately, whilst expected and assumed, transfer is difficult to realize. Perkins and Salomon (1994) draw on abundant evidence to show that, very often, the anticipated transfer from learning experiences to new settings does not occur.

The reasons proposed for the poor transfer of knowledge and skills differ according to theoretical persuasion. Those who view learning from a cognitive perspective assume that knowledge and skills are internal properties of the individual and, as a consequence, are concerned to identify the instructional conditions that most effectively allow their utilization in external contexts.

An alternative, and now more widely accepted view, emanates from theories of situated learning, which argue that much of what is learned is specific to the situation in which it is learned, that is, the nature of the situation and circumstances in which knowledge is acquired is likely to influence the subsequent deployment of that knowledge in other situations and settings. In this view, learning is inseparable from situation. Therefore, a far greater understanding of the social, cultural and technical context in which learning takes place is a prerequisite for developing more effective learning environments (Brown *et al.* 1989). Claxton (1996) thus argues that the sense that people make of their experience is a function of the knowledge, beliefs, schemas and attitudes, derived from previous, culturally situated, experiences, that they bring with them to the new event. This internalized situated learning context is integrated with, and developing in interaction with, the external situated learning context, together forming the learning environment. Learning is thus context embedded. In summary, the interpretation of the problem of transfer from this point of view is that the search is not for how knowledge or skills are transported 'whole' from one setting to another, but for how learning and performance in one setting prepares one to learn the rules, habits and knowledge appropriate to a new setting (Resnick and Collins 1994).

*Teaching for transfer*

Most research on transfer has been undertaken from a cognitive perspective and typically draws on a broad distinction between near and far transfer. Near transfer refers to the application of the same knowledge or skill in very similar circumstances, such as when students meet the same kind of problems in an examination paper that they have dealt with in class. Far transfer refers to transfer between contexts that seem different or remote, such as the example of the chess master carrying over the notion of control of the centre from chess to political or military settings, cited earlier. Perkins (1995) concludes that a century of research has shown that near transfer appears to have better prospects than far transfer and that the latter requires more conditional, and deeper, disciplinary content knowledge.

Nevertheless, there have been positive outcomes of research on transfer from which can be identified the conditions when it is most likely to occur (Perkins and Salomon 1994; Anderson *et al.* 1996). These include: thorough and diverse practice, explicit abstraction, active self-monitoring, arousing mindfulness and use of metaphor or analogy. On the basis of such findings Salomon and Perkins (1989) synthesized the research on transfer by recognizing two distinct but related mechanisms, the 'low road' and the 'high road', which identify the 'when' of transfer – when it occurs and when it does not.

Low road transfer is characteristic of near transfer. It happens when conditions in the transfer task are similar to those of the initial learning context and result in well learned automatic responses in the new setting. They reflect habit, extended practice of skills with little reflective thinking. The distance of transfer depends on the amount of practice. Whatever cognitive element is learned should thus be practised, in a variety of settings, until it becomes automatic and somewhat flexible because of the variety of contexts (Wolf *et al.* 1990; Blagg *et al.* 1993). Another way of increasing the likelihood of transfer is to make the learning context closer to the desired application context, as in simulations, for example.

High road transfer, by contrast, depends on the mindful abstracting of knowledge from the context of learning or application and a deliberate search for connections. Characteristically there is a deliberate search for common patterns, consciously formulated abstractions and general principles or procedures. These then become the elements for transfer. The abstractions demanded in high road transfer are representations with some generic quality or pattern that can be represented symbolically in the mind of the learner. For example, the term 'vertebrates' is more abstract than the huge and bizarre range of fish, birds and mammals that can be observed. Similarly, 'pressure = force/area' generalizes multitudes of everyday physical happenings. The abstractions have necessitated de-contextualization, are devoid of contextual specificity and take the form of rule, principle, label or schematic pattern. Abstraction thus leads to transfer by yielding a re-representation that subsumes a greater range of cases (Hattie *et al.* 1996).

The evidence would indicate that transfer is unlikely to occur unless intentionally planned for in the way that materials and contexts are structured. Teaching programmes that leave transfer up to the learner are less effective, as illustrated in Blagg *et al.*'s (1993) rejection of Bo-Peep theories of transfer – 'leave them alone and they'll come home'. Teaching for transfer requires careful thought and high levels of pedagogical skill. The assumption that skills transfer easily is simply not tenable.

This same conclusion is also applicable to the notion of work experience in undergraduate programmes as prescribed by Dearing and in the extent to which new graduate employees can learn, and transfer, skills in new employment settings. The effectiveness of 'learning on the job' aligns well with theories of situated learning but the work context also needs careful structuring because the impact of aspects of the organizational culture on learning and transfer can be very powerful, as is evident below.

## Developing skills in employment

Research findings on the reactions of graduates to the transition from higher education to employment have been extremely consistent (Nicholson and Arnold 1989; Smith *et al.* 1989; Spurling 1993; Graham and McKenzie 1995). Firstly, graduates experience a culture shock because they are seldom prepared for the change from working competitively as an individual to working as a member of a cooperating team. As such, they find it hard to adapt. Neither do they understand the company culture and structure. Handy (1985) has argued that the way each organization functions is different, yet Spurling (1993), for example, found that even after several years service with large industrial companies some graduates had only a vague notion of how the company was operated. Johnson (1991) examined the causes and consequences of the resultant stress of culture shock in small and medium sized enterprises (SMEs) and identified role ambiguity, relationships at work, and position within the organization as prime agents.

Part of this problem may, of course, be that graduates lack the skills to deal with these aspects of employment. For example, Nicholson and Arnold (1989) found that graduates were unaware of any generic skills that may have been acquired in higher education. When they compared the skills transferred from higher education with those acquired since joining the company, many, such as social and interpersonal skills, written communication and organizational skills, had been acquired in employment. An effective means of overcoming culture shock and the attendant stress (Kemp and Foster 1995) is the integration of academic and work-based learning, which received very strong support in the Dearing Report.

The second set of consistent findings is that the ambitions of many graduates outrun their experience as they move from higher education to employment, which leads to impatience and frustration. This frustration is exacerbated by the creation of inflated expectations, often engendered in the recruitment process. 'Unrealistic recruitment brochures and processes can sometimes build up expectations to ridiculous levels' (Graham and McKenzie 1995), which, unless met, can lead to graduates leaving the company.

The use of ambiguous terms in brochures can also lead to problems of interpretation. The competency framework used in brochures and initial screening processes is less than clear when broad and general terms are used. Stasz *et al.* (1996) concluded from their research that: '. . . very general terms like problem solving, communication, teamwork, and attitudes are too broad or ambiguous to be of much use to employers for either screening or training'. Smith *et al.* (1989) also argued that it is important for employers to identify the skill requirements of different jobs with some precision, but admitted that it is difficult to identify ways of adequately measuring them.

The clarity of employers' claims about graduate opportunities can also impact on what Evans and Heinz (1995) call: 'the challenge and rewarding experience in the passage to employment itself'. They claim that to a large degree the quality of this experience will determine their success in developing longer-term occupational goals. Transition from higher education to employment is thus aided when clear messages are given about the opportunities that exist in the workplace.

Thirdly, there is evidence of the misallocation or mismanagement of early tasks and roles. Graduates tend to perceive their skills to be higher than do their managers, who therefore give graduates less challenging work (Schein 1964; Arnold and McKenzie Davey 1992). As a consequence, levels of satisfaction decline and, at worst, the attributes for which they were recruited are lost or forgotten because the demands of the work environment are not conducive to their display.

It is clearly in employers' interests to develop new graduates quickly and successfully into effective employees and this tends to be achieved, in larger companies at least, by placement on structured development programmes in their first two years of employment. However, types of training provision vary in objectives, format, content, variety of assignments, site and the extent to which they are built around specified competencies or influenced by professional bodies. Further, performance appraisal tends not to be given sufficient attention and is often flawed in practice (Barlow 1989; Redman *et al.* 1993). Despite such variability there appear to be few, if any, evaluations of the differential effectiveness of training provision.

The extent, and the implications, of culture shock, unmet expectations, frustration and misallocation of roles and tasks among early career graduates is not clear. Neither is the apparent overreliance of employers on higher education to provide generic skills. However, the apparent mismatch between employers' 'wish lists' of the skills they demand from higher education, and what they themselves provide, is worthy of further study.

## Student perspectives

The search for ways of achieving effective transferability of skills and knowledge has focused largely on pedagogical issues – but what of learners' perspectives? Until recently, students' views of their educational experience were of interest to relatively few educational evaluators (Green 1994a). The survey of students' experiences and expectations of higher education commissioned for the Dearing Report (1997) is therefore valuable in this respect. Students rated getting a job, or a qualification for a job, as the most important reason for going to university and amongst the main opportunities they wanted was to develop new or existing skills. This latter was given more priority than conventional academic outcomes such as intellectual growth and stimulation. The majority reported improvement in most of the key skills identified in that report such as communication, teamworking, planning and using initiative. Less than three in ten reported improvements in numeracy, however.

Although the survey presents an interesting broad-brush picture, it is, unfortunately, of little value. There is no clear theoretical, or other, rationale for the choice of questions or skill lists, the depth of analysis allows little or no possibility for deeper exploration and the empirical status of the volunteer sample is unclear.

Although considerable research has been undertaken describing students' approaches to, and strategies used in, learning traditional academic tasks (Marton *et al.* 1997), very few studies have considered students' acquisition of core skills, their reaction to the teaching of such skills or the degree of skills transfer. The studies so far undertaken have relied exclusively on students' perceptions rather than on independently assessed outcomes. What evidence there is indicates that when skills courses are taught students are generally positive, find the content useful and believe that their skills have improved as a consequence (Tate and Thompson 1994; Greenan *et al.* 1997; Ng *et al.* 1997). Nevertheless, there is also evidence that some students are resentful of these courses if they are taught in their final year, as they feel that they limit their opportunities to acquire disciplinary knowledge (Dunne 1995).

Holman (1995), in a study of first year undergraduates, attempted to identify how skill development occurs. Students reported that this occurs in two ways – tacit and negotiated development, which is characterized by unconscious, non-reflective acquisition, and rational development, where skills are acquired in an individualistic, planned and conscious manner. The latter was found where students were undertaking skills modules, which allowed them access to vocabulary that enabled them to label their actions, articulate which area of skill required development and to plan a course of action. Holman thus recommends teaching strategies that enable students to formulate an understanding of their own skills and how to develop them, to increase their awareness of different types of skill and to encourage reflection – a recommendation similar to that of Tate and Thompson (1994).

The successful teaching, and acquisition, of generic skills must depend, in part, on the attitudes and motivation of students, yet to date there have been few research attempts to explicate the student experience in this area. Nor have existing studies investigated student responses to the acquisition of individual skills through differing modes of course provision. Answers to such questions are needed not only to identify successful practice in higher education, but also to be able to respond to what some see as the inflated demands of employers.

## Summary of major themes

In summary, despite severe misgivings by some theorists, the displacement of academic, by operational, competence in higher education appears well underway, in policy at least. As so often happens, however, policy is outrunning practice in this area. What little evidence there is shows that implementation of the teaching of generic skills is very patchy, of variable quality and largely undertaken by individual enthusiasts. Prescription has also outrun conceptualization. The term generic or transferable skills does not connote homogeneity. It hides substantial differences in definition and labelling and is shrouded in semantic confusion. Worse, although arguments for their utility may have some face validity, typical lists of skills are theoretically and empirically threadbare and the implicit assumptions about their context independence and transferability probably untenable.

Employer perceptions of their needs and wants are frequently portrayed, but largely through the proliferation of inflated 'wish lists' of desirable skills. Few studies have considered the perspectives of the new graduate employees themselves on such facets as transition to the workplace, skill requirements and use in differing work contexts, opportunities for continuing skills development and, crucially, in the light of the light of theories of situated learning, the impact on their learning of organizational cultures and contexts.

Empirical studies of student perceptions of generic skill provision are also rare, and the results patchy, some indicating positive, and others negative, perceptions. Missing too are empirical data on student experiences, and perceived outcomes, of different modes of skill provision.

In the light of these analyses, the overarching purpose of the study reported here is therefore is to gain enhanced understandings of the acquisition and development of generic skills in both higher education and employment settings, from the particular perspectives of those involved – university teachers, students, employers and recent graduate employees. Key to the achievement of this purpose will be the following strands:

- A focus on a justified set of transferable skills. Hereafter these will be called generic skills, the rationale for which is set out in Chapter 2.
- A theoretical framework that distinguishes generic skills, core skills and disciplinary knowledge in higher education settings, so that differing patterns of course provision can be delineated.

- Consideration of the role of contexts in:

  (i)   the development and take up of skills courses in higher education settings

  (ii)  the perceptions of learning and skills utilization and utility among students on undergraduate courses and in work experience schemes, and among graduate employees in early employment

  (iii) the training schemes planned and developed in major companies.

Details of the rationale, purposes and research approaches adopted are set out in Chapter 2.

# 2
# A Conceptualization of Skills and Course Provision

The overall aim of the study was to gain enhanced understandings of core, that is transferable, skills acquisition in higher education and employment, in order to inform, and indeed improve, its provision. However, as we illustrated in Chapter 1, the word 'core' is shrouded in semantic confusion and contested meanings. Reflective of this, although our original data collection instruments were framed in terms of 'core' and 'transferable' skills, typical responses from teachers, and many students, showed clearly that they defined 'core' as relating to disciplinary skills, and 'transferable' as non-disciplinary, generic skills. To further complicate matters, the same skills were being taught as core in one discipline but as generic in another. For example, communication and presentation skills in departments of drama and law are seen as essential disciplinary – that is core – skills, whereas these same skills in other departments are taught as generic, transferable, skills. Employers, on the other hand, largely conceived 'core' as 'transferable' skills. These very different reactions to the same terms are not difficult to deal with analytically, as we indicate later when discussing descriptive and interpretative validity, but they do create potential difficulties in reporting. Thus, in order to enhance clarity and consistency, the term 'core' will hereafter be used to refer to disciplinary skills and the term 'generic' to represent the so-called transferable skills that can support study in any discipline. This distinction maximizes ecological validity, in accurately reflecting shared meanings in higher education, and the use of the term generic is consistent with international usage.

The first stage of the study focused on mapping the field, by providing a clarification of contemporary policies, practices, priorities, conceptions and expectations in both higher education and employment settings. In the second, concurrent, stage, examples of employer-led initiatives in skills development in higher education settings were identified and evaluated.

The first stage required information from four different sources – teachers in higher education, their students, employers and early career graduates.

For teachers, the key questions concerned their knowledge and understanding of core and generic skills; how they conceived their development and their place in the curriculum of higher education; how they planned, delivered and assessed them; if, and how, they differentiated the planning and teaching of them; and what constraints, if any, impeded their teaching of these skills.

The extent to which the teaching of skills is effective depends, in part, on the attitudes and motivation of the student body. It was therefore important that data be acquired from students on their understandings of generic skills, the importance that they afforded them and their perceptions of the quality of skills teaching and of their own learning.

Employers have led the fight to integrate generic skills into the higher education curriculum but there is remarkably little information about policies and practices designed to sustain, enhance or develop these skills in employment settings. It was therefore necessary to ascertain in this study the perceptions of employers on the role of skills in recruitment processes, policies on training and skills development and the means by which graduates are socialized or enculturated into particular company organizations.

Employers' perspectives may differ considerably from those of their employees. In order to ascertain employees' perspectives, the study focused on the reality of the first two years of graduate employment. The questions of central concern here included the opportunities, and contexts, provided for the use of existing generic skills, the type and usefulness of any training provided for their development and the value and perceived transferability of the knowledge and skills acquired in their university career.

The data for the second stage of the study were acquired from evaluations of two very different employer-led initiatives – the Team Development programme funded by BP, and the Shell Technology Enterprise Programme, further details of which are presented in the following section.

## Sampling

The sampling frame developed to achieve these data is shown in Figure 2.1. The higher education sample comprised 32 lecturers, and their students, in 16 departments in four institutions of higher education, that is, teachers from four courses in each institution. A complete list of the courses sampled is presented in Appendix A. Two of the four institutions were 'pre-92' universities, one was a 'post-92' university and the other was an aspiring university. Both of the latter institutions had been in receipt of substantial awards from the Enterprise initiatives. The 16 departments were selected to represent a mix of vocational and non-vocational disciplines. Vocational departments included architecture, pharmacy and engineering, with departments such as English and French representing non-vocational disciplines. Others such as art, geography, computer science and mathematics could be regarded as either vocational or not, depending on the nature of the course and students' aspirations.

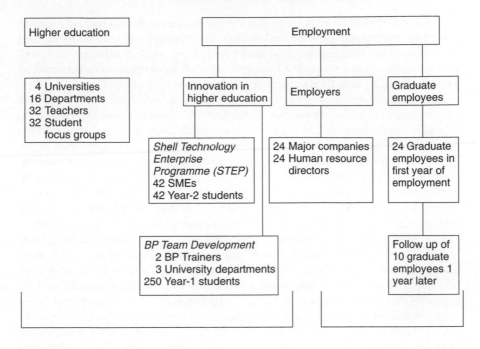

Data: Questionnaire – Interview – Observation –          Questionnaire – Interviews
Course Materials

*Figure 2.1*   Sampling frame

Given the aims of the study, the main criterion for the choice of courses, and thus of tutors, within institutions and departments was that each included the deliberate intention to teach generic skills in their courses. This information was made available either by central university bodies, such as teaching committees, or by heads of department. In either case the sample was, of necessity, selected on the basis of peer recommendation.

Data on course provision, including aims, content, delivery modes and assessment demands, were acquired through pre-course interviews with the tutors, together with an analysis of departmental and course/module literature. Data on teaching processes were collected by observation of several of the sessions of each course. At the end of each observation, be it a lecture, tutorial or other form of group learning, interviews were held separately with teachers (of between one and one-and-a-half hours duration) and focus groups of between four and six students (of between one-half and three-quarters of an hour), to gain their reflections on, and perceptions of, teaching and learning outcomes in relation to generic skills. (An example of the semi-structured nature of the interview is provided in Appendix B – the final interview schedule for the teachers.) In addition, 40 per cent of all students studying the 32 modules completed a questionnaire. This covered two aspects of skill provision: first, a direct focus on the course or module just undertaken and perceptions of skill development in this context; and second, a wider range of general issues relating to skills teaching and learning. These more general questions were devised to provide a background to the observation, and focus group interviews (see Appendix C).

Two separate samples were chosen to represent employers and graduate employees. The employer sample comprised the Human Resource Directors, or their equivalent, of 24 large national and multi-national companies, chosen from the FTSE 100 list to represent a range of employment types. The sample included manufacturing, petroleum, pharmaceutical, financial, central and local government, legal and service employers. In each case an interview of some one and a half hours covered three broad topics – recruitment procedures, training provision for skills development and the enculturation of new employees into the organization (see Appendix D).

The sample of early graduate employees was deliberately selected from a broad employment base because research and governmental literature had indicated that skills development in early employment is likely to vary according to the size of the company. Twenty-four graduates employed by a mix of larger companies and small and medium sized enterprises were selected for interview. The interview focused on the opportunities and contexts provided for the use of their existing skills, the type and usefulness of in-house training, where available, and their perception of the value and transferability of the skills acquired in their university career. Ten of these graduates were followed up one year later to ascertain changes, if any, in their skill use and development.

The sample for stage two was composed of two major employer initiatives in higher education – the STEP programme of eight-week vacation work placements in small and medium enterprises (SMEs), with a specific emphasis on generic skills, and the BP programme focusing specifically on team development. In the initial stages of the STEP evaluation, ten students and ten employers who had experience of the programme were interviewed, on the basis of which a competency framework was developed, which was then trialled with a cohort of 40 students. The impact of the BP courses was evaluated separately in three departments, one with a small group of seven volunteer chemistry students, a second involving 150 first year law students and a third with 58 first year computer science students.

# Models of course provision and generic skills

## *A model of course provision*

A necessary precursor to achieving valid answers to the research questions posed was the development of justifiable models of generic skills and course provision. The identification of patterns of course provision, in terms of the knowledge and skill outcomes planned for and taught, and the general

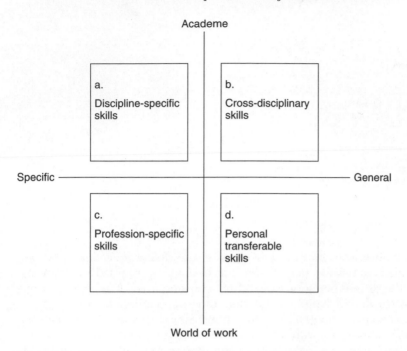

*Figure 2.2* Skills in higher education (Barnett 1994: 62)

teaching approaches adopted, has attracted little theoretical attention. In one of the few attempts to conceptualize this, Barnett (1994) argues that the modern university curriculum can be understood in terms of two super-imposed axes, as shown in Figure 2.2. One axis is formed by curricula, characterized by whether they derive from the internal agendas of the aca-demic community or the external agendas of groupings in the wider society. The other axis is formed at one pole by curricula that are specific to definite epistemic interests, usually discrete disciplines, and at the other pole by general aims transcending discipline-specific interests. However, this model fails to differentiate substantive and syntactic knowledge in a discipline and sets transferable skills outside the discipline framework. Yet, as Otter (1992) among others, has noted, in reality subjects or disciplines are often the vehicles through which these skills are learned and developed.

Drummond *et al.* (1997) consider only broad structural factors in their identification of three approaches to developing skills in higher education curricula. These are: embedded or integrated development, parallel or stand-alone development – often called bolt-on courses, and work placements or work-based projects that include sandwich and professionally approved courses requiring students to spend a period of time in the workplace.

The model developed for this study distinguishes five areas of provi-sion: disciplinary knowledge, disciplinary skills, workplace awareness, work-place experience and generic skills, as shown in Figure 2.3. Epistemologists

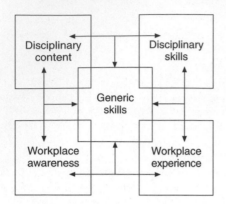

*Figure 2.3*   A model of course provision

disagree about how many different types of knowledge there might be but two have attracted most analysis, the first being propositional or 'knowing that' and the second being procedural or 'knowing how'. Ryle (1949) popularized this distinction and argued that they were independent domains. More recent analysts disagree, however, pointing out that one cannot opt for performance knowledge without also understanding that one has 'acquired' propositional knowledge in the bargain, and vice versa (Fenstermacher 1996). As such, the two domains are now seen as distinct but interdependent.

This epistemological view is shared by psychological and curriculum analyses of the nature of knowledge. Anderson (1983) explicitly accepts the distinction between 'knowing that' and 'knowing how' in his conceptions of declarative versus procedural knowledge, whereas it is implicit in Schwab's (1964) notions of substantive versus syntactic knowledge. Schwab's concern was to describe the conceptual structures of the disciplines. He defined substantive knowledge as consisting of the facts and major concepts, and the ways these are organized into frameworks for guiding future enquiry. Thus, in physics the concepts of atom, electron and subatomic particle are understood in terms of an organizing framework called the kinetic theory. Syntactic knowledge, on the other hand, identifies the procedural aspects of a discipline, including ways in which verification and justification of new knowledge are established. These skills would thus include the heuristics, methods, plans, practices, procedures, routines, strategies, tactics, techniques and tricks of the discipline (Ohlsson 1994).

Epistemological, psychological and curriculum theories indicate that substantive and syntactic knowledge are interdependent and are thus identified as such in the top two elements of the model.

The relationship between core, or syntactic, and generic skills is, however, complex. There is enormous variation across disciplines about what are considered the necessary core skills. In some disciplines, some generic skills are taught as core skills, as was indicated earlier, whereas in others these same skills are considered as generic and may be taught in separate 'bolt-on' courses. So the same skills can be taught either as specific discipline-related or as more flexible generic, skills. This is one of the reasons why the central element of the model is shown intruding into the other four elements, illustrating the extent of their relationships.

Both disciplinary knowledge and skills, and generic skills, can be acquired through work experience, achieved either through direct placement in the workplace or through some kind of workplace simulation. These are represented by the bottom two elements of the model.

The rationale for workplace experiences is underpinned by both logical and psychological arguments. To employers, work-based placements are a logical necessity to help students develop attributes that will enable them to be successful at work. They allow the development of specific work-related skills and provide a foretaste for workplace culture, which should help graduates to be more effective, more quickly (Harvey *et al.* 1997). The Dearing Report (1997) accepted this logic by asserting that there should be increasingly active partnerships between higher education institutions and the worlds of industry, commerce and public service, and that further development of work experience opportunities required action from both employers and institutions. Nevertheless, disagreements exist about the length of such experiences. Harvey *et al.* (1997) report their employer sample as arguing that to be worthwhile for both student and employer the placement should ideally be for one academic year. However, others have reported successful outcomes from much shorter, well structured, placements (Seagraves *et al.* 1996; Dunne 1997).

The psychological arguments for work placements crystallize around the problems of transfer of learning, a process largely assumed in notions like personal transferable skills. However, as was shown in Chapter 1, skills do not transfer easily and there is theoretical dispute about the reasons for this. The psychological and the logical overlap in theories of situated learning, as both stress the importance of the learning situation or environment in knowledge and skills development. Proponents of theories of situated learning argue that the nature of the situation and circumstances in which knowledge and skill are acquired will influence the subsequent deployment of that knowledge and skill in other situations and settings (Lave and Wenger 1991; Greeno *et al.* 1993). Thus, for students to learn to use skills as practitioners use them, they must enter that community and its culture, that is, learning is seen as a process of enculturation. Brown *et al.* (1989) advocate an approach they call cognitive apprenticeship, which supports learning in a domain by enabling students to acquire, develop, and use cognitive tools (skills) in authentic domain activity, in much the same way that craft apprenticeships enable apprentices to acquire and develop the tools and skills of their craft through authentic work at, and membership in, their trade. This view, that situations and social partnerships influence how knowledge is structured and used, has obvious implications for course provision, particularly in vocational subjects. It also provides a powerful theoretical rationale for the value of work experience schemes.

Attempts within university courses to provide authentic or simulated learning settings are represented in the model by the two elements of workplace awareness and workplace experience. Courses using a workplace awareness approach aim to enable the application of theoretical knowledge in simulated 'authentic' environments that approximate the activities of the workplace. Curriculum provision identified by the workplace experience element incorporates direct links with the workplace and is largely integrated into vocationally oriented courses as work placements. These vary considerably in length, frequency, purpose and approach (Winter 1994; Ryan *et al.* 1996; Seagraves *et al.* 1996). There are many such links between companies and higher education institutions, including those that provide degrees in a mixed, in-company and on-campus, mode. Sandwich degrees with placements of varying duration have, of course, existed for over 30 years, all with the aim of linking the theoretical and practical.

The connections between the elements of the model indicate the potential links and variants that are possible, given different course purposes and intentions. In this model there is no assumption about directionality. So disciplinary knowledge can, for example, be acquired in the institution for subsequent use in the workplace, or vice versa; in education degrees, for example, much disciplinary knowledge is learned in classrooms. Neither is there an assumption about the possibility of transfer. The arrows identify possible lines of transfer but, as has been indicated earlier, transfer may not occur unless planned for.

The validity of the model rests on its isomorphism with current psychological theories of learning, contemporary scholarship in epistemology, the agendas of employers and government, and the modes of course provision in higher education. Indeed, the utility of the model rests on its ability to identify patterns of course provision, and these are considered in Chapter 4.

## A model of generic skills

Our analysis of the conceptualization of core and generic skills in Chapter 1 led us to the conclusion that the lists of skills typically used are theoretically threadbare and rarely contain the perceptions of those who are expected to deliver them in higher education. The perspective adopted in developing a model for this study was framed by our broad aim of informing and improving provision in higher education. However, the evidence on institutional innovation, including that from Enterprise in Education initiatives (Biggs *et al.* 1994), indicates that curriculum and pedagogical change is extremely difficult to achieve and is more likely to be effective if a 'bottom–up' rather than a 'top–down' approach is adopted, in order to enable teaching staff to take some ownership of initiatives and of vocabulary. In the light of this evidence it was necessary, in developing our model of generic skills, to supplement an analysis of existing literature with a pilot

| MANAGEMENT OF SELF | MANAGEMENT OF INFORMATION |
|---|---|
| • Manage time effectively<br>• Set objectives, priorities and standards<br>• Take responsibility for own learning<br>• Listen actively and with purpose<br>• Use a range of academic skills (analysis, synthesis, argument, and so on)<br>• Develop and adapt learning strategies<br>• Show intellectual flexibility<br>• Use learning in new or different situations<br>• Plan/work towards long-term aims and goals<br>• Purposefully reflect on own learning<br>• Clarify with criticism constructively<br>• Cope with stress | • Use appropriate sources of information (library, retrieval systems, people, and so on)<br>• Use appropriate technology, including IT<br>• Use appropriate media<br>• Handle large amounts of information/data effectively<br>• Use appropriate language and form in a range of activities<br>• Interpret a variety of information forms<br>• Present information/ideas competently (orally, in written form, visually)<br>• Respond to different purposes/contexts/audiences<br>• Use information critically<br>• Use information in innovative and creative ways |
| MANAGEMENT OF OTHERS | MANAGEMENT OF TASK |
| • Carry out agreed tasks<br>• Respect the views and values of others<br>• Work productively in a cooperative context<br>• Adapt to the needs of the group<br>• Defend/justify views or actions<br>• Take initiative and lead others<br>• Delegate and stand back<br>• Negotiate<br>• Offer constructive criticism<br>• Take the role of chairperson<br>• Learn in a collaborative context<br>• Assist/support others in learning | • Identify key features<br>• Conceptualize issues<br>• Set and maintain priorities<br>• Identify strategic options<br>• Plan/implement a course of action<br>• Organize subtasks<br>• Use and develop appropriate strategies<br>• Assess outcomes |

*Figure 2.4* A framework for the development of generic skills

study of all departments in one university. This involved interviews with the heads of 33 departments, observations of students undertaking courses in skills and extended discussions with staff who were already promoting these skills in their teaching (Dunne 1995). These data highlighted that the vocabulary used was important in tutors' understanding and acceptance of terms, that different skills were perceived as important and significant in different departments and that, as a consequence, typical lists of skills presented by employers were seen to be inflexible.

The model that was developed from these analyses is presented in Figure 2.4. It consists of four broad management skills – of self, others, information and task. These skills are generic in that they can potentially be applied to any discipline, to any course in higher education, to the workplace or indeed to any other context. The set of subskills included within each of the four areas is intended to serve as a set of examples of learning outcomes, rather than as a rigid set of skills to be achieved in each university department or any employment setting. So, if used as a tool for planning, teachers can amend or adapt these sets for their own course purposes and curriculum. There is, therefore, an in-built flexibility in the model. The skills presented as examples in Figure 2.4 reflect the vocabulary of academic staff teaching skills courses. Nevertheless, they include many of the skills contained in typical lists of employer demands.

## Analysis

Details of data analysis are contained in the following chapters. Throughout the analyses descriptive and interpretative validity were checked by the return of transcriptions, and interpretations, of interviews to respondents for checks on accuracy wherever possible. These analyses are presented in the following order:

- Chapters 3 to 5 focus on higher education. Chapter 3 charts teacher conceptions of core and generic skills and Chapter 4 identifies patterns of course provision. This is followed by an analysis of student perceptions in Chapter 5.
- Chapters 6 to 8 focus on aspects of employers and employment. Chapter 6 presents the findings from stage two of the study, on employer-led initiatives in skill development, and Chapter 7 portrays employers' perspectives, prior to a consideration of those of new graduate employees in Chapter 8.
- Finally, we discuss the findings and their implications in Chapter 9.

# 3

## Beliefs and Conceptions of Teachers in Higher Education

Barnett (1990) argues that higher education is facing a crisis to do with the way in which we understand higher education, the fundamental principles on which the idea of higher education has traditionally stood, and the way in which these principles are being undermined. As indicated in earlier chapters, debates about roles and principles are likely to be undermined by what could be characterized as a further crisis: that of the poor conceptualization of the central concepts and the terminology relating to generic skills, which means that change in this area may be premised on shaky foundations. Although problems within the rhetoric are clear, there have been no empirical studies on the conceptions and understandings of those who are actually involved in generic skill provision. Yet the conceptions of teachers are likely to be crucial in determining curriculum change and innovation. Fullan (1991: 117) states that 'change depends on what teachers do and think – it's as simple and as complex as that'.

In this chapter, a brief outline of literature on beliefs and conceptions of teaching is examined as a background to the issues of generic skill development. This literature suggests that change is highly dependent on beliefs and conceptions. For this reason, curriculum change that is not consistent with belief systems may be difficult to bring about. The rest of the chapter is devoted to the beliefs, conceptions of teaching and attitudes to change of the 32 academics involved in the study, thereby giving a picture of why it is that change relating to generic skills may not be easy.

The role of beliefs is thought to be central to what teachers provide for students, and to how they perform. Angeles (1981) describes how teachers interpret, explain and structure their thoughts and practices through what he calls their 'educational world view'. Such a view is echoed by Schoenfield (1985), who contends that beliefs shape cognition, even when people are not consciously aware of holding those beliefs, that is, when they are implicit.

Research on teachers' *implicit* theories has been characterized by Clark and Peterson (1986) as attempting to make *explicit* the frames of reference through which teachers perceive and process information. This is on the assumption that a teacher's cognitive and pedagogical behaviours are guided by, and make sense in relation to, a personally held system of beliefs, values and principles. They also argue that what teachers say and do is mediated by contextual constraints. In short, contexts can in various ways, either enable or constrain the enactment of teacher theories in practice.

Studies of teacher beliefs or conceptions and their relationship to practice at tertiary level are few and theoretically unsophisticated. Biggs (1996) identifies two broad theoretical traditions. The objectivist tradition is based on the dualism between knower and known; knowledge exists independently of the knower and understanding is coming to know that which already exists. Teaching such decontextualized knowledge is a matter of transmitting it and learning is accurately receiving it, storing it and using it appropriately. This view is, he claims, still the dominant theory of teaching and learning in present use. Within the second tradition, based on constructivist theories of learning, it is claimed that meaning is created by the learner, not imposed by reality or transmitted by direct instruction. Thus the learner, rather than the teacher, is seen as central in the creation of meaning. Although this seems to be the dominant espoused theory in terms of learning, Biggs claims that it is not a common theory-in-use in higher education. Studies by Fox (1983), Dall'Alba (1990), Samuelowicz and Bain (1992), Gow and Kember (1993), Prosser *et al.* (1994), and Trigwell and Prosser (1996) all present findings that broadly conform to Bigg's classification. It is also agreed that teaching by transmission is far more prevalent than, for example, teaching with the specific purpose of changing student conceptions.

A common concern in these studies is the need for, and the difficulty of, changing teachers' conceptions. It is believed that conceptions are heavily connected to emotional and motivational conditions, as well as to value-loaded belief systems. For these reasons, they are resistant to substantial restructuring (Pintrich *et al.* 1993; Bromme and Tillema 1995).

To summarize, studies of teachers' conceptions in higher education have been limited to descriptions of the espoused theories of small samples of lecturers, on the assumption that teaching practices are underpinned by such conceptions. To date, this assumption has not been tested by observing actual practice, despite indications that the relationships between beliefs and practice are mediated by a range of contextual factors. Common conceptions have been identified and these have been categorized into a crude teacher versus student-centred dichotomy, leading to the conclusion that teachers in higher education have limited conceptions of both teaching and of learning. These findings may, however, have as much to do with procedures for sampling, data collection and analysis, as with conceptions of teaching.

To achieve a better understanding of conceptions and beliefs about teaching, about the role of generic skills within this and about attitudes towards change, all 32 teachers in the sample were interviewed. It was anticipated that interviews would provide complex data with a wide range of individual perceptions, conceptions and personal views set within the context of their own teaching. They were also asked to complete a questionnaire in order to provide background data to the interviews. In the descriptions below, interview and questionnaire data are taken together so as to build up a consistent picture.

The areas covered are:

- beliefs about the purposes of higher educaton;
- views on structural change of courses – modular degrees and assessment;
- conceptions of learning and teaching;
- core skills, key skills and career development;
- attitudes to change.

From all the responses gained, there was little evidence of clear distinctions between teachers at 'new' universities in comparison to 'old', nor of marked differences between younger staff and older. There was evidence, however, of clear trends in responses.

# Beliefs about the purposes of higher education

The concept of generic skill development relates, at least in the rhetoric, to the more utilitarian approaches to higher educaton and graduate preparedness for employment. If it is deemed important for there to be a cultural shift in terms of the purposes of higher education, with a significant change in emphasis towards employment skills or employability, then it might be expected that this view would be shared by academics. It was therefore of interest to know the views of those academics who deliberately incorporated elements of such skills into their teaching.

Table 3.1 outlines views on the purposes of higher education, taken from questionnaire data. All teachers indicated (predictably) that higher education should provide disciplinary knowledge and skills. Just over half think that universities should promote academic excellence above all else. Although two-thirds believe that education should be provided for its own

*Table 3.1* Trends in beliefs about the purposes of higher education

| | Strongly agree (%) | Agree (%) | Disagree (%) | Strongly disagree (%) |
|---|---|---|---|---|
| **The main purposes of higher education should be to:** | | | | |
| provide education for its own sake | 38 | 28 | 28 | 6 |
| provide disciplinary knowledge and skills | 66 | 34 | – | – |
| promote academic excellence above all else | 19 | 38 | 44 | – |
| equip students with skills for employment | 34 | 59 | 6 | – |
| prepare students for the world of work | 28 | 59 | 13 | – |

sake, almost all consider that students should be equipped with skills for employment and that preparing undergraduates for the world of work is part of their role. This, however, does not give any indication of the ways in which such preparation should be achieved; it could mean that the most traditional of academic provision is perceived as appropriate for this purpose. Written comments indicate that skills for employment may be important but emphasize the role of disciplinary knowledge, and that 'higher education is not vocational training and should remain distinct from the latter'.

All the teachers agree that employers should be encouraged to speak out about what they want in graduates and none feel that they should refrain from commenting on undergraduate provision. However, they are more cautious about their being involved in decision making on the provision of programmes of study, with 29 per cent believing that this should not occur.

From interviews, it seemed that few teachers were accustomed to articulating their beliefs. Asked about the purposes of higher education, one academic replied:

> That's a very difficult question. Almost certainly [a degree] is to do with broadening the mind in a very general sense. I don't think it's to get people good jobs, that's not my own personal view. I think it's primarily about education, but not necessarily education within a specific discipline.

The comments presented below illustrate a variety of beliefs about the purposes of higher education, including personal, social and intellectual aspects:

> I think, well to me, it's education in the broad sense of the word. It's about developing the mind, about acquiring specific knowledge and critical abilities, and then it's about growing up, and [a degree] is a very special thing to do.

> . . . it's all about self-development and being aware of society and culture.

> . . . actually learning about learning rather than just acquiring learning.

> I don't actually think it matters too much what you do for three years as long as you do something which is challenging in some sort of intellectual sense.

> I really want them to remember that it is not competitive . . . It allows them to acknowledge for themselves that they won't be the best at everything, and that there will be people around who will know more, and that if they don't know they can ask.

> . . . there is a process of [personal] maturity that has to happen and there is also a process of intellectual maturity, and the teaching or the learning at higher education level is about that process of intellectual maturity . . .

I can think back to my own time and things that were always important to me were the very strong messages people gave to me, affirming that I could learn things and their belief that I would do well. Those are the things which have sustained me over the years, not really academic content at all.

There was only one succinct but comprehensive statement from an academic who seems well rehearsed in pursuing a somewhat different stance:

Clearly there are a variety of purposes which at one end can be personal agendas, individual development; but I suspect for society as a whole that the principal purpose of undergraduate programmes must be to enhance the skills of the students so they can contribute more effectively when they enter the world of work. That, I am sure, is the government's principal agenda and I suspect it is often very much the student's principal agenda too, in that they hope that having an additional significant qualification will enhance their marketability and ultimately improve their life chances in the job market.

## Views on structural change of courses: modular degrees and assessment

A consequence of the increased intake of students in higher education has been a wider variety in student needs. This, in turn, has led to the recommendation to universities to provide modular, rather than linear, degrees so that students can study across disciplines and accumulate credit as and when they are able. The change to modular degrees also provided an opportunity to rewrite content and give attention to new requirements and outcomes such as generic skills.

A few of the teachers interviewed did not consider modularization to be a major issue, or were supportive to the extent that: 'we're stuck with them [modules] now, so we'll have to get on with it'. Only one academic demonstrates a real commitment to modularization (and to a style of imagery and jargon that has not been embraced by others):

Many degrees are Fordist in their nature. They consumerize the student and the student just gets a black model two Ford [car], just a degree. The modular degree is post-Fordist and offers selection to the consumer, the student, but it also offers flexible specialization of the staff member . . . I think the linear degree has long had its day, they are too inflexible, they are authoritarian and they are inexpert.

Many commented on the promotion of better description of courses, with attention to skills and learning processes as a consequence of rewriting for modules, but otherwise with a total lack of reconceptualization of content or of teaching methods. As further outlined by the speaker above:

. . . to go from one to the other you have to redesign. In most departments in Britain they have just divided up their old linear courses. You
have got to re-conceive a module, you have got to think of the topic of
the module and you have got to thematize it . . . I see no deficits except
the fact that it makes the staff work a bit harder.

Although the majority of these university teachers support innovation and
change in general, interviews highlighted that many believe the move to
modularization to be constraining, inflexible and inviting an ethos that
works against learning. It is perceived as aggravating the potentially negative aspects of assessment, so that students are encouraged to work only for
the final assessment and to move on to the next module with no consideration of its links with others:

. . . when it finishes they will leave that module and put it at the back
of their mind, they'll go onto the next one . . . I think that's the nature
of assessment, that more often than not students learn to pass the
assessment rather than think about the learning.

In addition, it is considered that there is less time for extended or progress-
ive feedback in a system where students are constantly moving on to the
next module:

I think we are going backwards. We are now in a situation where we
have a limited amount of assessment. The tendency is to load the
summative aspect at the expense of the formative. If you take now
compared to two years ago, we do less formative assessment and therefore less feedback on progress . . . it must leave them undirected.

It is felt that it becomes difficult for teachers to encourage or build links
between modules. Where, for example, generic skills are taught in level one
modules, supposedly as an essential foundation for the future, students may
be given no opportunuties to practise and develop them further in the
course of a degree. It is also stated that it is becoming increasingly difficult
to plan for any aspects of continuity and progression in teaching or learning, although a skill-mapping exercise across one department suggested
that, at least for modules taken within the department, it would be possible
to maintain better control over this.

Questionnaire responses highlighted some further issues of assessment
and its purposes. Table 3.2 outlines that few believe that a major purpose
of assessment should be to satisfy the requirements of a 'normal curve'.
Fifty-eight per cent suggest it is not about the provision of summative grades,
despite the feeling of being pushed into this by modularization. There is
considerable support for the provision of information on student progress
and provision of feedback, especially on learning processes. Developing
individual potential in learning and enabling students to evaluate themselves are also seen as important. These figures suggest an element of
espoused theory, rather than theory in use: although many of the teachers

*Table 3.2* Views on the purposes of assessment in higher education

| | Strongly agree (%) | Agree (%) | Disagree (%) | Strongly disagree (%) |
|---|---|---|---|---|
| **The main purposes of assessment in higher education should be to:** | | | | |
| provide summative grades | 25 | 19 | 47 | 9 |
| satisfy the requirements of a 'normal curve' | – | 13 | 47 | 40 |
| provide feedback on end-products | 31 | 50 | 19 | – |
| provide feedback on learning processes | 44 | 53 | 3 | – |
| develop individual potential in learning | 62 | 34 | – | 6 |
| enable students to evaluate themselves | 56 | 34 | 9 | – |
| provide information on student progress | 59 | 28 | 13 | – |

observed were innovative, there remains a strong emphasis in departments, and within institutional structures, on more formal and traditional forms of assessment where summative grades are of real concern. In the terms of Samuelowicz and Bain (1992), this would be an example of the difference between an 'ideal' and a 'working' conception of teaching.

Angeles (1981) explains possible reasons for this. He describes how the outcomes of learning must correspond to the original purpose of education if a 'world view' is to be consistent and functional. Angeles suggests that this is unlikely to be the case. He takes the example of a physics teacher who, in a traditional paradigm, views the purpose of education as the development of critical thinking and problem-solving skills (Entwistle 1984). However, a traditional epistemological approach assumes that learning is a quantitive increase in knowledge (Ramsden 1992) and that understanding will increase in proportion to the quantity of facts learned. Hence teaching is premised on the promotion of methods to increase knowledge, whether through traditional lectures or through innovatory advanced technology. Involving students in the *process* of science is considered an inefficient waste of valuable instructional time.

In this context, assessment is the measurement of the quantitative increase of knowledge. Teachers have to satisfy the stated objectives required for graduation and provide enough factual knowledge for students to succeed in standardized examinations; so long as students pass these examinations, it does not matter if the stated purposes of education are not achieved.

Similarly, many academics demonstrated that they are used to assessing products, not processes. Processes are expected to contribute to the end product and it is this final outcome that counts towards degree accreditation, not assessment of the processes themselves. The present pressures for accountability and quality reinforce this situation. Some of the case studies in the next chapter do, however, reflect attention to a variety of different forms of assessment, feedback and self-evaluation.

*Table 3.3* Perceptions of characteristics and abilities of 'good learners'

| | Strongly agree (%) | Agree (%) | Disagree (%) | Strongly disagree (%) |
|---|---|---|---|---|
| **Good learning is characterized by students who:** | | | | |
| exhibit high level skills in writing | 19 | 53 | 28 | – |
| exhibit high level skills in oral communication | 19 | 56 | 25 | – |
| are able 'problem solvers' | 59 | 31 | 9 | – |
| are able to evaluate their own progress | 50 | 31 | 19 | – |
| can 'think for themselves' | 66 | 31 | 3 | – |
| demonstrate understanding of basic concepts in a discipline | 69 | 31 | – | – |
| can memorize facts and information | 13 | 38 | 31 | 19 |
| can relate theory to practice | 56 | 40 | 6 | – |
| can apply disciplinary knowledge/skills in practical contexts | 69 | 22 | 9 | – |
| can perform at high levels in examinations | 9 | 31 | 44 | 17 |

## Conceptions of learning

As a background to investigating conceptions of learning, the questionnaire was used to propose some of the features that might be displayed by 'good learners'. These are outlined in Table 3.3.

'Good learners' are thought to be those students who can 'understand basic concepts'. This is rated the most highly, followed by the ability to 'think for themselves', to be an able 'problem solver' and to apply learning in practical contexts. High-level skills in writing and in oral communication are not so highly rated. Performing at high levels in examinations (61 per cent disagree), and the ability to memorize facts and information (50 per cent disagree), are considered by far fewer academics to characterize 'good learning'. Again, an element of the 'ideal' as opposed to the 'real' is evident, as the assessment systems in the main, in the institutions studied, reflect the essential need for written, memorization and examination skills and techniques.

From the interviews, it became apparent that a major problem in asking academics directly about how students learn is that it is not, in general, an issue that they are used to addressing: 'I just don't think I know how people learn', 'I don't know the answer to how students learn except to say that I am quite persuaded that they learn in very different ways'.

Several talk about their module or course in terms of how the learning is planned and how this relates to their provision for learning, or to their role as teacher:

- In terms of generic skills:

  They are not brought back to drink at the trough again and I think that is why over time they narrow into a small rut of learning techniques which they don't really get out of. I think good messages fade with time if you don't return to them, this is why you [must] have a spiral curriculum in skills – you keep coming back.

- Learning by doing, they learn more than by being told. This [module] is all about training rather than teaching, preparing them for things that will actually happen, preparing them for specific events, meetings, doing different things. Then learning from feedback . . . explain where they've gone wrong, or where they've gone right . . . making sense of why it did. I don't feel that I teach, I feel that I train, trying to raise an awareness, but I don't know if you can draw a specific line between the two.

- A comment such as: 'We've shifted the time to dealing directly with students . . . to me that is quality of learning' does not address directly *how* students learn but implies that face-to-face communication is important. In this department, there has been a decision to reduce the amount of work to be handed in and marked, as well as the staff hours that used to be spent on preparing model answers, in order to achieve personal contact with students.

- The following statement was one of the most clear, and the intentions for learning deliberate and planned. Yet it is concluded in a tentative manner:

  Well, in as much as it is something you learn through doing, yes it is very much a hands-on course with a certain amount of support and a step-by-step approach, with revision if you like. You learn these things through practice and when I wrote the [work] book I deliberately had some repetition, sections where they had to do it without looking back at the instructions, so I feel that I made an attempt at trying to take account of how I think people learn.

- One member of the sample demonstrates that he has thought deeply about the organization of teaching and learning experiences in relation to his own discipline. It would be easy to interpret his discussion as an example of an academic not wanting to let go control of learning but the issues may be more important than this, as they reflect tensions in the provision of learning experiences, which are not easy to resolve:

  I think it is a very difficult area. If understanding in a subject area is about forming big pictures and perhaps forming very clear ideas of relationships between different areas, then you need help with that process. You've got to form your own big picture, but somebody has actually got to do a lot of sieving for you. And the problem is that it is very easy for us to deliver something to students which is actually simply the pieces of the jigsaw. What we don't give them is the picture on the cover which they are supposed to make out of these pieces. So they think they're doing something because these bits fit together.

On the other hand, if you say to them, 'well here is the big picture', then they will say, 'well I don't need to know the jigsaw because I'll just use the picture'. So there is something in the interface between this, the big picture has got to be delivered at the beginning, slowly in some way, otherwise they don't bother to put the bits together; on the other hand the picture has got to be there, otherwise it's nonsense.

Within these views, the organization of learning figures strongly. An area that is not specifically talked about is that of transfer of learning. Transfer is considered by many educationalists and psychologists to be one of the most crucial aspects of effective learning, at every level of education and training – in school, in higher and further education and in the workplace (see, for example, Blagg *et al.* 1993; Brown 1994; Eraut 1996). The notion of transfer is also enshrined in the term personal transferable skills. Yet 'transfer' of learning is not something that is familiar to many of these academics. This should not be considered surprising, as discussion of such issues is not a part of the academic culture.

The concept, however, is one that was addressed implicitly in the context of modularization, as outlined above. Also, some of the courses observed, and the context of these courses in relation to progression and development, give evidence of planning for transfer: that is, through the gaining of new skills to be applied at a later point, through knowledge and skills being developed in increasingly complex contexts or through acquired skills being developed in the context of more complex knowledge bases.

It is not easy to determine whether this is evidence of deliberate planning for transfer, of spontaneous and unexamined beliefs about learning or of the nature of organization of knowledge within a specific discipline. In this context, Eraut's (1997) notion of the 'cost' of transfer might be one that is as important in higher education as it is in the workplace, where this concept was first explored. If learners are not able, or are not enabled, to transfer knowledge and skills across contexts – if learners do not make connections between their learning experiences and are not required to practise, apply and reapply skills – then it may be that the value of many experiences is lost. In economic terms, an implication of this could be that learning that is 'lost' is money that is wasted for students.

## Core skills, key skills and career development skills

The teachers for this study were selected to represent courses with an explicit focus on generic skills. At the time the study was set up, the term 'core skills' was widely in use to denote such skills (conceived as non-discipline-specific and potentially transferable to the workplace). For this reason, academics were interviewed not about about 'generic' skills, but 'core' skills. However, as discussed in Chapter 2, 'core' skills are most often seen by academics as those that are central to their discipline. This does not reflect the utilitarian, employer-led or vocational view but rather the common meaning of the word 'core' as something that is 'at the heart of' or 'central to . . .'. As most academics perceive their teaching above all in terms of their discipline, it is not surprising that disciplinary skills are seen as the core skills: 'To me it would mean the things that are an integral part of what they ought to be doing for their particular subject area'.

For some, there is a clear distinction between discipline-specific and more general cross-disciplinary skills:

> I think there is a difference between core skills and personal transferable because, as I understand it, personal transferable skills could relate to any discipline, they could be things such as capacity to take notes, organize yourself for study time, that sort of thing, but core skills I would see as being discipline related. I would see the core skills as having an intellectual discipline element.

Whether discussed in terms of 'personal transferable' or 'core' skills, the connection with disciplinary study remains firm: 'I see the ability to research, get their materials together, get their argument together and select their topic as essential core skills, which of course will be transferable, but I am thinking here in terms of the discipline.'

The term 'core skills' is considered by others to have the same meaning as 'transferable skills': 'I personally would see them as being exactly the same things', or differences between the two are seen as 'a grey area' or 'murky ground'. Most of those interviewed feel reasonably comfortable with the concept of transferable skills: 'Well I guess that they are skills that you can acquire in higher education that are transferable to the world of work or indeed non-work, not discipline specific' or 'I would use the word transferable skills for things such as how to organize themselves when doing an oral presentation, to time management, data handling and IT. These are things that make them employable in areas outside their field of study.' One academic admits: 'I am on a learning curve with these things.'

The term 'core skills' can be seen to have a variety of almost diametrically opposed interpretations, which is probably not helpful in bringing about change in higher education. As explained in Chapter 2, this feature led to the adoption within the study of the term 'generic skills', so that some of the confusion might be avoided.

The term 'key' skills (see National Vocational Qualifications for 'key' skills; Dearing Report 1997) is already becoming more widely used. Included in key skills are communication, numeracy and IT. A large proportion of the teachers interviewed consider that higher education should be responsible for ensuring that all graduates have these kinds of skills. They believe they should take some responsibility to ensure that graduates are highly literate (75 per cent), have basic skills in numeracy (66 per cent) and have a foundation in IT skills (72 per cent). Departments do emphasize IT skills and many have special provision for this. Some academics feel that literacy and numeracy in particular should be achieved by schools and that this is not the responsibility of higher education. Many believe that the widening intake has led to problems that they would prefer not to have to cope with. To overcome such problems, one of the institutions in this study was developing basic foundation programmes, available to all students.

When asked about the integration of key skills from the national framework into programmes of study, two-thirds thought this might enhance student learning, though only half indicated that this would be worth encouraging. Just over half believed that this would conflict with existing provision. Three academics did not respond to this question, beyond stating that they knew nothing about such qualifications.

Student career development is an area that relates closely to awareness of employer requirements and skill acquisition. Ninety-seven per cent of these teachers felt that career development should be fostered within departments; 62 per cent considered that it should be integrated into programmes of study, although 20 per cent thought that it should be kept outside academic learning. Over half also felt that students should be persuaded to pursue this independently, a comment being that individuals should 'exercise autonomy and show initiative *re* their career'.

## Attitudes to change

It became clear during the course of this study that changes in the curriculum or in its manner of delivery are not always supported by all members of staff in any department. Statements such as the following were not unusual: 'How dare you assume that we all agree. I fundamentally and categorically do not believe that these skills have anything to do with a university degree.' This person, despite his feelings and against his better judgement, had been teaching a course that was dependent on generic skills. The same person later stated: 'It's not the students who need these skills, they've probably already got them. It's us, we simply don't know how to teach them [skills].' What on the surface seemed like a strong belief in a need to maintain traditional standards, he admitted later as a personal insecurity.

However, a central issue remains, as voiced by one teacher:

> Increasingly what we are asking them [academics] to do is to get interested in the psychology of teamwork or the assessment of verbal presentations and so on, or enhancing people's portfolio of interpersonal skills. They are just not the right people to do it, they have got no interest in it, they are not prepared for it, they are not trained for it. I think there is an enormous tension therefore between the kind of

*Table 3.4* Trends in beliefs about change in higher education

| | Strongly agree (%) | Agree (%) | Disagree (%) | Strongly disagree (%) |
|---|---|---|---|---|
| **Higher education should, in general:** | | | | |
| take account of the changing needs of society | – | 56 | 34 | 9 |
| defend a traditional approach to educational provision | 13 | 25 | 53 | 9 |
| change radically in response to differences in recent intake | – | 34 | 66 | – |
| respond to the needs of individuals | 44 | 50 | 6 | – |

people that we have got in HE and the kind of expectations that the government has of what HE ought to be delivering in terms of student capabilities.

Table 3.4 suggests that teachers may often be somewhat cautious about embracing change. Many from among this group of teachers (43 per cent) do not feel that higher education should take account of the changing needs of society; two-thirds do not want radical change, although a similar number would not defend traditional approaches either. Responding to the needs of individuals is, however, seen as important. One academic comments: 'A "quality" degree programme provided for able, articulate and motivated students will always produce excellent output and should not be influenced by transient trends/fads in the thinking of government/society.'

A few suggest that a real drive for change is essential: 'We have to change, to further the mind sets of students and staff.' The role of enthusiastic staff is seen as central within departmental efforts:

I had to drag quite a few of my colleagues along with me. You have to have a bit of good luck in having two or three people around and [you need to] nurture them, support them and encourage them. If they ever get despondent, I suppose one can go in and say, 'hey, you are really doing pretty well after all' – a bit of team spirit I think. Everywhere you will find a few enthusiasts and missionaries, but to make the thing really work across the board, in all courses for all students, you need a cultural shift.

A further problem is that some individuals feel they do not know how to go about promoting change: 'TQA [Teaching Quality Assessment] gave us a terrible shock. We do actually want to better the way in which we teach.' The need for knowing about models of teaching and learning is discussed in this context. There is a perception that knowledge and information about teaching will enable colleagues to understand the necessity for change and how it might be attained.

There is little evidence in this group of teachers of planning for the future through knowledge of models of change, whether institutional, departmental or personal. Nor is there any indication of knowledge of learning theory or the use of models of teaching and learning. Phrases such as 'student-centred learning' or 'autonomy' seem to have crept into the vocabulary of some of them. But it is difficult for individuals to develop meaningful interpretations and connections with conceptions of teaching and learning and the nature of disciplinary study if, as in the words of one member of staff: 'HE institutions are simply not set up for this kind of discourse.'

Other kinds of institutional tension are also described as creating problems: 'The paradox is that our younger staff here are more committed to research than our older staff and I think the problem might be getting worse.' The current criteria of the research assessment exercise mean that researchers are more highly valued than teachers. Those in our sample, all of whom were recommended for their practice in teaching, had mixed views on their own role with respect to teaching and research, as shown in Table 3.5.

Seventy per cent of the sample see themselves as researchers; 90 per cent see themselves as teachers. Hence the majority of this group consider they have both identities. This is said by them to create tensions, and these tensions are reported as greater in some departments than others. Table 3.6 outlines some perceptions of the relationship of research to teaching.

*Table 3.5*   Perceptions of roles

|  | Strongly agree (%) | Agree (%) | Disagree (%) | Strongly disagree (%) |
|---|---|---|---|---|
| **Do you perceive yourself primarily as:** | | | | |
| a researcher | 25 | 45 | 30 | – |
| a teacher | 33 | 57 | 5 | 5 |

*Table 3.6*   Perceptions of the relationships of research to teaching

|  | Strongly agree (%) | Agree (%) | Disagree (%) | Strongly disagree (%) |
|---|---|---|---|---|
| **Staff involvement in personal and/or departmental research:** | | | | |
| will enable better quality teaching | 28 | 50 | 19 | 3 |
| will detract from the provision of teaching | 3 | 9 | 62 | 28 |
| is essential to a career | 53 | 38 | 6 | 3 |
| creates a tension with provision of quality teaching | 25 | 31 | 40 | 6 |
| is the prime motivator of this department | 28 | 40 | 28 | 3 |

Over three-quarters of these academics believe that research will lead to better teaching. Only 12 per cent think that research will detract from the provision of teaching, but more than half feel that there is a tension between the two. Ninety-one per cent consider that research is essential to a career, and 68 per cent feel that research is the prime motivator within their own department (half of these were from the 'new' institutions). Several are adamant that change in teaching practices will not be seen as important unless the emphasis on research is lessened, or until research on teaching is valued by all the disciplines and within the research assessment exercise. One academic in a traditional university was positively discouraged from writing about teaching because it was seen as 'low status' research.

In a prior study (Dunne 1995), it became evident that staff providing skills-based courses often felt isolated, unsupported and criticized for attending to teaching rather than to research. Similar comments were made in this study and the issue was raised that there is no extrinsic reward for working at teaching: 'I suspect my colleagues would say there is very little recognition for teaching. You don't get chairs for being innovative in the curriculum or for producing really successful programmes, but that is another big agenda.'

Questionnaire responses suggested that developing skills-based courses was time-consuming and that it demanded greater attention to course planning of outcomes and the processes of learning than more traditional modules.

## The relationship of beliefs and conceptions to practice

In general, stated beliefs could not be used as predictors of those who are likely to promote generic skills and how this would be achieved. In cases where skill teaching is explicit, where there is little disciplinary content because of a focus on skills, where a course is named, for example, 'transferable skills' and where such skills are assessed, teachers are more likely to support a utilitarian approach to higher education. Hence practices may, but do not always, provide evidence of beliefs about higher education.

Commitment to certain kinds of teaching approaches and skills comes from different expertise or motivations and almost every academic in our sample tells a different story. Some of these are outlined below:

- Entirely personal – a serious illness and associated counselling pursuaded one teacher that close attention to individuals in interactive contexts, and the encouragement of cooperation and teamwork, had to be important.
- As a consequence of professional development through, for example, working in higher education in Australia or the US.
- As a consequence of prior expertise – those who have come from industry may be particularly concerned with preparing students for employment

but have different convictions about the importance of generic skills. For example, perceptions that:

(i)   a traditional focus on knowledge is the most important aspect of a degree, though generic skills are a useful 'by-product' of the processes by which students are expected to learn, such as teamwork
(ii)  generic skills underpin a student's ability to function well throughout university as well as in the workplace and are therefore emphasized early in the degree programme and are assessed to reinforce their importance.

• As a consequence of the nature of the subject – one teacher saw his own subject and department as lacking status and was determined to remedy this through gaining a strong reputation and recognition for skills development.
• As a consequence of the nature of the institution – a commitment to raising the status of the institution as a whole, with generic or transferable skills seen as a vehicle for doing this.

Each of these is apparent in the personal practices of teachers or in the institutional and departmental commitments.

Beliefs and conceptions about teaching and learning gained from interviews may, or may not, be reflected in practices. Contexts such as those imposed by modularization or large numbers mean that teachers may not operate in their preferred way. Those who are most aware of their own beliefs seem often to be those who have struggled, or who are still struggling, perhaps with little support, to bring about fundamental change. Those who are most explicit about their own beliefs and practices are those who have had most occasion or need to talk or think about them. This may occur in the context of being a departmental or university representative, or in relation to a higher degree. In several instances it was reported as happening because a spouse or a close friend is a school teacher or a psychologist, and talking about teaching occurs outside the place of work.

## Discussion

In recent years, higher education has been subjected to many changes; access has been widened, accountability and efficiency have become key concepts and structural changes such as modularization have been achieved. However, developments in teaching and, in specific, the requirement to promote generic skills, seem to remain problematic.

The situation is not helped by the term 'core skills' having a wide range of individual interpretations and associated practices. Stalker (1996) took, from the German philosopher Adorno, the notion of an 'unfulfilled concept', indicating one that: 'is not sufficiently coherent in the abstract to be fully "realised" in practice'. The term 'core skills', with its many interpretations, or with its lack of clear conceptualization in the four institutions under study, would seem to exemplify this notion.

Description and understanding of these difficulties and confusions may not, in themselves, enable a more focused approach to change. Indeed, recognition of difficulties has led two groups to abandon aspects of the terminology: Industry in Education (1995) no longer uses 'core skills' as a descriptor because of the range of interpretations; the 'Graduateness' project (HEQC 1996) does not pursue 'personal transferable skills' because of the difficulties associated with transfer and the connotations of skills. 'Key skills' is a term that is now widely taking over. The main problem is that changing the vocabulary does not change the conceptual and practical difficulties underpinning the whole area and it probably exacerbates the lack of clarity.

Some academics may be open to change but, at present, institutions and individuals within them seem ill-equipped to deal with what must be central to progress – how students learn. None of the changes in higher education have been premised on a framework for student learning. If it is important that academics should become more deeply involved in changes in the processes of learning and teaching then attention needs to be paid to ways in which this can be achieved and to providing appropriate support in the development of change. While university teachers find it difficult to talk about how their students learn, and seem unused to examining their own beliefs about teaching, learning or the purposes of higher education, it will remain difficult to build a culture where teaching and learning, and the role of generic skills within this, become explicit and a focus of attention.

There is little doubt that academics have strong, and varied, views about the role of higher education and their lives within it, even if they are unused to articulating these. It is also apparent from the teachers within this study that there is a deep commitment to students. There is evidence of much time, effort and thought being put into the design of teaching and learning contexts and the preparation of materials. It is not surprising that, in the main, academics do not find it easy to talk about the ideas and opinions that underpin their teaching; they are not trained to do so and they have not been expected to do so. Most practice is premised on implicit beliefs and conceptions. It seems that a professional and widely shared language for teaching, and explicit conceptualization of practices, would be useful in terms of fostering awareness of individual provision as well as for institutional planning and development. Many of the teachers involved in this study claimed that they enjoyed the challenge of responding to questions that they found difficult.

Several stated that the interviews and questionnaires made them think a great deal more deeply about their beliefs, conceptions and practices. In some cases, deeper understanding of their own practice and its impact on students has enabled them to value more highly what they are achieving; others have been prompted to alter and to develop their teaching.

It is these practices, and student perceptions of it, that are explored in Chapters 4 and 5.

# 4

# The Practices of University Teachers

It was shown in Chapter 1 that current research evidence on course provision in generic skills is patchy, despite current initiatives being implemented by the DfEE. It was further argued, in Chapter 2, that descriptions of implementation efforts will be of little value unless informed by a theoretical perspective that elucidates the relationship of generic, core and disciplinary knowledge and skills. It was to this end that our model of course provision was developed. This chapter thus focuses on the patterns of course provision observed in the four institutions. It also examines the degree to which the teachers' intentions and beliefs as described in Chapter 3, are reflected in their practice.

Details of teachers' practices were acquired from several sources, including appraisal of course documentation, observations of each course (usually on three occasions) and interviews with the teachers both before and after the observed sessions. When it was not possible to observe students being taught, because they were on placement or working independently from teachers, increased time was given to interviews, to observation of, for example, student-led teams, and to assessment of end-products. The data were analysed as case studies within the framework of the model of course provision.

The analysis resulted in a typology of six patterns of generic skill provision. Each of these patterns is defined, and then exemplified by reference to: (i) course contexts, for example, mission statements, departmental policy, demands of lead bodies, and so on; (ii) intentions and practices – goals, constraints, teaching strategies; and (iii) assessment and transfer.

## Patterns of skills provision in higher education

The six patterns are set out in Figure 4.1.

- Pattern 1 – skills provision is within the distinctive substantive and syntactic knowledge of the discipline, which are seen by the course providers as

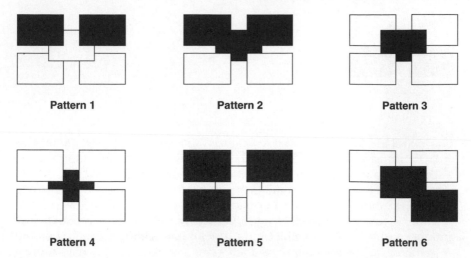

*Figure 4.1* Patterns of course provision in higher education

the core skills of the subject. Generic skills such as group work, reflection, communication, library use and so on may be used or encouraged to enhance the academic study but are of an incidental nature.

- Pattern 2 – substantive and syntactic knowledge of the discipline is developed through the purposeful acquisition and use of specific generic skills. The latter are the means by which learning of the disciplinary knowledge is encouraged and enhanced. Disciplinary and generic skills are considered of equal importance.
- Pattern 3 – there is an emphasis, explicitly, for students to acquire generic skills embedded to a greater or lesser degree in the practice of the discipline. The latter is the vehicle for skill development. The outcome of the course is clearly to acquire generic skills, developing disciplinary knowledge is of minor significance.
- Pattern 4 – the focus is exclusively on generic skills, to the extent that the disciplinary knowledge and skills acquired or used could be of the students' choice or could be entirely unrelated to disciplinary study.
- Pattern 5 – the focus is on substantive knowledge and its application, particularly in those subjects that are vocational. Insight into the workplace is through occasional contacts with employers, visits to the workplace or simulations. There is also some provision for generic skills.
- Pattern 6 – there is an emphasis both on generic skills and raising awareness about the requirements and constraints of the world of work. The context for skills utilization and development is 'real' work experience in a workplace setting. The focus on disciplinary knowledge and skills will vary depending on the purpose of the experience.

## Pattern 1

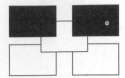

The Year 2 module *Introduction to Children's Literature* provides students with skills derived from the interests of the academic community; these are the disciplinary knowledge and skills characteristic of English literature, including skills such as interpreting and organizing information about texts, writing to justify a point of view and persuading through rational argument. The teaching in the department is underpinned by an extensive research programme and there is an emphasis on developing quality, commitment and an enthusiasm for the subject. Students are expected to: '. . . read a great deal . . . and think hard about the nature of literary criticism', but above all to develop: 'a fair degree of independence'.

The department adopts traditional means for students to develop substantive and syntactic knowledge structures of the discipline. The term 'core skills' is taken to mean these structures of the discipline, as the head of the department explained:

> . . . core skills I would see as being discipline related . . . we're looking for them to read, take notes, organize and argue. What I stress very much . . . is getting them to organize their data, leave out the irrelevant data, focus it, . . . see what's relevant and shape it into argument.

The lecturer aims to: 'provide essential information, examples and arguments, and suggest critical approaches to literature'. With 120 students taking the course: 'one cannot accommodate small group discussion work . . . so my strategy is to give theory in the lecture . . .' Books are recommended, in areas of literary criticism and theory, and books on children's literature. The lecturer provides substantive knowledge about the nature of narrative and literary criticism through the study of children's books; also about reader response. In addition, he informs the students about the syntactic nature of the discipline and about recognized forms of writing essays; the latter is seen as a means of restraining undisciplined creative writing. Thus students are enculturated into the structure of the discipline, in ways reminiscent of master–apprentice relationships.

The lecturer's intentions revolve around developing the independent thinker, within the context of children's literature: 'providing information and structuring the information that students have already got'. The 'core skills' he was hoping to develop reflect those of the department, stated in terms of the discipline: 'There are two forms of core skills – theoretical knowledge and practical knowledge. The theoretical knowledge is the theory of how to talk about text. The practical skill includes how to do it.'

Whereas the lectures provide theoretical knowledge, workshops offer students: 'experiential learning . . . the practical skill of how to *apply* theory to actual texts . . . and the practicality of talking about the text'. Both develop students' literary awareness; the skills underpinning them are essentially those of analysing texts and are concerned with the 'management of information'. There is an emphasis for students to be self-reliant (skills of 'management of self'), to develop personal opinions and to question the views expressed in books. There is also an expectation that they should 'manage time effectively' and be sufficiently confident to 'deal with constructive criticism'.

Observations at different times during the module provided evidence of the intentions of the lecturer in practice:

- It is clear that the approach to the teaching of substantive and syntactic elements of the discipline was complementary. During one lecture, students were told about 'the shape of narrative and theory of picture books' and then led on to ways of making meaning whilst reading text. In the workshop session, students read children's books to appreciate further 'the concept of text – what we can glean from the words used'.
- Another lecture provided theoretical ideas about the analysis of Kenneth Grahame's *Wind in the Willows*, used as a vehicle to discuss such issues as symbolism and characterization. It was stressed that any text is capable of generating an analytical approach, as would a serious text such as *King Lear*.
- The lecturer reiterated what was valued on the course and what would be assessed in examination. Students would be expected to: 'demonstrate your knowledge of a text – ways of thinking about it – and evaluate your own capacity of thought – your own generated thoughts. It has to be a mixture of what others think and what you think.'
- During lectures, the language of discourse reflected a rigorous intellectual pursuit of the discipline, but also there was an enjoyment factor. Students commented on the pleasures derived from reading.

Formative assessment is provided for students on their essays; feedback given on their ability to interpret information, present information and ideas competently, use information in innovative and creative ways, use information critically, justify a view and persuade rationally.

Summative assessment is by a one-hour examination, which requires students to demonstrate knowledge of children's literature and to discuss related social, cultural and literary issues. Students are '. . . given credit for knowledge . . . , but more credit for a demonstration of original thinking'. In essence, the examination tests the student's ability to think independently about the substantive element of the discipline and its application.

With regard to transfer, because writing within the module is contextualized along conventional lines, it is debatable whether writing activities can be regarded as generic. The 'management of self' skills – developing critical thinking and independent judgement – were planned to have transfer value to other courses within English literature. These thinking skills were developed through challenge and any shift in perspective was acknowledged as being within the cognitive frameworks provided by the lecturer. Thinking and writing skills were contextualized and the module was recognized by staff and students as non-vocational. The lecturer's purpose was to maintain the 'purity' of the subject as he emphasized: 'the subject of English literature is not a focus or carrier for those skills (that is, communication and interpersonal skills) . . . [students] don't like the fact that they are having to *use* the subject, and prefer to enjoy it.'

The process of applying theory is regarded as more important that substantive content and is: '. . . weighted 60–40 towards how they learn, to what they learn'. This balance reflects the importance placed upon thinking skills, especially independent critical reflection.

*Other pattern 1 courses*

The module *Analysing Architecture* is a compulsory part of the Year 2 programme in architectural studies. Seventy-one students took the module. The purpose of the module was to provide ideas and 'vision' for students to use in their design work and to encourage them to develop their intellectual abilities. The module did this by providing a conceptual framework of themes, through which students could analyse architecture in a consistent way. Students were encouraged to reflect on architectural concepts, so that the theory of: 'the strategies on which beautiful buildings have been based' is provided for them to make links with their own generative work.

The term 'core skills' was taken to mean the central tenets of the discipline, substantive knowledge as the ability to design buildings and the conceptual frameworks to aid this. These frameworks are: 'the means of making a bridge between analysis and students' own designs' and include: 'architecture as identification of place', 'space and structure' and 'geometry in architecture'. Teaching was influenced by the idea that cognition is associated with practical action. (This is of importance because it reflects the philosophy of Dewey (1946) and Layton (1991) about the enhancement of cognition through practical tasks.) Thus the lectures were strongly associated with studio project design work and with weekly exercises for students to consolidate their understanding. Oral and written feedback on these exercises was given regularly to emphasize the substantive element of a 'recognized way of doing things'. The written examination for this module also reinforced the role of substantive knowledge.

The lecturer maintained that others have: '. . . characterized architecture as problem solving but at the fundamental level architecture is about making propositions, like writing a novel, rather than solving a problem like mending a leaky roof'. It was thought that all skills practised within the module were of a 'situated nature', that is, they were contextualized, but could be transferred to other courses in architecture.

# *Pattern 2*

In a department of computer science, a Year 1 module involved 45 students in a project specifically designed to develop generic skills alongside technical computer skills. Students worked in groups of seven to eight, selected by staff so that each group contained a range of expertise. The project was student-managed, with an expectation for individual initiative but emphasizing the function of, and responsibility towards, the team. Team meetings were essential to achieve this. Each group had to provide weekly written progress reports and an end-of-project written report, to present orally to an assessor. The only information that students received was:

* a one-page overview of the project and outline of project rules;
* a one-page article (an abstract) to act as the basis for the task;
* a description of expectations for written 'weekly deliverables';
* a loan-list of books on generic skills and subject knowledge;
* information on each term members' particular expertise;
* one page describing team-building activities and 'what you can do to avoid becoming a team';
* a sheet on assessment procedures, including peer assessment.

The aims of the module were two-fold:

1. To ensure that students could apply prior theoretical knowledge of computer programming to a practical design (developing a set of technical skills).
2. To enable students to 'develop confidence and responsibility, and a set of skills that will remain with them for the rest of their lives' (generic skills).

The lecturer's intentions were for each group to produce a technical end-product, but also to focus on group processes. The groups were responsible for project management, organizing the task and completing it on time for a team presentation. Students were expected to learn to value others' skills and those with knowledge not shared by the team were expected to take on a peer-tutoring role. The structure of the task meant that group interdependence was reinforced.

Members of staff were available for consultation but considered themselves superfluous if students were responding properly to the task set. Staff did not necessarily respond in the ways that students desired; this lack of response was deliberate. Each group was known to have the necessary expertise to solve any problems and the intention was that students should read judiciously and think for themselves.

There was concern that the deliberate change in teacher role for this project, from 'leader and provider' to 'observer', could be perceived by students as 'backing out' of teaching. The designer of the course maintained that it was more to do with change in power relationships and that students had to realize that they, alone, should be responsible for learning. Much time and attention was put into setting up skill and knowledge bases before the project started, so that students *did* have all they needed to undertake the task and to solve problems for themselves. Tutors commented on the difficulty of maintaining the 'observer' stance and resisting the temptation to help students when they were struggling.

The course aims were supported by departmental aims and objectives. Observations of practice provided evidence of aims being fulfilled:

- Students were questioned rigorously during their presentations. For example, why group members had not been helped, why individuals had not asked for help and how in the final stages there was still misunderstandings of subject matter. There was praise for students who provided evidence of clarifying responsibilities, devising strategies for group coherence, delegating tasks, and so on.
- Students were also asked to defend actions and justify viewpoints; the lack of ability to do this was taken by assessors as an indication of gaps in understanding or involvement. It appeared unlikely that individuals or teams could remain unaware of their strengths and weaknesses at the end of a feedback session. Feedback also served the purpose of 'feed forward', possible because of detailed assessment of students' written submissions and notes made during the final presentation session. Final debriefing allowed students to review the project in the light of feedback; during team presentations there was much self-reported evidence of taking heed of what they had learned.

Students reported being enthusiastic from beginning to end, experiencing a sense of challenge, albeit at times coloured by frustrations. They appreciated the group composition and available expertise, simply because of gaps in their knowledge. Many reported that the practical difficulties were more problematic than anticipated, the tension was exciting and the teamwork thoroughly worthwhile. Many were sure that they could not have managed alone and reported learning from each other, in terms of knowledge and skills, revising past knowledge and talking through ideas without pressure.

Monitoring of the exercise was through the staff observers acting as 'auditors', checking for progress in occasional visits to team meetings. Auditors also read the weekly team submissions, which documented the development of the product and the learning processes of individuals and team.

However, there was no feedback to students until the project was completed. Auditors only gave guidance on misunderstandings when this was considered essential.

Each student was rigorously assessed on understanding and participation demonstrated throughout the project. Any apparent gaps in understanding were pursued by tutors through their analysis of 'audited' sessions, from written submissions or from discussion. Individual and group performance in the final presentation, including response to questioning, was included in the final project grade. A final debriefing, with all teams together, was used to pursue positive and negative aspects of their work.

Assessment focused on the learning processes as well as the final product. Students had to justify their decisions and actions in relation to both and were left in no doubt of the adequacy of their performance in relation to the assessment criteria. To emphasize self-evaluation, students were expected to monitor their performance as individuals and as team members, using criteria provided for successful groupwork. It was essential for students to comment on the contribution of peers to the team. Peer assessment sheets aided this review. Self-evaluation was also considered important in relation to meta-cognitive skills – understanding how team performance had an impact on the quality of the end-product and how they were responsible for the consequences of their actions. Summative assessment reflected the emphasis on generic and technical skills, and on individual and team progress.

|  | Generic skills (%) | Technical skills (%) |
| --- | --- | --- |
| Team | 30 | 30 |
| Individual | 20 | 20 |

Transfer to other settings, and application of prior knowledge, was central to the module aims. The workplace was frequently mentioned (for example, in terms of accountability and deadlines), so that the need for transfer was constantly reinforced. Transfer was also emphasized in relation to a second year project that was designed to build on this first year experience, in particular with regard to 'management of others' and 'management of information'.

*Other pattern 2 courses*
For a series of workshop sessions, a department of law made clear to students the differences between disciplinary skills, disciplinary knowledge and generic skills. The latter were emphasized within the variety of activities in which students were involved, the expectations for application of a range of interactive skills and the demand for active participation in workshops. The monitoring and assessment of generic skills alongside the legal disciplinary skills reinforced the centrality of both kinds of skill development.

A module, *Computer-assisted Learning in Pharmacy*, focused on teaching students new biological concepts, for example, about cell structure, and also challenging their misconceptions about disciplinary knowledge. Laboratory simulations of physiological experiments were provided and the content knowledge of lectures already attended were reinforced. Although the considerable involvement of students using computer-assisted learning (CAL) packages is regarded primarily as a means to learn new substantive knowledge and laboratory procedures, students were simultaneously acquiring the generic skills of IT and communication.

## Pattern 3

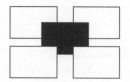

The purpose of one second year module *Spectroscopy, Including Nuclear Magnetic Resonance* is not at all obvious from its title. It consisted of three lectures and workshops and provided substantive knowledge of spectroscopy theory for 110 students. More importantly, its main purpose was to develop transferable skills, specifically in data handling.

The lecturer thought 'core skills' were the substantive and syntactic knowledge of the discipline. He believed that 'practical application' could be subject specific or generic, depending on the context, for it: 'sits on the interface between the two'. In planning the course, the lecturer was concerned to improve teaching quality (a university mission statement) and to: 'build on the philosophy of generic skills being important'.

The primary purpose of the lecture is seen as providing content knowledge, as a vehicle for generic skills:

> The course is [about] . . . the use of various forms of spectroscopy to analyse compounds, like drugs . . . The subject matter is scientifically hugely interesting . . . [but] there is not a need for this technical knowledge. So I viewed it as an opportunity to use the module as a vehicle for transferable skills.

The purpose – to develop certain generic (transferable) skills – was made explicit to the students on a hand-out: 'specifically which ones I hope they will acquire during the session'. These included: working collaboratively in groups, selecting relevant data from a mixed data bank (that is, using information critically), analysing data in different forms/representations (for example, from tables and graphs), oral presentation skills and reflecting on subject matter and skills used.

In the workshop sessions, students were given sheets of spectral data to interpret. Working in small groups, the task was to solve problems about spectroscopy. Some were text, some graphical, some diagrammatic: 'Throughout the session I stress that it is not only the subject matter knowledge that the groups have which enable them to solve the problems, it is the utilization of their group resources.'

The lecturer described that this meant that while one person tried to solve one aspect of the data, another might analyse a different section, rather than all members of the group looking at all data together. Also, weaker students could be helped by stronger students. He thought that developing data analysis skills meant:

> . . . being presented with a sheet of complex data, different data in different formats and different scales, and to be able to disentangle from that, materials which are important from ones which are not important. I think that is one skill which is generic and is important.

Skills of reflection were encouraged but, because lectures provided little chance for reflection, he: 'provided notes for them, and handouts to fill in, during the lecture'. Because the subject matter was complex, he illustrated his lecture with computer projections of animation videos, which build up concepts piece by piece. These picture sequences enabled reflection after the lecture. Students who had not assimilated the material were encouraged to communicate with staff through e-mail. The workshops provided a means of developing presentation skills and analysing data, a further means of helping students to reflect on subject matter.

Evidence collected during observations substantiates that the course provided students with activities about how to learn, in addition to what had to be learnt:

- Students were reminded during lecture and workshop of the importance of learning strategies, of reflection and group functioning: '. . . you might well want to spend a few minutes talking now, about how you will organize your group, even before I give you the data'.
- Handouts clearly stated the strategies that the students could use to solve problems, and clearly stated the core skills that it was hoped they would develop.

Feedback, as oral commentary on students functioning within a group and their collaborative skills of problem solving and data handling, was given during workshops: '. . . there is a comment, there is feedback, but not a mark.' In the examination, marks were given only for disciplinary knowledge and its application. Given the emphasis placed on developing generic skills, it is surprising to find that they were not assessed directly: 'They are not formally assessed in terms of a mark being attributed to them, separate from the (subject content) knowledge.'

One reason for this lack of formal recognition of generic skills was the problem in ensuring: '. . . an objective system for marking generic skills. I think we find it much easier to assess subject matter knowledge and to assess thinking around that subject matter knowledge, and its application to new areas . . . but the acquisition of generic skills is less easy for us to objectively assess.'

The intention was for the generic skills rather than the disciplinary skills to be transferable. The module promoted the idea that developing data handling skills and group collaboration was applicable to other courses and for lifelong learning. Spectroscopy instruments are far too expensive to run, and too time-consuming to warrant students' first-hand experiences. Therefore, the simulation practicals allowed students to carry out experimental data analyses and develop specific problem-solving skills.

## Pattern 4

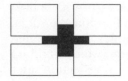

A department of geography made a significant change in curriculum provision when it was decided to entitle a set of three modules: *Transferable Skills.* The teacher who initiated the first move towards this major step recognized that not all members in the department were sympathetic to the change. Funding gained from an Enterprise project, and the additional staff input achieved by this, made it more acceptable, as did the perception that a grounding in such skills might have an impact on the quality of students' work. Institutional reorganization to create a modular, semesterized system also allowed an opportunity for development and change. Significant support from a new head of department, especially in terms of a commitment to funding, and external recognition of the quality of these modules, with additional funding attracted as a consequence of this, has ensured the continuation of these modules.

The three modules are now conceived as being core to the geography curriculum and therefore compulsory to all single honours students. Their purpose is explicit in all course documentation and the aims are two-fold:

1. To enhance students' capabilities as geographers – by, for example, focusing on study techniques or presentation skills that underpin geographical learning and will improve performance in essays, reports, projects, examinations, and so on.
2. To promote generic skills that relate to 'life after finals' and that have more of an emphasis on future careers.

Continuing positive feedback in departmental reviews has resulted in generic skill modules becoming more highly regarded by a greater number of academics within the department: 'colleagues who, 10 or 15 years ago, would have had a very different set of priorities in mind'. The module designer explains that: 'we have worked very hard at making them attractive to students because if we didn't, this could fall very badly on its face. The students come to do geography; they don't come to do skills . . . We have been determined to see it succeed.'

The actual provision of these modules remains with a small team of staff:

> You need a core team – a small number of enthusiasts who are both committed to working from a student's point of view, but also to persuading their colleagues that this is 'a good thing' . . . I had to make sure it worked because had there been serious signs of failure, I think some of my more sceptical colleagues would have taken advantage to say: this skills thing, I told you would never work.

Despite the success of the course there is still further development needed:

> There is still some way to travel . . . We have to change, further the mind-sets of students and staff . . . I still believe the agenda in higher education teaching is set largely by the research interests of individual staff rather than the needs of students . . . Which isn't to denigrate the disciplines, because it is the excitement of the discipline and the importance of what it can contribute that [provides] a motivating context for students to work in.

The design of modules has been influenced in particular by the large numbers of students – a yearly intake of some 120 undergraduates. For this reason, teaching was designed to make use of a variety of methods, which ensured coverage of material and some close teacher contact. Use is made of large group lectures and small group tutorials. A major input comes from a range of purpose-written handbooks used for independent study.

It was recognized that a separation of generic skill provision and disciplinary teaching might prove problematic and this was taken into account in the overall planning process. One advantage of separate provision is that it does not get lost by being embedded in the curriculum; it is explicit to students and other academics (internally and externally), as well as to auditors and assessors. Further, it is easier to control input and to ensure coherence and progression.

Every aspect of generic skill provision is explicit, in that the titles of themes and descriptions of content outline nothing other than skills. It is considered essential, none the less, that there should be a geographical flavour to text or to examples. For example, statistical data to be incorporated into a poster presentation (for which the only purpose is practice in visual presentation) relates to geographical comparisons. In addition, geography staff teach all generic modules, in order to emphasize to students that these skills are valued by geographers.

The content covered in modules includes:

* Module 1 – study skills, for example, approaches to learning, reading, notetaking, writing skills (planning, drafting, editing for effective writing, styles), word-processing, basic statistics.
* Module 2 – laboratory skills, for example, organization, experimental design, safety, graphicacy (visual presentation, diagrams, line drawing).
* Module 3 – verbal presentations, for example, preparation, delivery, review, group work (team roles, committees, meetings).

Perhaps the most important feature of assessment is that each transferable skills module is weighted equally with other geography modules: 'if you are not explicitly assessing the skills, students don't give them the attention that they deserve'. Modules must also be passed before access to the next stage of the course is allowed. It is intended that this should signal their importance. Students are required to complete assignments and tests, to give oral presentations, to conduct a group research project (with a report) and compose a CV and job application form.

The major problem for the designer of these courses is the form of assessment within mainstream geography modules:

> We are faced with the fact that we are assessing, essentially, the knowledge. We are giving 57s in geomorphology and 62s in urban policy, and I still wonder what this means for employers who really want to know: 'Are these people good at working in a team?' 'Are they effective communicators?' 'Can they write well?' 'Can they organize themselves to do an effective piece of independent research?' And what we are saying is, geomorphology – 57. So we have still got a long way to go.

With regard to the question of transfer, attention has been given to mapping the continued availability of skill practice and development in geographical modules throughout the degree programme. It is apparent, however, that generic skill provision organized through disciplinary-based content is comparatively fragmented and erratic, and is dependent on the interests of individual teachers. There is, however, a selection of modules and field courses which ensures that students will have to use their generic skills in new, subject-related contexts. This is considered of utmost importance in demonstrating to students that the transferable skills modules relate to disciplinary study. Observation and interviews with students suggested that, by the second year, they were beginning to perceive the links and were aware of the ways in which they needed to transfer and adapt skills to new and more complex contexts. The applicability of skills to the workplace was also reinforced in the sections of the module that dealt with job applications, CVs and 'what geographers do'. Transfer of generic skills is considered important because:

> Only 10 or 15 per cent go into professional work which is highly related to the knowledge they have obtained in their degree. After that you get into a range of careers which have a geographical element but it is not

very powerful. Beyond that there has been an element of preparation in the degree programme which is very useful but essentially they are not applying geographical skills.

*Other pattern 4 courses*

The use of free-standing courses, possibly taught by teachers who will have no further contact with the student and delivered out of the context of any discipline, is an approach that was widely adopted but soon abandoned in one institution. However, such courses may be appropriate in some contexts. For example, British Petroleum (BP) provided a short 'Team Development Programme' for students in several departments within one of the sample universities. This had the main function of making students aware of the need for team skills in the workplace. It was unrelated to any discipline in its use of outdoor exercises, although some university teachers are now working at ways in which student learning from the programme could be embedded into disciplinary study through the use of team and group work. More details are given on this programme in Chapter 6.

In education the module *The Professional and Community Education* essentially prepared students for 'lifelong learning'. It offered them opportunities to acquire a fundamental change in attitude towards others and to experience being a member of a group: for example, developing skills of being aware of the needs of others, of supporting others' learning and skills of negotiation. There was also an emphasis on developing skills associated with 'management of self'. Substantive knowledge was not offered formally and was negotiated with each student. Teaching strategies supported learner autonomy.

## Pattern 5

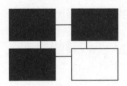

A Year 3 module *Building Design* caters for 64 students. Teaching is in the form of an apprenticeship for modern practice and students have to write a building brief and design a multi-storey building for a pretend 'client'. The context is a simplified simulation of real life; the demands of the 'client' are recognized as important, but the students work individually, whereas in the workplace there would be a team of consultants.

Underlying modules in architecture, there is a clearly articulated view about the nature of the discipline; about the tension between a knowledge base (an understanding of cultural and human needs and technologies of building) and aesthetic awareness: 'in architecture, imagination and logic,

freedom and responsibility, are not in opposition: they are in creative interdependence. The disciplines inherent in building have to be mastered if
they are to be transcended . . .'

The second tension is the balance between the rigour of academic pursuits
(including an emphasis on the history of architecture and architectural
precedent) and workplace awareness. The syllabus reflects this, guided by
an extensive research programme and strong links with practising architects.
For example, undergraduates can assist experienced architects with projects
on a commercial basis and visiting architects act as tutors or judges assessing design projects. Students' interests are protected by the lead body, the
Royal Institute of British Architects (RIBA), which can influence the syllabus. For example, in response to the criticism, in the *Strategic Study of the
Profession* (RIBA 1992), that architects were not good at relating to clients
and specialists, the module purposefully stresses the need to listen carefully
to clients, and that discussion as an 'intensive interaction' is vital.

Objectives of the module focus on training to apply substantive disciplinary knowledge and a creative element to design. The former includes:

> . . . knowledge of building types, and solutions to building problems
> which other people have done under other circumstances – we would
> call that a knowledge of precedent, . . . about the way people use build-
> ings and their needs, . . . and a grasp of building technology; various
> aspects of structures, the environment, construction materials, economics
> and so forth . . .

These technical aspects provide a particular perspective and act to restrain
undisciplined creativity. The restraint is emphasized:

> Projects can tend towards fine art, as happens in other schools of
> architecture, but here the students need to know how to create *real*
> buildings, not diaphanous paintings of the unreal. There is no point in
> developing the blisteringly unrealistic, even if creative, if at the end
> they can't get a job.

The syllabus reflects the competing paradigms of traditional architectural
practice – those of sociotechnical expert and creative artist – and emphasizes the commitment to workplace awareness. Links made with potential
employers are purposefully embedded in the module and the role of visiting professionals is seen as vital. They ensure appropriate challenges to
the students and provide a picture of current architectural thinking. The
picture – of the trends and attitudes of employers – is referred to as the
'credibility factor', contemporary ways of seeing, thinking and working, as
discrete from academe.

The module revolves around project work. Students are required to design
a building. The strategy for teaching the design process is essentially one
of constructively criticizing each student's work on a regular basis throughout
the course. It is vital for students to learn to defend their designs and argue
for the way they interpreted their briefs. Thus, at times the lecturer's role was

supportive, 'sharing perspectives' with students, whereas in critique sessions it was to elicit a justification and or an explanation for students' designs.

One vital element in the apprenticeship, generally taken for granted, is learning the specialized design language of the profession, for example, 'cladding', 'shell and core', 'split floor plate'. The importance of specialist discourse is thought to 'reinforce the identity of the profession' and learning to use the vocabulary is an important 'core' skill.

Observations provided evidence of the lecturer's intentions in practice. Students were initially told how to write a brief, as a statement of building needs. They had to listen to a 'pretend' client's detailed requirements. Working in small groups they practised writing design briefs, as a response to the client's needs. They had to rationalize their suggestions.

During one critique tutorial, students practised their presentation skills in front of a small audience of internal and external critics (visiting architects) and their peers. They needed a knowledge base and a professional language for dialogue. Students were given ample opportunity to respond to the critics' challenges, to justify their point of view. After the critique, one student acknowledged the value of the discussion, which he thought would help him to reflect on his design decisions. He explained: 'You cannot say "because I want it to be" – you cannot be simply stubborn – you have to argue the point.'

In the final critique session, judgements were made on the quality of students' drawings and models, including the extent to which the design met the client's needs, and on their: 'capacity to sell the scheme to a sceptical client – their credibility and plausibility'. Visiting architects challenged students, for example: 'Can you see any other uses for this area?', 'What if you had orientated the building differently?' – questions needing a sound professional knowledge to answer and an ability to argue. For example, one student used his model to show interior details to justify his design, and another did so with reference to an historical precedent.

The influence of visiting architects provided students with experiences required by the workplace and the lecturer thought the module to be an education towards vocational employability.

The lecturer planned for regular formative evaluation during tutorials – constructive critical feedback as described above. The module teaches specifically how 'to persuade rationally to an audience'. Periodically, as work progresses, students display their design and describe how far it has evolved. The essence of these small group presentations is one of helpful discussion.

Formal assessment of the module is a single mark for the final oral presentation of a student's design:

> . . . primarily it is about the quality of the design. But it also takes into account particularly effective or ineffective presentation . . . One can't say that half of the marks go the design of the building and a third go to something else . . . It is a single mark . . . it is a feeling, subjective, but on the part of usually three people, who come to some agreement.

Thus there is recognition of substantive and syntactic knowledge, as represented in the final drawings and models. Even though considerable emphasis is placed upon effective presentation, and abilities to explain and justify one's perspective, there is no specific mark for demonstrating these skills.

The module, prompted by its professional context, encourages those skills concerned with 'management of information', 'of task', 'of self', and 'of others', specifically transferable to the workplace. For example, the skill of 'how to choose and use appropriate media' is vital in learning to present one's design: 'They have to learn whether it should be done on computer, free-hand or by model, by orthogonal drawings ...' The skills of 'how to gather information from appropriate sources' and 'how to listen' are also vital within the module and to the workplace.

The skill of writing a design brief is important because it reflects the student's interpretation of a client's wishes. Listening carefully to needs and then using information critically to solve design problems are vital transferable skills:

> The students have to weigh evidence, because of the nature of the subject – architecture is open, not like engineering ... design decisions are infinite and therefore the students have to respond to problems when information for making decisions is incomplete – it always is!

But, above all, students have to learn to substantiate and justify their decisions. They are told that their ability to do so is a basic professional requirement, as are those skills of 'management of self', especially time management.

There are no plans to increase development of generic skills, to provide an education for job flexibility: '... I am not convinced that a course as intensive as ours, that is so closely tailored to producing people who design buildings, is a particularly sensible one for those who want a general education of some sort, that is, non-vocational.' One consequence of such a perspective is that there is little effort to 'dis-embed' the generic skills from architectural contexts and students were generally unaware that the skills they were using had potential use outside the discipline.

*Other pattern 5 courses*
The purpose of a third year module *Practice of Pharmacy* is to contribute towards the professional aspects of pharmacy. It is highly vocational. Lectures provide pharmaceutical knowledge and about the law as it relates to medicine. Practical sessions are held in a mock-up pharmacy, even equipped with telephones, to enable students to query the legality of prescriptions (staff take on the role of doctor), and a controlled drug register. This simulation of practice teaches how prescriptions are to be dispensed in real life, through carefully structured exercises. Practice at problem solving and, if necessary, repetition of tasks, lead to high degrees of accuracy.

Substantive knowledge is extensive and strictly vocational, approved by the Royal Pharmaceutical Society of Great Britain. Teaching allows students to apply their understanding of patients' needs and legal and professional requirements to the sale of drugs in conditions that mirror the workplace. There is an overriding influence on students' learning through the modelling of correctness by the teacher. Her role is unique. She is a Boots teacher practitioner, working two days a week in Boots The Chemist's pharmacy and three days a week in the university. The workplace could be hardly better represented.

Assessment of practical skills used in the formulation and dispensing of medicine occurs during each class and by practical examination. The performance of students requires accuracy and, as in real life, has to be completed within specified time limits. Considering the stressed importance of communication skills it is surprising that these are not assessed.

Another Year 3 clinical pharmacy elective, *Pharmaceutical Care Planning*, is also highly vocational. Twenty-eight students take this module, which, in a practical way, teaches students how to write care plans for patients when working as a hospital pharmacist.

The workplace, and current health team practice, is embedded in problem-solving activities. The lecturer was until recently a teacher practitioner and her colleague works each morning in a hospital pharmacy. Students examine imaginary and real (confidential) case studies of patients to consider the personal, social and drug issues that have to be considered in formulating holistic care plans. Simulations were simplified, for real life scenarios are often too complex for students to analyse. The syllabus is defined by the Royal Pharmaceutical Society of Great Britain.

Core skills are seen as the substantive knowledge – dealing with drug therapy, aspects of human physiology and psychology, and scientific aspects of pharmacy. The knowledge base also includes understanding of pharmacy law. Some skills were thought to be of a generic nature, in 'management of information' and 'management of self', and particularly in 'management of others', where students are taught to work cooperatively, respect others' views and defend and justify their views and actions.

Assessment is of the written care plan. There is no attempt to assess individual communication skills when presentations are given.

A further example in a department of engineering was unusual. Although based in the workplace, the intention was awareness-raising rather than provision for extended or assessed experience. Over a semester, engineering students undertook about ten days work in a school, supporting technology and working with children of any age between 4 and 15 years. These undergraduates, many of whom had come from a background of independent and grammar schools, went into the placements with the intention, for example: 'of providing pupils with a better experience of learning' and: 'changing what happens in schools'. They soon realized that life in school is a great deal more complex than they had appreciated; interviews showed significant changes in perception and attitudes over the weeks.

This *Independent Study* module was viewed by the organizer as an exercise in generic skills: self-management – including punctuality, correctness of dress and modes of speech, taking responsibility, giving responsive and positive input within a new context – the kinds of activity that students in this department might seldom otherwise undertake. Engineering skills were seen as essential background but it was the ongoing evaluation of self-management skills, written up in the form of a weekly review and final report, that was assessed.

## Pattern 6

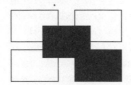

In a department of fine art, there had been a history of relationships with local businesses and organizations that made use of the talents of under-graduate artists, including participation in school and community arts projects. Students had also been encouraged to take on commissions, engage in competitions and participate in foreign exchanges. They were given advice and assistance from the institution in all these areas but any participation was entirely voluntary. Problems began to emerge: student absence from other aspects of degree provision, pressure on assignment deadlines and, on occasion, stress from taking on responsibilities and managing time outside academic work.

At this time there was a growing interest in transferable skills in higher education by several members of staff. There was also recognition that fine art graduates, on leaving, were finding it increasingly difficult to get commissions or professional work without previous experience. As a consequence, Enterprise funding was gained to enable development of vicarious work-based activities into a professional studies programme. In the first stages, an optional module was run; this later became compulsory at level two and is now supported by a second compulsory module at level three.

It was well understood that making the *Professional Studies* module compulsory would give rise to complaints and difficulties. Students, in the main, enter a fine art degree with an expectation to develop as artists. An internal research evaluation confirmed this view and made it clear that students wanted technical knowledge and skills, the opportunity to develop creative potential and to refine critical and aesthetic judgement and 'as much time as possible in the studio'. A tension resides in the fact that, as explained by one of the module designers, students perceive fine art as a vocational degree, but 'in a *literal* sense, in that you have a vocation to do something . . . they have this burning desire to be painters or sculptors'. Managing a work placement sets up a different agenda, but is likely to reflect a more realistic approach to survival as an artist after graduation.

The second year module consists of a series of lectures from professionals in art-related careers, followed by a project executed outside the academic environment: organizing an exhibition, being an artist in a school, taking a placement in a museum or gallery, taking commissions and working in community and public arts. Students were given a 'project directory' with a list of 15 possibilities, prenegotiated by staff and requiring a group of between one and ten persons.

One example of a project was the requirement for a 30-foot mural in a Go-Cart Centre: one organizer, one designer (15 points each) and a team to paint (five points each for two days' work). Fifteen points-worth of projects must be accumulated to pass the module. Students can either apply from the list or can put in their own proposal. All initiatives must be approved by a tutor and the project 'point value' agreed in advance. Making use of guidelines in the Professional Studies handbook, students complete a proposal form to outline the area of work. They estimate the length of the project, stating when and where it will take place, the resources needed, transport arrangements and a health and safety statement, where appropriate. Students also have to write a statement on expected outcomes, reasons for wanting to participate in the project and long- and short-term benefits. With tutorial support, learning contracts, called 'study agreements', are agreed and personal outcomes negotiated.

It is intended that the programme will allow students to develop a professional attitude and an understanding of fine art outside the institution. They will also experience the demands of professional obligations, such as sound time management, effective communication, sensitivity to the needs of others and working efficiently within a resource framework. These kinds of skills are presented explicitly to students as 'transferable' skills. In contrast to this view, the course designer perceives 'core' skills as discipline-based: 'very particular skills adapted for the profession – key skills like critical reflection . . . but it's subject specific . . . The ability to be visually aware, visually literate, have command over visual materials'.

Assessment was through documentation of experiences and could take a number of forms – a written report, diary with critical commentary, a portfolio of work, photographic record or a seminar presentation. Self-assessment was emphasized and a written critique could be used to contribute to summative assessment. Students were generally pleased with the learning from this exercise but found it difficult to cope with not being given feedback on their artistic achievements. However, this was not the purpose of the module.

Transfer of skills between contexts is considered problematic, but is being addressed at present:

I don't think our students are aware of what they know in what contexts. I don't think they've fully grasped the connection until they get a degree. That's why we have now been focusing on the value of feedback. It's something I'm very keen on, and has actually changed our programme delivery. We spend more time in tutorials concentrating on the acquisition of skills . . . students are encouraged to reflect in a one-to-one or group interview about what they've learnt . . . I don't think we put enough resources into the process.

*Other pattern 6 courses*
Groups of students from different universities were involved in The Shell Technology and Enterprise Programme (STEP). This promotes vacation placements in small and medium sized enterprises. Undergraduates were engaged in projects that required them to take responsibility for the application and acquisition of knowledge and skills. They had the opportunities to use and develop generic skills, especially communication, problem solving, task and self-management. They were also expected to show an awareness of the culture, the rules and the constraints of the workplace. In particular, they were expected to monitor their own skill development and to review their progress. This programme is discussed further in Chapter 6.

## Discussion

In this chapter university teachers were found to expend much thought and effort into the design and content of their courses. The outcomes of these deliberations, in terms of the patterns of skill and knowledge intended and taught for, was analysed utilizing the model of course provision developed for this purpose. The analysis resulted in a typology of six patterns of course provision, each of which has been described. These patterns are varied and indicate a number of important features.

Firstly, teachers perceive 'core' skills as those central to their discipline; thus the majority of courses required students to develop subject-specific and/or vocationally specific skills. The impact of the move to modularization has also resulted in courses that, to varying degrees, use subject disciplines as vehicles for developing wider personal skills. For example, a student in English, whilst being enculturated into the method of analysing text and shaping argument, was also developing skills of self-reliance and time management; a pharmacy student learning spectroscopy skills did so in part through developing analytical and data handling skills.

In planning vocationally orientated courses, there was equal concern with the quality of academic rigour as with realistic provision of workplace awareness. Nevertheless, very few planned for those skills associated with attitude and motivation, in spite of the known importance of affective influences on cognitive development (Boekaerts 1996). One of the few was clinical pharmacy where students are taught to care about the particular. In Barrow's words (1987: 194): 'one does not teach people to care; one cultivates the values, emotions and understanding that enable them to care.' Thus, developing attitudes and caring behaviours in students is seen within a context of subject knowledge and is considered complementary to those of higher order skills, such as decision-making, in constructing care plans. The fact that one cannot make an effective care plan for a patient without deep-level subject knowledge, illustrates the complexity of relationships between knowledge, skills and eventual workplace performance.

Modules that stressed the importance of developing generic skills often found it necessary to convince the students of their worth in relation to the core skills of the discipline. This was exacerbated by a reluctance to assess generic skills that, as will be seen in Chapter 5, was an important factor in student choice.

Lack of assessment was often grounded in perceived problems of achieving objectivity and, in some institutions, to a lack of flexibility in university examination policy. Similarly, given the claimed importance of generic skills in modules and degree programmes, it was surprising that they were not more often considered as a component in final assessments.

On another aspect of assessment, there were extreme differences in feedback policy and the way in which it was perceived to be useful to learning. In some modules there was immediate feedback to students, whereas in others feedback was delayed to provide time for students to re-think, for example, their design strategies. There was purposeful denial of some kinds of feedback, particularly where self-evaluation was conceived by tutors as the focus of learning. Students often found this difficult to accept, either because their conceptions of learning were inextricably bound to disciplinary study rather than a skills framework or because they did not like (or found it uncomfortable) to self-evaluate without the comfort of a tutor's judgement.

One of the major features highlighted in this study is the variety and complexity of conceptualization and practice with regard to skills development, the extent of its embeddedness within a discipline and the relationship of skills to the workplace. Such differences occurred within the same subject, within the same department and at different stages within a degree programme. The delineation and elucidation of this complexity has, of course, been made possible through the utilization of our model of course provision. This achievement not only provides validation for the model, it also presents opportunities for further development and use as, for example, a curriculum planning device for designers to transform purposes into practices. Staff development initiatives incorporating the use of the model have, on the basis of user evaluations, been very successful.

# 5

# Student Perceptions of Skills Development

Research on students' experiences of higher education falls into two main areas, depending on the definition of 'experience' used. It may relate to the impressions students have of a course, and their reactions to it, or it may be used in a more theoretical way, meaning the factors that influence students' perceptions of education and, as a result, have an impact on their ways of studying.

Research into higher education before the 1970s focused almost exclusively on the perspective of the teacher; it omitted the centrality of the student in the teaching and learning process (Hounsell 1984). Since the mid-1970s a coherent body of research has developed on students' approaches to learning, on how these affect outcomes and on the effect of the learning environment on strategies used. For example, Marton and Säljö (1976) claimed to observe two types of text processing, which they termed 'surface-level' and 'deep-level'. In the former, the student was suggested to use rote-learning strategies (a reproductive conception of learning). In deep-level processing, a student was more concerned with comprehension (associated with higher levels of understanding). It was found that students who consistently used a deep approach retained more of the information over time and performed better in end-of-year examinations. A similar approach was taken by Svensson (1977), who described two ways in which students organized text information: 'holistic', where they were concerned with understanding the whole text, including searching for the intention of the author; and 'atomistic', where they focused on memorizing details and specific sequences of the text, but not the overall message. The terms 'deep' and 'surface' have been further developed by Entwistle (1984), who concluded that students' intentions play a vital part in determining how they deal with information presented to them.

Research into students' conceptions of their own learning is largely based on the findings of Säljö (1979) who devised five categories. These are learning as:

1. A quantitative increase in knowledge.
2. Memorizing what is required.
3. Acquiring facts and procedures for subsequent use.
4. Abstracting meaning.
5. An interpretative process aimed at understanding reality.

This research has been replicated and the findings are now well established. Marton *et al.* (1993) contributed a sixth category, that of 'changing as a person'. The importance of this category is that, as it suggests, learning is a developmental process; students may evolve from a position of perceiving 'right' answers to one where knowledge is recognized as relativistic, each student having a considered commitment to particular point of view. These categories are markedly similar to the academics' conceptions of learning outlined in the previous chapter.

Motivation and orientation towards education (whether vocational, academic, personal or social) are thought to play an important part in determining how students will go about the learning process. With increasing recognition of the importance of context and the learning environment in determining students' approaches to learning, Laurillard (1993) found that students alter their approach to learning depending on their orientation towards the task and on their perceptions of the teaching they receive and the task in hand. Students also react to a situation as they perceive it (which is not always the way that teachers or researchers define it). Performance may depend: 'not only on ability, motivation and skills but on whether the student decides they are needed or not, in a particular situation' (Ramsden 1987). Beaty *et al.* (1997) have shown that different orientations mean different goals. For example, a goal of 'having a good time' will influence approaches to learning in a different way to one of 'self-improvement'. Another factor influencing learning is assessment and Ramsden (1991) found that the form of assessment used could have an impact on whether students took surface or deep approaches to learning. Harvey and Knight (1996) also suggest that students are more likely to adopt deep approaches if they are not overloaded with work, where they have some freedom and where the work can be invested with some relevance.

In the specific context of skills development, Holman (1995) compared three different first year undergraduate courses and found that students reported skills development in two ways: either as 'tacit and negotiated', when skills were apparently acquired almost unconsciously, or as 'rational', when individuals developed their skills in a planned and conscious way. This was most prevalent when they undertook skills modules and used learning contracts. Holman states that these experiences gave students access to a vocabulary that allowed them to label their actions, to articulate which skills required development and to plan a course of action.

As part of a research programme on notions of quality in higher education, a survey of 4000 staff and students in 16 universities and polytechnics was undertaken by the Quality in Higher Education Project (Harvey *et al.*

1992). Results indicated that the key factor in the assessment of quality was what came to be called the 'total student experience'. Features such as students feeling involved in the learning process, within a coherent and structured programme that inspires them and gives them confidence, were reported as paramount. Similarly, students being able to understand programme aims and objectives, and with assessment testing whether these specific aims and objectives had been met, were highly rated. At the time of this survey, assessment of workplace learning was not considered important in measures of quality, and teamwork was given a low rating. These particular features have been emphasized more strongly in higher education over the last few years.

The Dearing Report (1997) has recently provided information on student experiences in terms of impressions and reactions, reviewing students' opinions on life at university in general. A total of 1270 randomly selected students, from 73 academic institutions, participated. In a comprehensive survey they were asked, amongst other things, about their reasons for coming to university/college, their opinion about teaching and assessment and what skills they had developed so far during their course. Over half rated getting a qualification to pursue a specific career as most important, whereas only 25 per cent gave intellectual reasons. Students also rated the opportunity to broaden their horizons and meet new people, and skills development, as more important than academic items, such as experiencing intellectual growth and new ideas. Reasons given for choosing particular courses were grouped as 'intellectual', 'pragmatic', 'instrumental' or 'fatalistic'. Despite the predominance of 'instrumental' reasons for coming to university, the majority (71 per cent) opted for their particular course for 'intellectual' reasons. Only 5 per cent chose a programme because it was most related to their preferred future occupation.

With regard to teaching and assessment, the survey illustrated the range of methods used. Although traditional methods such as lectures (experienced by 98 per cent) and tutorials (91 per cent) were almost universal, newer learning methods were mentioned, albeit to a lesser extent. For example, almost half experienced computer-based learning and 15 per cent had been on work placements. Similarly, traditional methods of assessment, in the form of essays (87 per cent) and written examinations (86 per cent), were most common. Oral presentation, a variety of coursework activities and tasks relating to learning in the workplace were also assessed, though marks gained for oral presentation, in particular, were not necessarily included within a final degree classification.

The skills that students indicated they had developed were grouped into three categories, academic (for example, analytical, computing), personal development (for example, self-motivation, using initiative) and enterprise (for example, communication, teamworking). The skills listed appear somewhat arbitrary and it is not clear how they were selected. Terms such as communication are too vague to be meaningful and it could also be argued that some so-called skills, such as 'self-confidence', are not skills at all. The survey may provide a general overview of the current situation in higher education but there is no reason to believe that those who volunteered to complete the survey provide a good representation of the student population at large. A further criticism of the study could be the lack of any obvious theoretical base upon which to premise questionnaire items and to select skills.

## Gaining student views

Questionnaire data for our study were gained before the results of the survey outlined in the Dearing Report were available. There are similarities in some of the questions asked but a major difference is that the questions for our study relate to known courses with known outcomes. They also allow exploration of qualitative relationships between, for example, student beliefs about the purposes of a degree and motivation towards skills development. Alongside qualitative data, the questionnaire provides more than just a survey; it also allows the exploration of explanatory factors for student responses to specific courses.

Details of student perspectives on skill provision were collected not only from a questionnaire, but also from focus group interviews. All students studying the 32 modules were invited to complete the questionnaire. Student teaching groups ranged from four to 150; most contained between 20 and 50 undergraduates. For each group, between 10 and 85 per cent of the module intake returned questionnaires, giving a total of just under 400 students, who represented a range of vocational and non-vocational modules in each institution. The difference in return rate was due, in the main, to the context of teaching provision: for example, some teachers invited a group to complete questionnaires within taught time (and return rates were high); others had little, or no, direct contact with students who were studying independently (and return rates were low). Most academics felt uneasy about imposing any burden, feeling that questionnaire overload was already problematic for undergraduates.

The questionnaire covered two aspects of skill provision: first, a direct focus on the course or module just undertaken and perceptions of skills development in this context; and second, a range of broader issues relating to skills teaching and learning. These more general questions were devised to provide a background to observation and to interviews. They covered areas that were expected to impinge on perceptions and interpretations of provision, such as: familiarity with the terminology of skills, opinions on what employers consider to be the benefits of graduate education and on what they see as lacking in graduates, the purposes of gaining a degree and the kinds of learning experiences by which they are motivated and at which they perceive themselves to be successful.

Focus group interviews – usually with between four and six students – were used in order to explore specific content and processes that had been observed, as well as to gain more general perceptions on teaching and learning. This chapter reviews each of these sets of data and relates the acquisition of skills to features such as student conceptions of teaching, learning and skills development, personal motivations, the nature of course provision and the teaching and learning processes observed. The questionnaire data is presented first but on occasion is supplemented by interview material to support or develop findings and issues.

## Questionnaire responses

Almost all questions were open ended, that is, there were no prompts or suggestions as to possible answers. Categories of response were developed from the range of student replies. The figures presented in the tables below represent the number of times any point was mentioned, as students were free to give more than one response. As there were almost identical numbers of questionnaire returns from each institution, data are presented as a mean of the eight observed courses from each of the four institutions studied, thereby allowing institutional differences to be considered when appropriate. Differences apparent at the level of individual courses will be outlined later in the chapter, in the context of teacher intentions and course provision. Tables of findings present a continuum from 'most traditional' institution to 'least traditional' of the sample – in terms of history of, and approaches to, generic skills development. The traditional institutions are among the 'old universities', which, in general terms, are those least likely to adapt and change at speed, and in this case neither had been involved in Enterprise schemes, which might have encouraged the development of skills-based efforts.

### Familiarity with terminology

Students were asked if they knew the meaning of the terms 'core skills', 'personal transferable skills' and 'lifelong learning', and to provide a definition if they did. As with the university teachers involved in the study, we were interested in conceptions of the terms 'core' and 'personal transferable' skills, in the extent of recognition and understanding of their meaning and in differences between them. Students were also asked about the term 'lifelong learning' because of its associations with ongoing learning, training and skills development, as well as its being a widely used catchphrase. Table 5.1 outlines the number of students who responded to each term. Almost all responded to at least one, few responded to all three.

Lifelong learning seems to be the term that was most readily understood and for which there was little conflict of meaning; there were, however, different emphases in response. For some, lifelong learning is associated with a general, automatic, ongoing process: 'the fact that people never stop

*Table 5.1* Students familiar with terminology (percentage responses)

| | Institution | | | | Mean (%) |
|---|---|---|---|---|---|
| | Most traditional (%) | | Least traditional (%) | | |
| | 1 | 2 | 3 | 4 | |
| Lifelong learning | 55 | 45 | 42 | 60 | 50 |
| Core skills | 48 | 33 | 64 | 65 | 49 |
| Personal transferable skills | 37 | 41 | 64 | 50 | 44 |

*Table 5.2* Comparisons of conceptions of 'core' (C) and 'personal transferable' (PT) skills (percentage responses)

| | Institution | | | | Mean (%) | |
|---|---|---|---|---|---|---|
| | Most traditional (1 plus 2) (%) | | Least traditional (3 plus 4) (%) | | | |
| | C | PT | C | PT | C | PT |
| Generic | 21 | 27 | 28 | 28 | 24 | 27 |
| Career/job-related | 7 | 12 | 4 | 12 | 5 | 12 |
| Course specific/ subject-oriented | 15 | 3 | 15 | 1 | 15 | 2 |
| Personal | 1 | 12 | 2 | 8 | 1 | 10 |
| Life | 8 | 2 | 9 | 1 | 8 | 2 |

learning, even after academic study', 'You will learn things all your life, in any situation. Learning has no end.' For others, there is an emphasis on continuing formal education: 'continually taking courses or updating knowledge'. Others relate the term to aspects of self-awareness and motivation: 'You never stop learning. The amount you learn is dependent on how hard you try, how much help you get, what opportunities you get and your ability to do what you take on.' The term is also associated with the notion of keeping pace with a changing world: 'It means that things develop and never stop and that one has to adjust to them, learn about new developments and innovations.'

'Core' and 'personal transferable' skills have a variety of meanings to students. There is considerable overlap in description. Similarities and differences in conception of the two terms are outlined in Table 5.2. Responses suggest that about half the students perceive either 'personal transferable' or 'core' skills, or both, as akin to the category that we have now labelled generic skills. Definitions and examples given for each term were often almost identical: 'Skills that can be used across a range of disciplines', 'The skills developed as a part of learning, regardless of the area, for example, data handling skills, reading, writing, communication skills, and so on'. Further examples covered group work, teamwork, communication skills, presentations, group speaking and so on. Basic skills were included in this group; for example, word-processing, basic competence with numbers, English language. Overall, about one-quarter of the definitions and examples given for 'core' skills and one-quarter given for 'personal transferable' skills are included in the generic category (51 per cent altogether).

Career and job-related skills include those 17 per cent of responses that have an emphasis on employer requirements. Some are non-specific: 'presumably they are basic skills required to get a job', whereas others give examples similar to those for generic or basic skills: 'Essential skills that employers would expect to find, such as literacy, numeracy, language'. These are most often equated with personal transferable skills.

Responses touching on course-specific or subject-oriented skills (15 per cent) are, in the main, seen as being 'core': 'Skills which are fundamental and essential to the subject', 'Basic knowledge that [is] built on to become more complex. Essentially, I suppose, the bones of a subject'. This is similar to the interpretation of many of the teachers interviewed and again illustrates one of the central confusions with the term 'core' in higher education. Whereas 'core skills' are widely taken to be those skills that stand outside disciplinary study, many within higher education see them as precisely those skills that are bound to a particular discipline or represent and characterize that discipline.

Responses also show that some students picked up the 'transferable' element of 'personal transferable skills', sometimes specifically relating this to the workplace: 'Skills which are relevant in a wide variety of contexts and whose acquisition in one context is of benefit elsewhere, ranging from word processing to project management', 'Skills that can be transferred with the person from situation to situation or from job to job'. Other students picked up the 'personal' element of 'personal transferable skills': 'Skills acquired that apply to the individual and can be applied to a wide variety of circumstances, situations', 'Personal skills I have that I can use, not necessarily related to course/core skills'. A few students also refer to 'life-skills', most frequently in relation to defining 'core skills': 'Skills necessary for everyday life, intuitive, and though definable, difficult to teach'.

## Basic skills

'Literacy, numeracy, grammar, pronunciation, IT skills – none of these should be provided in a degree; by then it is too late.' Despite this student's

Table 5.3 The areas in which students believe that basic s
as part of a university degree (percentage responses)

| | Institution | | | | |
|---|---|---|---|---|---|
| | Most traditional (%) | | Least tradit (%) | | |
| | 1 | 2 | 3 | 4 | |
| Information technology | 63 | 35 | 55 | 50 | 51 |
| Numeracy | 19 | 28 | 24 | 75 | 37 |
| Literacy | 10 | 10 | 7 | 25 | 13 |
| Generic skills | 19 | 26 | 25 | 15 | 21 |

comment, all but two undergraduates from the entire sample believe that certain kinds of basic skill should be offered within a degree programme (Table 5.3).

Information technology is considered as important within degree provision by half the students; this is seen as relating to word-processing for assignments or presentation of a CV, the use of databases and spreadsheets, and e-mail, internet and CD-ROM packages. Forty per cent of this sample owned their own computer or had easy access to a computer outside the university; a similar number were unhappy with their institution's provision. Just 3 per cent suggested they found using a computer difficult. Of interest is that those who own their own computer are most likely to make use of university facilities, and to be critical of them.

Numeracy is seen as most important in one institution. This may reflect the less conventional student intake, many of whom may not have gained formal qualifications or may have low-level qualifications. It may also reflect this institution's policy – that all students lacking a certain level of mathematics may gain accreditation towards their degree, whatever their discipline, by studying a numeracy module. Possibly for the same reasons, literacy is also considered important within this institution. However, numeracy is clearly an area for concern, highlighted further in the context of a general question: 'What are you not so good at learning.' Overall, 22 per cent of all students give the response 'mathematics'.

Responses that included communication, report writing, presentation skills, teamwork, time management and so on, were classified as generic skills. They are noted as important by up to one-quarter of the sample students in any institution. In total, 10 per cent of students feel that too little attention is paid to basic, foundation skills, that there is too little staff support, that not enough time is given to thorough study or that having to devote additional time outside the degree content is not easy to fit in.

4 Purposes of gaining a degree (percentage responses)

| | Institution | | | | Mean (%) |
|---|---|---|---|---|---|
| | Most traditional (%) | | Least traditional (%) | | |
| | 1 | 2 | 3 | 4 | |
| Career/job prospects | 77 | 80 | 81 | 85 | 79 |
| Broaden knowledge | 31 | 26 | 42 | 50 | 37 |
| Social/life experience | 23 | 29 | 28 | 15 | 25 |
| Personal satisfaction | 16 | 4 | 24 | 30 | 19 |
| Intellectual satisfaction | 19 | 20 | 13 | 0 | 13 |
| Ensuring economic status | 14 | 10 | 3 | 10 | 9 |

## Purposes in gaining a degree

It was anticipated from pilot studies that undergraduates would have a variety of purposes in gaining a degree, and this has since been confirmed within the Dearing Report (1997). As with the teachers, student beliefs about the purposes of higher education (Table 5.4) were expected to have an impact on the ways in which they perceive degree provision.

Career and job prospects are rated by some 80 per cent of students in all institutions. However, only 48 per cent state that this was the *single* most important factor, the majority being in the 'new' universities. Many responses touch on the necessity of having a degree to compete in today's society: 'I have seen how hard it is for people without degrees to get a job' or 'employers prefer people who have a degree, therefore a degree improves career prospects'. Some students describe gaining a degree as a 'cultural expectation' or 'the done thing' and show awareness of the increasing numbers of degree-holders of the future. A small number appear cynical: 'playing the game the establishment requires in order for you to get anywhere in this world', or perceive the orientation towards work to be, for example, 'unfortunate'.

Broadening knowledge is considered important by over one-third, and particularly by those in 'new' universities. The 'experience' of being at university is particularly valued in its own right by one-quarter of students, with an emphasis on personal satisfaction in 'new' universities and intellectual satisfaction in the 'old'. For mature students, studying for a degree is often perceived in a somewhat different way: 'I had achieved as much as I could in my working life, but wanted to do more. The only way to further my ambitions was to gain a qualification.' It was seen as 'the fulfilling of a long-held ambition', as a means of becoming 'a useful member of society', as gaining experience of a system that would then be seen as available to their children, or that might broaden horizons or 'act as a spur' to other family members.

Gaining knowledge is taken as underpinning a university education but is perceived in different ways – either as the development of knowledge in specific and specialists areas, or in broader terms. The experience of going to university is, in itself, the most significant aspect of obtaining a degree to some, especially the younger undergraduates: 'I have grown up an awful lot through coping alone' and 'I feel more confident in my relationships with other people and coping with the big wide world.' The shibboleth of 'knowledge as power' was also quoted.

Comments on personal satisfaction often relate to the development of self-image: 'It's a personal thing – proving to myself that I can reach a high standard of learning', 'people in the past have always thought I was a bit thick.' Many such comments came from those who, as mature students, have been able to profit from more flexible entrance to higher education. 'I left school at 15 with no qualifications, leaving being told I would fail any exam as I had [failed] the 11+. I knew they were wrong!' A few show resentment at: 'leaving school with exam qualifications which would not allow me now to re-gain entry into the job market'. Self-image also relates to expertise – 'I like the idea of being able to do something that other people can't, being an expert' – and to prestige or status: 'being able to say, I can complete a degree!' Intrinsic intellectual satisfaction from academic involvement is evident in comments such as: 'I chose this course because it fascinates me. I was not thinking of any particular career' or 'I have an active and inquisitive mind. I am interested by the way things work so I like to learn how they do and why.' A perspective from mature students is again evident: 'I have done many jobs where I had little personal satisfaction from doing them. Therefore, studying a subject I enjoy, and will hopefully use one day in a job, is important to me.'

A desire to ensure economic status is rated by only one in ten, but for some is seen as crucial: 'Unfortunately what we earn does matter and I don't want to have to struggle like most of my family have to.' Not living off parents, not having to worry constantly about finance or supporting children going to university are all considered important, as well as 'doing a valuable job and getting paid accordingly'. A small number of students mention other purposes in gaining a degree: personal management, skills development or simply not knowing what else to do. Degrees in some disciplines were also seen as important in allowing access to further study or to professional qualifications.

Students were asked to outline any difficulties experienced in pursuing their stated purposes in gaining a degree. Almost 20 per cent of students give evidence of some kind of concern, 6 per cent being most worried that a degree will not lead to employment and 5 per cent being unsure that their chosen degree will be useful to them or a good preparation for the future. Four per cent report being hampered by specific personal difficulties

*Table 5.5*   Student perceptions of what employers consider to be the benefits of graduate education (percentage responses)

|  | Institution | | | | Mean (%) |
|---|---|---|---|---|---|
|  | Most traditional (%) | | Least traditional (%) | | |
|  | 1 | 2 | 3 | 4 | |
| Acquisition of disciplinary knowledge | 48 | 35 | 37 | 30 | 38 |
| General academic development | 28 | 39 | 56 | 35 | 37 |
| Application of knowledge | 28 | 38 | 15 | 20 | 25 |
| Career/job-related skills | 8 | 4 | 15 | 15 | 11 |

– family obligations, social problems at university or a perception of inadequate intellect. Just 1 per cent report financial difficulty.

## Student perceptions of employer views on graduate education

Although there is evidence on what employers expect and require from a graduate education (as outlined in Chapter 1), it was not clear whether undergraduates would be aware of these views. Table 5.5 shows that students expect employers, above all, to require disciplinary knowledge.

The kind of disciplinary knowledge that is perceived as being needed is described as 'sound', 'both theoretical and practical', 'up-to-date', at a high level and with the potential to 'open new opportunities for a company'. Application of knowledge, perceived as more important by those in traditional institutions, is considered to relate to graduates who have 'insight', who can 'solve problems', who can 'think in an ordered manner' and who have the ability to learn new skills and knowledge as well as to apply existing knowledge.

General academic development covers areas such as 'having a developed mind', 'maturity of thinking', 'open mindedness'; having the ability to discuss, argue and show respect for the opinion of others; having commitment, initiative and independence or 'being disciplined, hard workers with high aspirations'. Comparatively few students expect career and job-related skills to be of importance to employers; the majority of those who do come from the 'new' institutions.

Despite an emphasis on subject knowledge and academic skills in the responses above, more than half the sample feel that job-related knowledge and skills would be seen by employers as lacking in graduates (Table 5.6). The need for 'work experience', 'knowledge of the world of industry and the

*Table 5.6* Student perceptions of what employers see as lacking in graduates (percentage responses)

|  | Institution | | | | Mean (%) |
|---|---|---|---|---|---|
|  | Most traditional (%) | | Least traditional (%) | | |
|  | 1 | 2 | 3 | 4 | |
| Job-related knowledge/skills | 57 | 52 | 61 | 45 | 54 |
| 'Real world' skills | 16 | 10 | 6 | 20 | 13 |
| Personal attributes | 7 | 12 | 15 | 15 | 12 |
| Generic skills | 15 | 14 | 6 | 10 | 11 |
| Subject knowledge | 4 | 12 | 0 | 20 | 9 |

organization of firms' and 'practical business skills – awareness, for example, of how a business or company works' – are mentioned. There are also references to the gaining of experience, some of which are negative in tone: 'practical skills, the stuff you can learn on the job if only they would show you' and 'experience, even though most graduates are capable of learning new things with relative ease (hence their degree), employers seem to want work experience so that they need not spend any time and money on training'.

Responses that are categorized as personal attributes cover areas such as a lack of 'sense of humour', 'care and consideration' and – most often – 'common sense'. 'Real world' skills refer to the lack of such experience in graduates, the irrelevance of some degrees to the 'real world', a lack of social skills or a general inability to interact. Generic skills include the inability to work and communicate with others, to present ideas clearly, to identify key issues or to transfer theory into practice. Mention of subject knowledge (especially from one of the 'new' institutions) is seldom related to specialized disciplinary knowledge but rather to basic language and numeracy skills, computer literacy or a lack of general 'background knowledge' or breadth – 'everyone is too science oriented'.

## Responsibility for career management

University careers services are concerned not only that students should be aware of the employer emphasis on skills but also that undergraduates should take their career development seriously throughout their degree, rather than making use of services, in the words of one careers adviser, in a 'last-minute panic'. In response to the question: 'Who is responsible for your career management at university?', many students replied that they did not know; many others did not answer the question, suggesting that

*Table 5.7*  Who is responsible for career management at university? (percentage responses)

| | Institution | | | | Mean (%) |
|---|---|---|---|---|---|
| | Most traditional (%) | | Least traditional (%) | | |
| | 1 | 2 | 3 | 4 | |
| No reply / don't know | 40 | 23 | 49 | 50 | 41 |
| Undergraduate him/her self | 30 | 22 | 24 | 15 | 23 |
| Tutor / academic counsellor | 22 | 15 | 10 | 30 | 19 |
| Careers services | 12 | 25 | 22 | 0 | 15 |

they did not know (especially as very few questions were left blank in this way) (Table 5.7).

Students show considerable concern about this issue, for example: 'Courses do very little (or nothing) to reinforce career development. The whole subject is ignored and left up to us – a great burden without any helpful guidance.' A very different comment from another student reflects not only an alternative belief about the purposes of higher education but also about the nature of the degree selected for study, in this case, English literature: 'What career? How many undergraduates know what they want to do, and what is the likelihood of them getting those jobs anyway? The object of a degree is further study, not three years to pick a job.'

Focus group interviews highlighted differences between careers provision for students and the opportunities that had been taken by individuals. For example, second year students in one group had no idea what kind of careers services were available, nor where to go to find them. A third year student who had completed his degree at the time of interview stated:

> The frustrating thing is the position I am now in. I am looking for any old job, but it's like there's no way unless you send out a press release saying: I can do all this. I think you might like me in your business because I can do this and have got these skills. It's so difficult knowing I am this kind of person . . . I *am* an employable person in this field but it is actually getting the idea across to the industry.

A fellow student responded: 'As soon as you go through a careers adviser, they send you all the information and it is down to you. It's down to you to write all those letters and say: "Excuse me, do you want me, hello". It is as simple as that.'

One of the problems is that careers services in the past have remained largely reactive, responding only to those students who made appropriate efforts to make use of them; there now seems to be some concern in these institutions to provide more proactive help. New 'career management' courses being developed in two of the institutions incorporate aspects of generic skills. Also, generic skills modules often include career-oriented skills (such as writing CVs, preparation for job applications and interviews), in order to raise students' awareness of their necessity. These modules seem to be very effective in drawing to students' attention what will be required of them in the process of applying for jobs, although the relevance is not always appreciated until later in their degree.

## Contexts of provision for learning

As generic skills development is often delivered via less traditional forms of teaching, is often less teacher-centred, demands more active and interactive forms of learning from students and often has a focus on processes, it is interesting to know in which learning contexts students believe they learn best. All students report a diet of lectures, individual work, seminars and/or tutorials; the majority have also experienced team or group work (96 per cent) and project work (82 per cent). Fewer felt they had been involved in student-led activities (45 per cent). From this particular group of students, 8 per cent from the two traditional universities had undertaken, or were about to embark upon, a sandwich year. Over 40 per cent, spread more evenly across the institutions, had undertaken a work placement or work experience associated with their degree subject. This finding, as with team and project work, is unlikely to reflect institutional provision as a whole but, rather, the kinds of departments that were involved in this study because of their commitment to skills development.

The contexts in which students state they learn 'most' varies between institutions, as outlined in Table 5.8, although there are also some clear trends.

*Table 5.8*  The contexts in which students perceive they learn most (percentage responses)

|  | Institution | | | | Mean (%) |
|---|---|---|---|---|---|
|  | Most traditional (%) | | Least traditional (%) | | |
|  | 1 | 2 | 3 | 4 | |
| Projects/teams | 52 | 41 | 33 | 55 | 45 |
| Lectures | 23 | 29 | 52 | 25 | 32 |
| Individual work | 30 | 30 | 34 | 20 | 29 |
| Tutorials/seminars | 41 | 29 | 12 | 10 | 23 |
| Work experience | 12 | 3 | 6 | 20 | 10 |
| Student-led sessions | 6 | 1 | 3 | 5 | 4 |

Forty-five per cent of students report teams and projects as the context in which they learn the most. This high figure is likely to reflect the sample of modules and courses selected and observed, wherein there was evidence of much good quality provision in these areas. It may also reflect the fact that at least one-quarter of these students suggest they are 'good' at problem solving and practical application of skills rather than rote learning, although interviews with students suggest that perceptions of 'being good' at something is likely to be a result of 'good' provision. However, 17 per cent also report these to be the contexts where they learn the least. This may reflect poor provision but is also likely to correspond with beliefs about the kinds of context that should be provided for degree study.

Almost equal numbers report lectures to be the most, or the least, useful learning environment. Individual work is well rated by 29 per cent, although 6 per cent do not value it. Tutorials or seminars are considered good learning contexts by almost one-quarter of students, although this is particularly within the traditional institutions; 15 per cent report these to be least good. Work experience and placements are favoured as contexts for learning by only one in five of the 48 per cent of students who had been given this opportunity. One-quarter of those who experienced student-led sessions reported them least good for learning, although they were appreciated by a few.

## Motivating factors in student learning

In terms of motivation, the subject being of interest is mentioned most often. Students enjoy their disciplinary study and, in the case of generic skills courses, interviews suggest that the subject content is often perceived as refreshingly different and useful. It is perhaps surprising, therefore, that subject content is not mentioned more frequently.

Overall, the figures in Table 5.9 suggest that students – not unexpectedly – feel themselves most motivated to learn within a variety of different contexts. The comparatively high figures for 'working alone' and the low figures for 'good teacher' in institution four may reflect – at least in part – the sample. This included students of fine art who, as a group, insisted that personal development as an artist can only be achieved through individual expression. There was no evidence of students being less appreciative of teachers in this institution than in the others.

Although there are complaints in interviews about the tension and stress they are expected to cope with, many students do admit to responding well to pressure. In higher education there are the conventional pressures of examinations or completing written assignments on time. The kinds of pressure in the modules observed were created most often by course demands that were closer to the kinds of demand of the world of work: making instant and accurate decisions in a simulation, working as an interdependent team on a short-term or a long-term basis, taking responsibility

*Table 5.9* Student perceptions of motivating factors in learning (percentage responses)

| | Institution | | | | Mean (%) |
|---|---|---|---|---|---|
| | Most traditional (%) | | Least traditional (%) | | |
| | 1 | 2 | 3 | 4 | |
| Subject of interest | 28 | 29 | 22 | 10 | 22 |
| Working alone | 10 | 3 | 16 | 30 | 15 |
| Good teacher | 22 | 16 | 15 | 5 | 14 |
| Under pressure | 12 | 19 | 16 | 10 | 14 |
| Teamwork | 9 | 13 | 9 | 20 | 13 |
| Relevance | 12 | 12 | 9 | 15 | 12 |
| Small group/tutorial | 13 | 6 | 12 | 15 | 11 |

for negotiating and completing a work placement. Each of these situations created pressure and anxiety. Interviews highlighted that appreciation of the value of this was sometimes dependent on a positive experience (including perceptions of 'fair' assessment for teamwork); but many students were able to perceive benefits even when they were not entirely satisfied with the outcomes: 'Despite all the faults . . . most of us are capable enough to see it objectively and think: well, we saw the disaster in some ways, but we have learnt from it. I think, because we are all trying to be quite positive about the experiences we've had, we can take it on in the future.'

Interviews also suggest that the quality of the teacher is more important than shown by the questionnaire data above. Students talk about being inspired by their teachers, about being drawn into areas for which they thought they had no interest (including generic skills), about teaching techniques and representing information in different ways (from the use of teddy bears to multi-media presentations), about teachers being well organized, making clear the learning objectives and so on. Students also report how they feel motivated to work harder, to do additional reading, to go beyond the narrowest expectations. A student who has changed courses explains: 'If you don't enjoy what you're doing, you don't go out and try and learn even more. Now [in the context of a skill-based module and an exciting teacher] I don't mind what I'm doing because I'm getting something out of it.' There is a frequent implication, supported by questionnaire data, that students feel they become good at learning what is made of interest to them; also that relevance (a motivating factor) is created by the way in which the content is taught as much as by whether it is instantly useful. The importance of the teacher becomes even more apparent in the context of questionnaire data on demotivating factors in learning, where general lack of student interest, the feeling of 'wasting time', lectures and seminars that are not of interest, lack of teacher enthusiasm and ill-defined tasks are all representative of perceptions of lack of quality in teacher provision. These teacher-related features account for 67 per cent of demotivating factors, thereby emphasizing the importance of the teacher role.

Twenty per cent of students feel that the surroundings in which they work have a marked influence on their learning. Dark, dreary, shabby rooms are not thought helpful, nor is a noisy environment. Home circumstances are often described as distracting, as are good weather or the activities of friends. The only other demotivators mentioned are too much pressure (8 per cent) and teamwork (3 per cent). Of interest is that just over half the students report a need to improve on a particular aspect of their degree study. Of this group, 86 per cent felt that the onus was on themselves to make more effort with their work.

## Outline of skills perceived to be most developed within modules

At the end of the questionnaire, students were provided with the generic skills framework (management of self, others, information and the task), outlined in Chapter 2, and were asked to tick the skills they had used or developed during the observed module. Almost all skills on the framework were ticked by at least 30 per cent of students. Table 5.10 shows the ten skills that were selected most often. A comparison is given with the percentage of students who tick each of these ten skills as being developed in other courses they are studying. The percentage of students who find each of these ten skills of particular importance is also shown.

*Table 5.10*  Outline of skills perceived to be most developed in observed modules (1), in other course provision (2) and ratings of importance (3)

|  | (1) Observed | (2) Other | (3) Important |
|---|---|---|---|
| Present information | 65 | 36 | 36 |
| Take responsibility for own learning | 61 | 43 | 34 |
| Use appropriate sources | 61 | 40 | 33 |
| Carry out agreed tasks | 58 | 32 | 10 |
| Manage time effectively | 57 | 33 | 50 |
| Identify key features of task | 53 | 33 | 13 |
| Gather information | 50 | 37 | 13 |
| Listen actively/with purpose | 49 | 31 | 7 |
| Respect views/values of others | 49 | 36 | 17 |
| Deal with criticism | 48 | 30 | 21 |

The selected skills range across management of information, of self, of the task and of others. The figures suggest, above all, that students are aware of skills development across these areas and that the skills descriptions offered to them were relevant and appropriate. There was little response to a request for adding skills that had been left out of the lists. Skills were marked more frequently in the context of the observed courses than other courses, but this may reflect these particular modules being fresher in the memory than others. It is clear, however, that undergraduates feel that the opportunity for skills development in the areas outlined by the framework is widely available.

Of interest is the lack of relationship between those skills reported as being developed and those considered as important by students. 'Listening actively' is one such example, with half the sample reporting its development within observed modules but only 7 per cent feeling it of particular usefulness or importance. 'Managing time effectively' was seen as the most important skill of all (50 per cent), followed by 'coping with stress' (39 per cent), 'taking responsibility for own learning' (34 per cent) and 'presenting information' and 'using appropriate sources of information' (36 and 33 per cent, respectively). No other skills were marked as important by more than one-fifth of the student group.

Considered least important on the framework provided were the ability to 'delegate and stand back', to 'take the role of chairperson', to 'organize subtasks' and to 'identify strategic options'. 'Using appropriate language', 'interpreting a variety of information forms', 'learning in new/different situations' and 'clarifying personal values' were also seldom ticked. The lack of usefulness of these particular skills in the eyes of students reflects the lack of attention given to them in the particular modules that were observed and, as such, these findings are not unexpected. The exception to this is the notion of 'reflecting on own learning'. Reflection is a word that is often uttered by teachers and presented to students as 'something that must be done', but which may be given little meaning or practical sense. The concept is thus likely to remain too vague to be useful. Some of the observed modules made specific attempts to promote reflection and the low rating here may indicate how difficult it is to make this a meaningful concept to undergraduates.

## Focus group interviews on course provision

Feedback from students in interviews indicates differing patterns of experience in relation to generic skills and, in particular, different levels of awareness and understanding of skill development. An interesting feature of the focus groups was the way in which they often developed into discussion and argument amongst the students participating, and examples of this will be given below. Student comments about specific modules are used to illustrate central concerns that emerged from this study: issues pertaining to the embeddedness of skills within disciplinary content, to expectations of degree study, to modular choice, to assessment and to the nature of effective learning.

## Recognition of embedded skills

One of the major contributors to student awareness of skills is the extent to which teachers are explicit about skill provision and the extent to which messages are confounded by approaches to disciplinary study. It seems that generic skills embedded within a discipline are not easy for students to recognize, especially if teachers simply make assumptions that students will perceive the skills and value them. Even when teachers *are* explicit and expect students to undertake processes that reinforce skill use, the messages may not be received if they are clouded by an apparent need to focus on disciplinary learning.

For example, one of the observed teachers – despite emphasizing skills such as note-taking and group work during workshop sessions, and attempting to be explicit about these features in the provision of note-taking sheets and the organization of collaborative groups – failed to enable students to recognize these as important. Essentially, students saw this module on spectroscopy as providing theory, the purpose being: 'to introduce us to the analytical methods and to the use of these techniques in real life'. They perceived skills as associated with learning subject matter and the workshops as opportunities to apply theoretical understanding: 'Lectures are to understand to a certain level – a basic understanding only. But you have to do the labs. [workshops] to make sense of the theory.' It seemed almost incidental that collaboration and group work – which the lecturer thought were the *raison d'être* for the module – were mentioned in the interview: 'We discuss the concepts in the lab. and look for them in the practical sheets and discuss in groups. We worked competitively, so had to learn about organizational skills, because if different individuals did different aspects of the work and then cooperated, the weaker students got better.' The students were enthusiastic about the teacher's style and organization, they enjoyed the content, but they did not appreciate that the processes that the teacher had provided, and valued, were what they were meant to be learning about. There was no kind of assessment, either formative or summative, of generic skills. Hence the examination on disciplinary content dictated the importance of what had to be learned.

Modules with strong vocational links do not necessarily alleviate this kind of situation, even when the reality of the workplace is a major focus. For example, architecture students perceived one such module to be about theoretical matters, developing ways of perceiving architecture: 'It's the ABC of architecture – specifically a different way of looking at buildings and the way of breaking down into component parts – why things are there – the reason.' One student suggested: 'You learn a different language –

getting a frame of mind from the outset.' They talked about the way architects work, about the discipline in terms of a struggle between conceptual understanding and the skill of eventually producing an acceptable design: 'the compromise in using knowledge and skills; it's handling conflict at a theoretical level'. Description of such skills remains firmly embedded in the discipline. The module could be seen to be developing some generic skills, albeit within the context of architecture, for example, 'using information critically', 'presenting information', 'taking responsibility for one's own learning' and 'reflecting on learning'. There was evidence to point particularly to the skill of 'conceptualizing issues', which is at the centre of the module's intent. However, because these skills and learning strategies were not made explicit, the students were generally unaware that they had such abilities.

In another architecture module, students thought the major purpose was to provide the required substantive knowledge needed to create a design: 'It's to lay down a foundation of knowledge, for when you respond to tasks – like technological information, historical and general information on buildings.' They were also well aware of the means by which designing was to be achieved, coping with the tension between being a sociotechnical expert and a creative artist. One explained the need to alter his design to deal with this: 'There are lots of changes now to be made, and at each change I have to argue the change so that, architecturally it is pleasing, and aesthetically it is pleasing.' The generic skills that students thought they were developing were, as the module intended, associated mainly with management of information and of task and with management of self. Comments in this instance did reflect their awareness of generic skills, although they remain embedded in the context of architecture; for example, the ability to: 'stand up and communicate even if you are under pressure' or '. . . to be able to defend yourself. You become a salesman – very sure of what you have done. This is the client's cheque book to be concerned about and in my design I have got extras and therefore have to argue what I have done. Even if you are not entirely convinced, you still argue your point.'

Many commented upon the need to take responsibility for one's own learning: 'You also have to learn to manage your time. After the initial tutorial I had to think about materials needed and the basic design – all in a week. I organized my week and by Friday I had all the ideas and then the weekend for drawing it up' or 'Being critical of self – because the subject is very subjective'. The necessity to develop skills associated with management of the task was also discussed, an ability to be rigorous about making choices and decision making: 'To think laterally and to sort out ideas. There are so many and you have to make choices continually.' One student provided a succinct summary of skills that he perceived as being developed: 'Analysis and problem solving – it all comes down to this. Design is problem solving . . . trying to get you to analyse your building, admit to an error or argue a case.' It could be argued that these kinds of skill are firmly embedded in the discipline, that they remain 'situated' in this context. None the less, the

extent of emphasis and the attention to recognition of skills is markedly
different to the previous example and the way in which students talk reflects this.

A module in pharmacy included simulations of practice to enable students
to become competent pharmacists. Students again perceived these sessions
as the means of making sense of theory given in lectures: 'the theory is
useful but difficult to take into the pharmacy as it is – this lab. provides the
means of doing that', 'The time pressure is in this "lab." – that's real!' They
also recognized the importance of skills of communication: 'How to read
and check the prescriptions . . . accurately read and interpret hand-written
prescriptions, like spotting interactions of drugs in a prescription', 'how to
talk to GPs and to patients. The telephoning is most realistic, and it is good
to have this skill.'

This was a vocational module providing disciplinary-based training for
would-be pharmacists. Similarly with the notion of reflection; there was
agreement that the course demanded reflection and that this was a valuable
aspect of their learning, but the concept was interpreted as a means of
checking for accuracy: 'In the lab., the supervisors look through what you've
done – then you have to reflect on what you have already done for preparation for this class, in your own time. You can check it – to get perfect.' The
intention of the module was to provide workplace awareness, as close to a
'real' situation as possible, and this is exactly what students perceived it
to be doing. Hence, communication was that required of pharmaceutical
settings, dependent on elements of pharmaceutical knowledge, rather than
a generic skill.

In this module, students were left in no doubt as to the centrality of
skills in the curriculum. This is also the case in modules for which the
focus of knowledge and development is clearly skill-dependent rather than
discipline-specific.

## Student expectations of degree study

Student expectations of what a degree should be about do have an impact
on their perceptions of provision and, as outlined above, the hold of disciplinary study is very strong. The advantage of skills being firmly embedded
within a discipline is that such modules do not run against expectations of
what is most usually perceived by students as the appropriate content of a
degree programme. However, an earlier study (Dunne 1995) highlighted
that the first experiences of university life and the culture provided by any
department can have a marked influence on student expectations. It was
suggested that provision of generic skills is most likely to be successful if
introduced early in the degree programme; there is similar evidence within
this study. The examples of student perceptions given below come from
modules where the explicit focus is on generic skills, without heavy use of
disciplinary content. There is evidence of considerable surprise at some of

the provision and at what is deemed by teachers to be relevant within a degree programme:

> ... part of it [is] you coming to terms with the problems that you will have, not having someone to feed back to you all the time ... I did think the first year was just about trying to get settled and familiar with your surroundings and then all of a sudden having to do this was quite a shock really. (talking about work experience)

Some students also found the generic content of their modules surprising:

*Marie*: To start off with I didn't think it was going to be very useful. I thought it was going to be a load of psycho-mumbo-jumbo sort of stuff. But now looking back on it, you can see that some of it has already helped and is going to help further on ...

*Susan*: He keeps it interesting as well. Even if [some part of it is] monotonous, you're still sitting there thinking, yes ... I'll get through this.

*Paul*: It's different and it's a break from all your other modules.

*Marie*: A good starter course for university. Helps you get going.

*Helen*: If I was speaking to anybody, I'd tell them to stick with it for the first few weeks and then you will realize it's worth doing. I was like, I just really cannot be bothered with doing something like this.

*Susan*: I remember starting with mind maps. I never got my head around ...

*Helen*: Yes, but that gave me the attitude that I thought: Right, I am somewhere new. I've got to try something different. So I thought, OK, I don't like this mind mapping, but I gave it a go to see what it's like.

Students from this module also discussed how their enjoyment encouraged them to look up additional information in the library: 'If you enjoy doing it, you're going to want to do the work, aren't you.' The enjoyment and motivation came from interest in new ideas and approaches, but also from the 'easy-going' and 'relaxed atmosphere' and the novel teaching approaches. They also appreciated that one of the teachers learnt everyone's names (within a module intake of 120 students): 'it makes it a bit more personal', 'you're not a number', 'it makes him more approachable as well'. The personality of the teacher and his skills in making students feel excited and involved were paramount. Alongside this, he ensured that the skills and knowledge promoted within the module were perceived as relevant; he created a relevance through his manner of teaching.

Just one student admitted that she would not have become involved if the module had not been assessed, but also stated: 'Now that we've done it, I think it was of great benefit and it was really good.' Another said that if it had been optional, she probably would not have selected it: 'but if I hadn't, then I would have kicked myself'. These statements raise two important issues – that of selection of options and that of assessment. Each of these issues is discussed in turn.

### Selection of options

Students were adamant, time and again, that they would not have selected a skills-based module if it had been optional. They also accepted that they were not in a position to judge what was of benefit until they had experienced it. Discussion with mature students suggested that they often opted for what they perceived looks most like a 'traditional' degree; having got into university they gain satisfaction from achievement in traditional academic terms. They also reported being highly committed to their chosen discipline. Younger students gave some evidence of not having the confidence to move beyond a selected discipline or the maturity to know what else might be of value to them. As an example, students selecting from a wide range of short options provided specifically to allow them to 'pick and mix' a broad-based curriculum, premised their choices on whatever 'looks easiest', 'won't take up extra time', 'has the shortest/easiest assessment' or looked as if it would directly benefit their present studies – not on enabling them to become more employable or a better learner or giving themselves a wider base of knowledge and skills.

Self-chosen modules may not always be the best approach to getting the most from a degree. In a discussion on whether there should be elements of choice within a compulsory module on generic skills, many students were also persuasive that this would not be appropriate as they might deliberately avoid what they were least good at doing.

### Assessment

It is often said that students are becoming more instrumental in their approaches to work, so that 'what is assessed becomes all that counts'. It was indicated in Chapter 3 that such a syndrome is perceived to be exacerbated by modular systems and associated assessment practices. There is evidence from this study that, in some circumstances, students will participate positively in generic skills courses without assessment, but it is likely that the pressure of large numbers will make this increasingly difficult to achieve. Assessment is likely to provide the main motivation for student involvement, whether the orientation is disciplinary or generic. This may seem a somewhat negative approach to study. It is also possible to view assessment in a more positive light. If, as highlighted above, assessment is the most effective way to ensure that generic skills are recognized, then a powerful means of addressing learning outcomes is via an assessment-led curriculum, that is, the assessment is devised to drive the aims of the course.

## Effective learning: challenge or stress

A frequent theme of focus group discussion was in relation to the nature of effective learning and how this can be promoted and supported. As many of the skills courses require students to take on responsibilities beyond what they had anticipated, much debate covers the extent to which the pressure, stress and time commitment is useful to their learning.

For example, one group of first year computer science students have to complete a problem-solving team project that is specifically devised to be difficult, time-consuming, almost impossible to complete without using the efforts of the whole team and largely dependent on drawing on knowledge and skills provided for them through the first two terms. Teachers do not intervene in the project work. They keep an eye on progress in the laboratories and via students' written course submissions. They are available for consultation but are unlikely to respond to many of the questions asked of them.

The volunteers for the focus group came to their interview in complaining mode but, during the session, a change of emphasis became apparent.

*John*: We seemed to get a crash course in about 30 different things.

*Ben*: If you're moving into the workplace you're going to be doing 12 different things. If you can do the basics of 12 different things instead of being very good at a couple . . .

*John*: People have been doing 17 hours.

*Mark*: People have been doing 12- to 15-hour shifts every single day.

*Ben*: I would have thought that you could have got all the work done in a nine 'til five day. But we've had to go beyond that.

*Claire*: Well, we're much more likely to get jobs.

*Mark*: I would say that the work we're doing will get us involved in industry . . .

*Ben*: It's working from a base of knowledge and bringing new skills into it.

*John*: It's like 'dropping you in'. You know how to doggy paddle but you've got to get your way out of this. It's almost like that.

*Mark*: It's a very stressful way to learn but a very effective way to learn. At the time you don't enjoy it all, but retrospectively you think, 'I really do value that experience'.

*Claire*: A lot of what we learned in the last two weeks was the sort of glueing part. We seem to have struggled with ourselves.

*John*: But it seems to be completely independent of everything they've taught us. They taught us up to a level and then we've literally had to drag ourselves through and bring each other up.

This discussion suggests that the teachers' intentions have been well met with regard to students' application of knowledge and skills, to understanding the relationship with workplace skills, to taking the responsibility (even if reluctantly) for their learning and to supporting each other as a team. In this example, the disciplinary context has not cut across recognition of generic skills. Requirements for self- and peer evaluation, and assessment of teamwork, ensure that skills development is not only explicit but is also made important. However, it seemed to be the opportunity to talk about their learning and to hear each other's views that allowed them to recognize and appreciate more fully what had been gained from their experiences.

Recognition of the benefits of working through difficult situations was frequently discussed. For example, after a difficult work placement, one student suggested: 'If you don't struggle within the situation that you are put in, you don't learn that much'. Another commented that being: 'thrown in at the deep end works'. In such cases, students are confronted by what needs to be done and have to take action. Coffield (1997) states: 'The experience of most people suggests . . . that learning is often difficult and disturbing and that growth often results from hard graft and disconcerting struggle.' Jackson (1986) claimed: 'No one except a sadist would advocate the introduction of discomfort and suffering into the educational process for their own sake . . . But the crucial question is: how much discomfort can be eliminated from the educative process without losing the risk of something even more important than relative comfort – education itself?'

Some students give evidence of finding it easier to cope with stress than others. One student suggested that being 'thrown in at the middle end' might be more useful. By this she meant that she was not averse to difficulty but would have appreciated more guidelines and teaching of generic skills. Herein lies a dilemma for teachers: to what extent do students need formal preparation in aspects of skills and to what extent can they learn from practical experience alone? How much sense can students make of any situation if they are not equipped to deal with it? Or is it the dealing with it that provides the learning?

## Discussion

At present, there is a prevailing rhetoric that advocates democracy, flexibility and freedom in student choice. Scenarios, such as that painted by Wagner (1996), of opportunities for lifelong learning best served by flexible systems (with, preferably, a breaking down of barriers between HE and FE) are widely considered to provide the best educational pattern for the future. However, there is also concern that changes in this direction – such as modularization and semesterization – are only 'superficially liberating' for students. Harvey and Knight (1996) argue that such open 'cafeteria' approaches allow 'no identifiable progression or conceptual development'. Ratcliffe *et al.* (1995) also suggest, from the American experience, that an unstructured accumulation of small units is not a useful preparation for the future. In the departments surveyed, there is little evidence of students moving outside a chosen faculty or widely supporting options designed to offer breadth and interest. Some of the departments we visited set out core programmes of study, which maintained control over learning experiences and made it difficult for students to range widely outside the selected discipline (although it seemed that such action was more likely to be justified in terms of issues of funding, rather than providing the best opportunities for learning).

Students may also be unlikely to espouse the 'new rhetoric' of the purposes of higher education and this is supported by the questionnaire data, which showed a strong tendency for responses to be conceived in terms of subject knowledge rather than skills. One academic comments: 'We are still failing to open our students' eyes to what they need to be fundamentally developing and practising and nurturing – what they need basically to get out of higher education.'

In many instances, the diet that students got strongly influenced what they perceived as important. Even when this diet was unexpected or difficult, they came to recognize its importance:

> To start off with, I thought: this has got nothing to do with computing. Why? And I sat here learning about how to take notes and talk to someone in an interview. But the point of getting a degree is so you can go and get a job. So if you haven't got any interpersonal skills – I guess that is what they're trying to teach you – then there's no point in getting a degree, because nobody's going to want to employ you.

This comment was further supported by others in the group: 'I think that's a relevant module for *all* courses', 'Yes, definitely'. But sometimes benefits are recognized only in the long term. One student interviewed at the end of her degree stated that generic skills modules should be: 'Definitely compulsory. Even though when you're doing it you don't know what you're doing at all. As you go through university, the things you've picked up and worked on are useful.' The problem for teachers lies in persuading students of benefits that are not instantly recognizable.

One way in which this can be achieved is through formal assessment of skills, thereby ensuring that students will take them seriously, at least in terms of gaining their degree. Assessment of skills requires teachers to be explicit about skills development and students to devote attention to it. When skills processes are emphasized by teachers but assessment is of syntactic and substantive knowledge, students are less likely to perceive the significance of generic skills. When skills remain embedded and implicit within disciplinary study and are not assessed, students are least likely either to recognize skills or to be eloquent, or even interested, in their description.

So-called bolt-on courses in skills are often criticized; they may not be taken seriously by students because they are not seen to be relevant to disciplinary study. In the modules we observed, it could be suggested that the best way of ensuring student recognition of generic skills is to teach them out of the context of disciplinary subject study, but within the disciplinary setting, with teachers of that subject and perhaps using disciplinary examples. What is then important are the ways in which these skills become embedded within disciplinary study in order to support and enhance it. The clamour from employers often suggests that students should be equipped with generic skills only because they are necessary in the world of work. In this sense, generic skills become a preparation for work. This kind of conception may, however, be inappropriate. In the modules observed for this study, an explicit focus on generic skills was almost always intended as providing a foundation that would be central to effective learning throughout higher education. First year students were introduced to generic skills so that they could use them, practise and develop them in new contexts, and in particular within disciplinary study. Generic skills modules are considered an investment by those who teach them. This investment may have the additional pay-off of providing graduates who are well equipped to deal with the requirements of work but the rationale is provided from within higher education and the major purpose is to enhance students' experiences of higher education.

Many students expressed gratitude for being involved in the focus group interviews despite, in some cases, having been 'unwilling volunteers': 'It's certainly helped me this morning. Hasn't it? [nods from the rest of the group] Just thinking about, just thinking things through more deeply, what we have learnt.' This suggests that ensuring opportunities for review and guided reflection on learning may deserve greater attention by teachers. One student suggested, in similar vein, that most important of all is: 'The skill of knowing that you know more as you go along'. It is this kind of self-awareness that could be equated with conceptions of individual 'empowerment'. This is a term used by employers (see Chapter 8) but not by anyone within the group of higher education teachers. It is, however, a concept explored by Harvey and Knight (1996), who believe that higher education should empower learners to be 'knowledgeable, skilful, comprehending and critical people'. It could be argued that all the observed modules, whether vocational or not, whether skills oriented or set within a discipline, had such aims as central. It could be argued that all were well on the way to achieving such aims. What was noticeably different between modules was the extent of attention to each of these areas and to the balance between them. Attention to this balance may be critical if it is important that all students should recognize the role of generic skills in higher education and beyond.

# 6

# Employer Initiatives in Higher Education

As outlined in Chapter 1, reports suggest that employers universally require graduates to possess a set of skills and attributes in order to be effective in the world of work. Not all employers are critical of graduate entrants, as evidenced in our interviews with human resource managers (detailed in Chapter 7). Many employers believe that universities are making positive changes, but also that some students are being better equipped for the workplace than others and that these are the students that they wish to recruit. The onus is generally placed on higher education to remedy the perceived weaknesses in skills development and the kinds of skills courses provided by academics, and student responses to these, have been reviewed in the preceding chapters. However, a few large, private companies have demonstrated that, rather than expecting higher education to undertake this unaided, they are prepared to take a proactive approach to skills development in higher education, running programmes devised as a practical response to delivering the transferable skills required of graduates. Two such existing initiatives were extended and evaluated as part of this research study:

- The Shell Technology and Enterprise Programme (STEP) has, over the last decade, been supporting a major programme of undergraduate vacation placements in small and medium enterprises (SMEs) across the UK. The purpose of this is to encourage work-based skills development. A further aim is to enable the eroding of barriers to the employment of graduates in small and local companies, so that graduates perceive them as places that offer opportunities and employers in such companies perceive the benefits of recruiting a graduate workforce.
- British Petroleum (BP) has been sponsoring the Team Development in Universities Programme over the last five years. This is an initiative to promote the use of team skills so that graduates are better prepared for the workplace. Expertise from the context of industry has been taken into a group of ten universities, to provide students with an experience of

teamwork and academics with the kinds of ongoing professional development in teaching skills advocated by the Dearing Report (1997).

The focus of this chapter is on each of the two programmes, providing a rationale for their implementation, the developmental and evaluative role of this study in relation to them, and associated outcomes. The focus for STEP was on the development of assessment and accreditation procedures for skills acquired by undergraduates during work placements in small and medium enterprises (SMEs). For the Team Development programme, the focus was on the acquisition of teamworking abilities that could be transferred to the world of work and on the integration of team skills into curriculum study. Both of these programmes clearly address the kind of skills development widely advocated by employers and the government. Each of these initiatives is described in turn.

## The importance of work placements in undergraduate degrees

The vision of the Robertson Report (HEQC 1994) is that an open and flexible education system will mean that traditional full-time courses become outmoded, as work-based internships, professional placements, periods of independent study, and so on, become intertwined within a degree. A realistic move in this direction is in the encouragement of more students to take up work placements – beyond those for whom it is already a compulsory vocational element of the course or a part of professional training. Recent interest in this area has been reinforced by the Dearing Report (1997). Two major reports (Harvey *et al.* 1997, 1998) have also emphasized the need for work experience for undergraduates. In the first study, year-long placements were recommended, as this is most beneficial to employers. The latest report is more cautious, suggesting that a placement must be, above all, a worthwhile learning experience for the student.

In the context of our study of large companies (detailed in Chapter 7), one of the main reasons for employer satisfaction with a new graduate intake is in relation to work experience. In some companies, work experience is used as a specific criterion for selection, which has led to 'targeting those universities where the majority of students do sandwich courses, because those students are certainly more employable than those who haven't had work experience'. When employers were less satisfied with the quality of new employees, lack of experience of the workplace was given as a specific reason: 'It's tying in with Dearing, in terms of work experience. Just more exposure to the world of work, to translate what you're learning at university . . . to try and apply some of that in a workplace environment.' A complaint was that graduates: 'have a completely alien set of expectations to start with, that bear absolutely no relation at all to the world of work'. Over half the employers in the sample claimed 'work awareness' to be the most desirable skill for new employees and a number pointed to the difference between 'work experience' and developing a 'useful awareness' of the world of work: 'It's not just experience of companies, it's being aware of what's going on around you. We're not expecting people to come with absolute knowledge of things, but what we do expect them to have is a feel for the market, what's going on in the world'.

# The Shell Technology Enterprise Programme (STEP)

In the light of such comments, the importance of a programme such as STEP is reinforced. STEP enables the provision of 8-week vacation placements in SMEs for undergraduates at the end of their second year. These placements are often non-discipline-specific and, although there is always a specific project to undertake, an emphasis is placed on the development of generic skills and on understanding the context of work. Organization is undertaken by agencies and universities across the country. Students are usually paid something over £100 per week, half from the employer, the rest from local agencies, with STEP funding administrative costs. Each year, increasing numbers of undergraduates are involved; last year some 1500 students were offered placements, with a total over the last 12 years of more than 8000.

## *The assessment and accreditation of skills*

Until this time, employers had been required to write an end-of-placement report on the undergraduate in their company and students had been expected to monitor their own progress by using a 'Skills Tracker' disk. There had been no formal assessment or accreditation of those undertaking STEP placements and it was not known whether this was something that could be of interest, of value, or would be feasible in practice. This project therefore engaged in a small-scale exploratory study with four major aims:

1. The detailing of attitudes of both employers and students towards the assessment and accreditation of workplace skills and competences.
2. The identification of skills and competences developed by students during STEP placements.
3. The development of assessment systems to allow for accreditation of STEP work experience, either within a degree programme or within the NVQ framework.
4. The trialling and evaluation of such systems.

To gain information on the first two aspects, ten students and ten employers from the South-West of England were selected for their recent experience of either completing a STEP placement or for having a STEP student in their company. To gain as wide a set of employer views as possible, given the small sample, companies were selected to represent a range of the kinds of placement offered (for example, market research, database organization, engineering), a range of size (from 3 to 200) and a range of locations (from city centre or industrial estate, to rural). Both employers and students were interviewed about their attitudes to assessment and accreditation and were invited to talk in detail about the placement activities and skills. Analysis of these interviews led to a set of practical outcomes.

First was the development of a set of 'grounded' skill areas, that is, premised on what students and employers had suggested was specifically available from, and appropriate to, the STEP experience. These skill areas were designed into a framework that could be used to underpin generic skills development in the workplace. This framework was then used as the basis of a competence log for students and an evaluative matrix to be completed by employers. Finally, these materials were trialled with a cohort of 40 STEP students and their employers during summer vacation placements. Findings in relation to each of these areas are outlined below.

## Attitudes to assessment and accreditation of STEP placements

Degree accreditation of placements was considered appropriate by eight of the ten students, but only if the placement had direct relevance to their degree subject (and this was seldom the case). This was also the reason for not wanting accreditation: the experience 'doesn't correspond closely enough to my degree'. In relation to competence-based assessment, five felt they had no idea what this meant; two claimed familiarity and gave examples; three were unsure but offered statements such as 'sort of key skills', 'skills, things that you can do', 'things like teamwork?' Similarly, most students felt unable to comment on accreditation via National Vocational Qualifications frameworks (NVQs/Key Skills), as they did not have enough knowledge to do so. The others were negative in their response: 'never thought of them [i.e. vocational qualifications] as relevant', 'no benefit to me', the 'snobbery factor' makes them of little use in comparison to a degree. The most positive statement was: 'I suppose any qualification would be worthwhile.'

Interviews highlighted the extent to which employers feel pressurized by time and by financial constraints; this seemed to influence their preparedness to assess students. Half would do this, so long as guidance was given, whereas the rest did not want to – because of the 'hassle', 'time-restraints' or 'lack of understanding. Four felt unfamiliar with the concept of competences, two had some knowledge and one stated that they are 'meaningless'.

With regard to accreditation via NVQs, three felt they did not have enough knowledge to comment; most were unenthusiastic, with some negative attitudes being apparent: 'not a useful form of accreditation', 'it would be wrong to comment... NVQs [are] not that good'. The most positive statement was: 'something I would be prepared to take on board if that came along with the scheme'. All were invited to scan an abbreviated list of the national framework for Key Skills Qualifications. Most of them ticked the majority of these skills, or groups of skills, as relevant to a STEP placement, but few felt that this was an appropriate approach to assessment or accreditation. It was seen as too difficult, too complex, too time-consuming, unmanageable and full of jargon.

Half the employers felt students were given up to 25 per cent of their time for learning opportunities beyond their personal project, for example, visiting other departments in the company; but this did not mean giving personal attention to the student. Two employers felt learning was not a priority and students took on routine office work for half of their time, without any expectation of new learning from this experience, other than perhaps gaining a realistic picture of what the workplace can be like. One of the problems in relation to assessment is that the employers' main interest is in what the student can bring to the company. Students' learning from the experience is seen as an automatic spin-off, but not as a focus for which the employer should take responsibility.

## *Developing a framework for the assessment of skills*

Interviews highlighted four key areas for skills development during STEP placements:

- communicating;
- focusing on aims/deliverables/products;
- taking responsibility through decision making;
- applying and developing knowledge/skills.

These were used to provided the outline for a work experience framework (see Figure 6.1), which could be broken into sets of skills and subskills.

The design of the framework, and the exact relationship between skills, was left intentionally fluid, because interviews provided no evidence of distinct pathways or relationships between skills, but rather of different links and patterns of development according to context. Nor, at this stage, was it possible to identify any differentiation of levels of skill, as often associated with competence-based frameworks. The word 'experience' was set at the core of the framework, in recognition of the fact that students talked first and foremost in terms of their experience. This is what they remember; this is what is important to them; but from this experience, they can be encouraged to probe more deeply the nature of skills development.

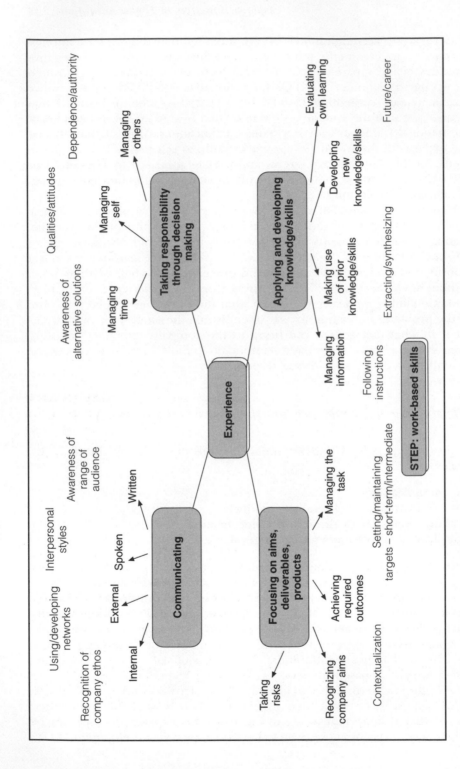

*Figure 6.1*  The work experience skills framework

## Means of assessment

The work experience skills framework was used to underpin the design of:

- a work experience skills development log (a set of preprepared record sheets in A4 booklet form) to provide students with a means of monitoring their own performance and development in relation to the key skill areas (see Appendix E, Format for log record sheets).
- a work experience skills matrix (an A3 tick-box format) by which employers could provide feedback to students on their progress and performance in appropriately selected skill areas.

It seemed important that any assessment initiative undertaken should not require a great deal of additional work for the universities, agencies or employers. The log was devised so as to be self-explanatory and, if completed properly, available as 'evidence' for assessment purposes at the end of the placement. The matrix was devised with the same purpose in mind. There was no intention that students should be formally observed, monitored or assessed during their placement.

## Using the frameworks: student outcomes and feedback

The skills log and matrix were trialled with a cohort of 40 STEP students. The materials were self-managed with almost no introduction from the university. Examples of skills on the framework were provided to both students and employers for guidance (see Appendix F). Student feedback on outcomes was provided via questionnaire and interview; completed logs and matrices were collected for analysis.

### The skills log
Student views on the skills log were unexpectedly positive, especially as completion was voluntary: 'Definitely a worthwhile experience', 'Gave a good overview of what I did. Glad I filled it in every week'. All felt it was useful. Comments included:

> It's so easy to forget what you've been doing and for it all to slip and to merge into one. At the end of the first week I could see it was going to be useful to me, especially for the final report.

> You see how you can split the whole job down into different areas . . . how skills you were acquiring were in completely different areas and it also gave you encouragement. If you didn't have much to say in one area, you could work on that one during the next week.

> That was the definite benefit, because you had to sit down and think about it . . . see where you needed to improve.

The log was appreciated for being portable, always available for reference and providing a convenient format and an easy-to-use overview. Some students recorded ongoing 'critical incidents'; others developed a routine for retrospective completion. The visual impact of the log was considered important (students talked constantly about 'seeing' how skills could be developed from an experience, 'seeing' relationships, 'seeing' what had not been addressed). Just two students reported the log difficult to use, because of the requirement to take their own decisions on how to complete it. However, this is exactly what they must get used to doing for themselves if they are to become independent as learners and workers.

The students felt that completed record sheets would be of particular use for future reference, both to 'look back on and see what was achieved' and because they 'provide a wide range of information useful in future applications to jobs': 'They have headings like this and sometimes you try and think back in your mind to pick up some examples: in which situation did I actually show I could do this.' It was also considered important that employers validated the skills as relevant: 'It gives you reassurance that you are not just saying it, somebody else thought you should have these skills too.'

On their return to university, students reported little direct use of placement skills within degree study, no matter which discipline they came from. However, some changes in perception and attitude were suggested. For example: 'I am more aware of skills that I have developed', 'I have realized the subject matter of a degree is less important than the skills learned', 'It's made me more satisfied with my course in that I've applied my economics in the real world which I'd failed to do before' or 'I think in writing my essays, I've become more critical, looking at them and thinking about how other people would look at them as well. When I was in the job [placement], I had to be aware of how other people were seeing me rather than just doing it for myself'. A growth in confidence was also widely apparent: 'Definitely feel more confident. Nice to know I can do an actual job and complete it successfully. I'm now more outgoing when I meet people', 'I encountered different people, which was nerve-racking at first, but as time went on, I became used to it', 'That's always been my problem, being a little bit, not shy, but standing back and watching. I had to go out there. I had to talk to people even if I didn't want to.' Such comments came from both female and male students.

The growth of confidence was also evident in log descriptions, as shown in the following extracts.

### Paul: communicating
Italics are used to highlight progress from 'reluctance' to communicate, to 'putting pressure' on the employer.

I have not been afraid to ask questions. Everyone is very friendly and helpful.

However, I have been *rather reluctant to contact other people outside the company* – I'm not sure really what I want from them.

I have met a lot of people this week ... I *have not been afraid to ask questions – it saves a lot of hassle* in the long run.

I have been *in touch with outside agencies* in a quest for more information.

I have communicated with my supervisor and various other people in the Board ... *to update people* on my progress.

I have *continued to update my supervisor* on my progress.

I have *had to regularly update my supervisor* on my progress this week and also *pressure him to check through the work* that I have completed already.

## Mark: taking responsibility: decision making

The language used by Mark in his log reflects the way in which he took control of his task:

I had to decide how ...
I decided to analyse ...
I have continued to manage ...
I have had to think carefully about the allocation of ...
I have continued to make decisions as to how to ...

### The employer matrix

The employer matrix was premised on the general findings outlined above: that employers have little time; that they do not find the vocabulary of key skills appropriate; that they are, in the main, averse to the NVQ framework; that there is a perception that students are sent to them in order to 'do a job', not for them to develop student learning, and that this is not their responsibility. For these reasons, a tick-box matrix was developed. This has simple vocabulary, few instructions and requires little reading and little time to complete. (On the other hand, it is deceptively complex, demands selection and thoughtfulness and requires attention to progress over time.)

Feedback on the matrix was gained only from students. Eighty-six per cent claimed the matrix to be useful in terms of outlining their skills and progress. They felt that employers were not so keen on the matrix. Only half of the students thought that employers would perceive this kind of record to be useful and one-third believed they would find it difficult to complete: 'hard to work out which boxes coordinated and were relevant'. However, this was, to some extent, deliberate in the design. A requirement to work at meanings and possibilities, especially if employer and student do this together, is likely to provide a worthwhile experience in understanding what a placement experience might offer: 'He [the employer] looked at the headings and really didn't know what to make of them.' However, by talking, 'deciding what we thought they meant' and using the examples, which were 'a great help', difficulties seemed to be overcome. In future, this kind of shared activity might be pushed more strongly. For this group of employers, there had been no requirement for joint activity of this kind, although it was suggested to students that it would be a worthwhile possibility. Despite the suggestion of difficulties, most employers did complete and annotate the matrix; each completed matrix provides a different picture of student skills.

From the students' point of view, difficulties in understanding related to the complexity of skills, as 'they all interlink'. Reading through the matrix with the employer was considered a great benefit in relating competences to a particular placement. Most students would have preferred to complete it in the presence of the employer but this was not achieved by any of them. Feedback suggests that some employers did discuss the student's progress in the context of the matrix in some detail, whereas others did not. Also, some gave the completed version back whereas others sent it to the university without showing it to the student. This may have been because it was completed after the placement period, but it then became somewhat distant from the student and perhaps less worthwhile.

One student felt the tick boxes: 'don't tell you enough. They don't tell you *why* you are good at communicating, just that you are.' This aspect is something that can be better built into expectations both on the behalf of employers and of students. Discussion between student and employer can further such understanding but student analysis of their own performance is what really counts and employer ticks on the matrix should be made sense of in the context of the log. One student particularly appreciated that: 'the whole point of it is that you can see it corresponds with your record sheets in the log'. For another, the main importance lay in the fact that an employer had highlighted his skills: 'in black and white – very useful for my CV and for finding out about myself'.

## The future: accreditation of STEP placements

It is intended that accreditation will be via a portfolio. Present STEP materials for self-review, presentations and written reports, and data gained from completion of the competence log and matrix, can be used as evidence for different purposes (Figure 6.2). Materials could be presented for either (or both):

• validation within NVQ or Key Skill Qualification frameworks;
• accreditation within a degree.

Neither form of accreditation requires assessment within the workplace. Identification of 'levels' of competence can be achieved via evidence gathered to demonstrate performance and progress and can be matched to national standards through the NCVQ and Key Skill frameworks. For degree accreditation, the writing of a summative, reflective essay allows a traditional form of graded assessment, for which it is realistic that those in higher education should take responsibility. It is hoped that evidence of learning within logs, accompanied by either kind of assessment, will reinforce reflective

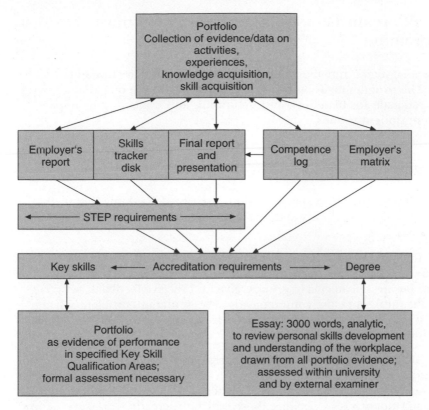

*Figure 6.2* Model for accreditation of STEP placements via portfolio

self-evaluation and the awareness of the world of work of the kind that employers desire.

At present, assessment of portfolios within NVQ/Key Skill Qualification frameworks would require individual student funding; degree accreditation would need university funding only for internal and external examiners. However, many universities still have no means of funding cross-disciplinary initiatives (and STEP students are intentionally drawn from a range of disciplinary backgrounds). This means that degree accreditation cannot easily be undertaken until flexible credit systems are widely available.

It is not appropriate to make generalizations from a small-scale study but this research does illustrate some of the difficulties of change, especially when students, academics and employers, and the cultures of universities and the workplace, are all involved. Students on STEP placements have demonstrated enthusiasm – not just for gaining an experience but also for learning from that experience, monitoring their own performance and responding to descriptions of competences that enable them to make sense of their skills development. This seems an essential foundation for developing strategies for the future.

# The BP Team Development in Universities programme

The second major initiative was a programme for the development of team-work. This programme is outlined in a similar way to the one above, providing a rationale for teamwork and describing and evaluating its impact on different student groups.

## *The importance of teamwork*

The ability to work in teams is another area of skills development that is highly valued by employers and was emphasized in our interviews in major companies:

> We find that people have no perception, straight from university, of team working. They need to be a team, to experience teamworking, solve business problems in groups, give and receive feedback, set goals for the future, practise communication, presentation, problem solving. So, it's all of the things that we need for groups to be able to do, for individuals to be able to do on site.

Team or group work is becoming increasingly important within higher education, not only because of employer requirements but also as a consequence of the increase in intake of students. As student numbers increase and staff:student ratios decline, there will be increasing pressure to find ways of delivering a similar curriculum to that traditionally covered. At the same time, there will be a need to maintain rigour and standards, to ensure the motivation of students and, in many universities, to ensure the continued output of high quality research. It is often assumed that pressure can be removed from staff if students become more independent as learners. Case studies (Dunne 1995; Gibbs 1995) suggest that, to encourage independence, there needs to be a great deal more attention paid to planning for the processes of learning. One of the ways of supporting independent learners can be through the use of groups or teams.

There is also a wide-ranging body of research on team and group work, both clinical and educational, and premised on theoretical perspectives, which suggests that groups and teams can provide a powerful context for learning. Theories of social constructivism (originally emanating from the works of Russian psychologist, Vygotsky, in the 1930s – see, for example, Vygotsky 1962 – and pursued by educationists such as Bruner in the 1970s onwards in the US and UK), now underpin much current thinking at the level of education in schools. This theory is equally useful at the level of higher education. The importance of learning in a cultural context is emphasized and, in particular, the central role of communication within this. Talking is perceived as a major way in which knowledge is constructed, developed and reconstructed by individuals and through which higher-level learning and understanding are promoted.

Each of these perspectives suggests that the development of team and group work is well worth supporting. However, as in the context of schooling (Dunne *et al.* 1991; Bennett and Dunne 1992), it often seems to be assumed that undergraduates are equipped with the skills to work in teams or groups, or that they can be easily learned *in situ.* Attention is seldom paid to training students to recognize and understand the processes, the roles, the tensions and the means of resolving them.

## The team development programme

The one-and-a-half-day team development course was designed for an industrial context. As part of a wider programme of community-based projects, the course was first run five years ago as a small-scale trial with students in one university department. Following the positive response, a programme was devised that now includes ten institutions across England and Scotland. BP also set up a training course for academics in these universities to run the same programme with students, initially with support from BP-funded trainers, but with the longer-term intention of universities being able to support their own.

The course uses a series of (mostly) outdoor problem-solving activities, with a specific focus on understanding the benefits of working with others, reflecting upon how each task has been performed and learning about the theoretical principles of teamwork and team review. The programme is based on a repeated sequence of two main forms of activity:

- A challenging practical task undertaken in teams, usually in the open air, and requiring planning, cooperation, problem-solving skills, creativity, attention to detail, and so on.
- A team review of the task, for the purpose of developing awareness of self and of the team, of strengths and weaknesses, of attitudes and motivations.

To ensure optimum learning from a short programme such as this, the activity/review sequence is repeated, usually up to six times over the duration of one and a half days, to give a good opportunity for practising skills and applying learning just acquired. It also allows any group to go through a series of stages of team performance (Drexler *et al.* 1988).

The programme has a series of theoretical underpinnings. It is designed around Kolb's (1984) 'learning cycle', a model frequently used in the arenas of training and 'experiential learning' (and by many of the human resource managers in our sample of major companies), but not so familiar in higher education. This 'cycle' outlines four distinct phases to learning: experiencing, processing, generalizing and applying (see Figure 7.1). Having a concrete experience does not, of itself, promote learning. It needs to be followed by analysis of that experience. 'Processing' is a reflective stage, encouraged in the context of teamwork by discussing the experience, sharing reactions and observing the reactions of others. Improved understanding of the experience enables movement towards 'generalizing'. This involves the integration of the new experience into prior learning and the development of understanding of patterns and concepts. 'Applying' is a stage of active experimentation, where understandings are used to plan a modified approach to the next experience. The structure of the course is designed to allow participants to go through these stages over and over again, so that awareness and understanding can be built on, and the model evolves into a continuous learning spiral.

## Tasks and reviews

Tasks last from half an hour to one hour. Being set in the open air means a change from the usual university environment and the associated expectations for learning. Each task demands a different kind of physical and mental activity and has a different emphasis on cooperation or independent input. Examples range from taking a burden and a team across a 'minefield' by using fixed 'stepping stones' and planks, or passing a team through a security network, to drawing an original map, executing a task when blindfold and designing and decorating a T-shirt to represent the team. Although the tasks are deliberately selected to support a range of purposes and interests, it is not the doing of the task itself that is important, but the learning that can be taken from the experience.

All review sessions are designed to follow a similar pattern: a period to write down personal thoughts and reactions about the last experience – what went well, what could be improved, what the writer will need to do differently (these questions correspond to the processing and generalizing stages of Kolb's cycle). This is followed by an interactive session where the tutor helps to draw out the lessons, managing and controlling the process but without dominating or imposing views. Reviewing areas for improvement enables planning for the next task. Review sessions are also underpinned by a model devised by Adair (1986), proposing three areas of common need when people work in groups: those of the individual, the group as a whole and the need to accomplish the task.

## Implementation and evaluation of teamwork courses

Within this research study, a number of team development courses was observed in a range of university departments. Three examples of these have been selected to provide brief case studies of courses that had different aims and purposes:

1. The course as designed in its original form and run by the trainers who had designed it (in a chemistry department).

2. An adapted version of the course to suit an individual department and its specific curriculum organization and run by the same trainers (law).
3. A BP-style course run by academics who had received training and were running the course without outside help (computer science).

The descriptions and evaluations cover courses run with, altogether, some 230 first year undergraduates. Each of the three courses is first described and examples of student responses are given. The extent to which each of the courses is integrated into the curriculum is then discussed, as the embedding of teamwork into disciplinary study is one way in which these skills can be practised and developed within higher education.

### The original course
The original-style course is limited to giving small groups of volunteer students a brief introduction to teamwork skills, sufficient for a mention on their CVs. One such course in a department of chemistry took place over a day and a half, with four groups of six or seven students. Tasks and reviews followed the format outlined above, giving plenty of opportunity for repeating the cycle and for building on experiences. There was no specific integration of skills learned on the course into the curriculum, nor any requirement that skills should be used or developed further after the course.

### The adapted course
A department of law collaborated with the BP-funded trainers to adapt the team development programme for specific curricular needs and for large numbers of students. A major focus was on how the teamwork programme could be integrated into existing courses so that it plays a central role in students' learning, rather than remaining peripheral. First year students (150 divided into groups of ten) were expected to work together over the course of the year within a system of workshops. Workshops were designed to improve the quality of the learning environment by moving away from didactic approaches and facilitating the development of both legal and interpersonal skills within the context of substantive law. The team development programme had three explicit aims: (i) to emphasize the benefit of effective teamwork; (ii) to establish a framework and process for tackling group projects in a positive way; and (iii) to start building an identity for each group of students working together.

The restricted length of the course offered (one day) and the size of the groups (ten instead of the usual maximum of eight), suggested that it could serve merely to introduce students to a structure for teamwork development. The importance of the training lay in whether they would be able to apply their learning to more academic problem-solving situations in law (for further detail, see Prince and Dunne 1998). To gain evidence of this, a year's longitudinal study was undertaken in order to monitor the impact of the course on student learning processes, with observational and interview data and the collection of students' written exercises and self-assessments.

Outcomes of this are discussed below in the context of integration of skills into disciplinary learning.

### The course run by academics

A trial in a department of computer science was monitored to assess the effectiveness of a programme led by non-experts. One of the critical features in providing team-building courses of this quality is the cost – much reduced if university tutors can undertake the work rather than using specialist consultants. The course fitted into a series of initiatives in this department relating to the use of generic skills. Earlier feedback had illustrated that, despite attention to skills and students valuing teamwork, being explicit about the kinds of skill they had gained remained difficult. The team development course was therefore seen as a means of reinforcing departmental aims for enhancing project work and building a greater awareness of skills, explicit vocabulary for their description and reflective abilities including self- and peer evaluation.

All 58 Year 1 students, divided into 12 project groups, were requested to attend. The course was modelled on the BP Team Development Course; it was, however, the first occasion on which such a course had been undertaken in this university without the direct involvement of expert trainers. The need to shorten the programme to a maximum of five hours, to fit in with other departmental commitments, created some difficulties. The main question was whether it would be possible to maintain a balance of activities in terms of potential difficulties within a task, as well as maintaining the 'bouncing ball' potential of tasks (Drexler *et al.* 1988), that is, with expectations that group dynamics will shift and change both according to activity and to length of time into the course.

## Student responses

Feedback was gained from written evaluation sheets completed by all students before leaving their team development course. Responses from all three courses were similarly positive. The course was described as an excellent, valuable, worthwhile, useful, interesting or a thought-provoking experience, enjoyable and fun: 'an interesting and constructive day', 'I am very pleased and satisfied'. Many wrote that it had exceeded their expectations. Students commented on the lack of formality and the 'non-pressured' environment, which contributed to the success of the day. The words of one student provide a good summary:

> Extremely valuable, enjoyable and I have many new experiences to take away with me and learn from. It has enabled me to value groupwork as a very enjoyable and productive method of carrying out tasks. I believe I am more able to work as a team member and have gained the ability to experience others' qualities and adapt them.

It was also suggested that the course should be compulsory for all first year students and that it had been 'an invaluable experience for someone from overseas'.

As had been hoped, courses enabled students to 'build a good working relationship' with the members of their group. One described how she: 'realized you get more out of everything' by working as a team; another stated: 'our problem-solving skills improved even in the course of the day. We all had individual approaches and ideas – but by the end of the course we all worked together.' The day: 'helped us to understand that working as a team means making sure everybody understands what is going on and that consideration and respect for others is important'. It allowed them to: 'appreciate each other's skills', to see: 'how to improve myself as part of a team' and demonstrated: 'how well we can function as a team'. It was equally valued by the computer scientists, already operating in teams, with recognition of those skills they would need to implement immediately in project work: for example: 'improving cooperation', recognition of: 'the importance of time management skills' and: 'how essential it is to PLAN!'

## Tasks

Tasks were also described in similar ways across the three courses – as fun, useful, interesting, varied and well designed, presented and organized. Students liked the: 'physical and mental challenges', felt it was: 'enjoyable and worthwhile being outside' and appreciated: 'lots of activities where we can get involved and not have to listen to long talks'. 'I thought it would be really boring and slow moving but in fact we were busy all the time. Time went really fast and I totally enjoyed myself.' Observation of the performance of groups highlighted, as would be expected, that the character of each group was very different; that students responded in a variety of different ways to the tasks; that all groups, at some point of the day, experienced both difficulties in executing a task and in analysing their performance and progress and that all groups had high and low spots, especially in terms of motivation.

## Review sessions

Reviews provoked more mixed responses, providing an example of how student perceptions of the same experience are likely to vary enormously. This mixture of response was apparent within each of the three courses. Positive comments on reviews included:

It was good reviewing the tasks within our small teams.

. . . most useful thing was the summary of how to work better as a team.

These can be compared with:

I liked the tasks but all of the talking about teams went on for too long.

It was quite fun but I thought evaluating every single thing you did was a bit unnecessary.

This is not unusual in feedback from team development courses but, as the reviews are central to the programme and to promoting student learning, there is an onus on tutors to ensure participation and progress in these sessions. It may often be that those who have a preference for being active, rather than reflective, are the ones who are least happy with reviews. However, self-evaluation and evaluation of team progress and of the barriers to progress are important; the review sessions are likely to highlight this and to suggest strategies for analysis and action.

The occasional comment on 'not learning anything' reflects a lack of understanding of what is available from review sessions. It may also be that statements on 'not learning' should not be taken at face value, as appreciation of learning may take place at a later time, after repetition or in a different context. This has also been evident from other groups of students and is well-documented in the literature on experiential learning (see Jacques 1991). It is also possible that the brevity of the courses meant that students were not drawn deeply enough into the processes of team development. Further, student conceptions of learning are often highly dependent on prior experience of learning, which, for many, have previously resided in the context of factual knowledge, subject disciplines and rote learning rather than that of self-development and analysis of behaviours. Changes in conception are not easy to achieve; some students respond more readily than others.

Differences in perception, attitude, motivation and action were apparent between students in each of the three courses. Some students had already experienced similar team development courses elsewhere. Again responses were different, ranging from an enthusiasm for developing and building on prior experience to the belief that, having 'done' the course, there was nothing more to learn (though there was no evidence of such students being more effective than others in their group). There was also little evidence that prior project work in groups had provided them with the skills, or the recognition of skills, promoted through the team development course.

## The integration of skills into disciplinary learning

As part of the normal academic provision in the chemistry department observed, students work in tutorial groups on problem-solving exercises. There is hearsay evidence, from staff who teach these students, that those volunteers who undertake the team development course are better equipped for this at the beginning of the year; it is also thought that differences soon fade. Unfortunately, there is no further self-evaluation required of team or group work skills, no assessment of these at any later point of the degree programme and no planned developmental approach to skill formation. With no further reinforcement, much of the potential of the course may be lost.

The extent to which personal and social outcomes would be valued had not been anticipated by the law department and this feature was reinforced by statements at the end of the year. The day was viewed as a precursor to law-based activities, as had been intended: 'brilliant fun, yet relevant to our work'. It was considered to provide 'a solid foundation for [the] future', 'it allowed members of groups to learn and work within an informal setting, before tackling more complicated problems'.

As a follow-up to the Team Development Course, each workshop group was allocated a task that required research on, and analysis of, a legal theme. The aim was to determine whether the students could easily transfer the skills they had learnt on the BP programme to a legal exercise. Across groups there was evidence of deliberate organization to make the best use of a team, to assess what was practical or possible given the time constraints, to divide the task into manageable units, to allocate tasks, to assess knowledge or lack of knowledge of individuals, to make use of individual strengths and weaknesses and to undertake peer tutoring where appropriate. In reviewing this exercise, there was evidence of taking seriously messages from the BP training: how they worked to team strengths (as assessed during the BP day), how they had: 'learned skills last week which they wanted to put into operation here', how organizational skills were the most important – allocating tasks to maximize coverage and minimize repetition – and how to ensure that all views were taken into consideration. A few who had demonstrated themselves lacking in confidence in speaking out during the BP day were now prepared to join their team effort.

A three-week teamwork simulation exercise on negotiation at the end of the academic year (managed entirely by students) became a major vehicle for students to demonstrate their skills. They demonstrated that they were able to manage their own team organization without demands on teacher time and that both legal knowledge and skills can be supported by team effort. The quality of writing for self-assessment schedules offered further reason for optimism about the processes of teamwork – at least at the level of students being coherent and explicit about their skills. Whether such coherence relates to their abilities to work in teams in the future is yet another question. Despite such encouraging results, a small number of students, although thoroughly enjoying the BP course, did not see any purpose to working in teams. They believed that subject content is all that matters and that it is best learned independently. When this kind of belief was very strong it tended to have a negative influence on the rest of their group.

As all first year students participated in the BP programme, and all completed workshops and the simulation exercise, there is no control group with which to make comparisons. It is therefore difficult to assess the impact of the training, either in terms of the quality of the learning of individuals or of the team output. There is no evidence that traditional examination standards are dropping as a consequence of students working in teams and having fewer contact hours with teachers, but this could be attributed to individual effort rather than the gains of cooperative working.

Transfer was stressed as central to course aims and the relationship of skills to the workplace was reinforced in project debriefing sessions. It was also emphasized that learning from the first year project would need to be transferred to a second year project where the teamwork and academic problems would be more difficult. It is hoped, by staff who teach these groups, that the benefits of the course will be apparent at this stage.

## Discussion

A range of initiatives between higher education and employers was observed during the study. Not all were successful. Bolt-on activities (such as practical problem-solving activities, games, simulations or lectures on 'how to give good presentations'), even if provided by a major company, were not necessarily seen as relevant by students. This was particularly the case when university teachers did not participate (even as observers) to demonstrate that the activity was valued, or did not reinforce learning from this context within disciplinary study. Also, assumptions that what works in training can be brought directly into universities may create false expectations. Using training activities without knowledge of the target students, the context, the constraints or the relationship of the activity to the curriculum, created difficulties.

Both of the programmes studied are widely valued by those who participate in them. The Shell project addresses and supports the needs of employers and offers students opportunities that might not normally be available within higher education. The BP programme is becoming increasingly collaborative and integrated within the curriculum of several of the university departments where it has been welcomed. Both programmes, however, are hampered by widespread resistance amongst academics to development and change and by university administrative systems that do not always easily support new initiatives.

Scrutiny of the outcomes of teamwork courses using outdoor exercises suggests that, despite their being fashionable, there is little evidence of any benefit in the context of training, either to the individual or to the company (see a meta-analysis of such courses by Hattie *et al.* 1997). Many courses use activities that are a great deal more physical and prolonged (even to the extent of creating popular concern for their appropriateness) than those used in the BP Team Development programme. The evidence from this programme in universities suggests that it is worthwhile, especially when reinforced within the processes used for disciplinary study, as in the example of the law department above. In the chemistry department observed, after a day and a half, students were pleased to know their peers better; friendship patterns may have shifted slightly: 'At least I'll say hello to him when I see him in the department now.' This may be positive but it is probably not an important enough impact to warrant the kind of attention and funding that is being put into it.

Many disciplines already pay attention to teamwork, for example in team projects, often for vocational reasons. Others use small groups as a means of students' supporting and learning alongside each other. Traditionally, many students are taught, or gathered together, in small groups for seminars or tutorials. Each of these situations provides a context for which the team development programme would provide a useful preparation to working together. It is likely to be most effective, however, when the curriculum and the learning processes expected of students have been designed specifically to promote teamwork. A major problem is that many university teachers are used to more didactic teaching methods rather than facilitative, interactive and student-centred ways of working. The study outlined above demonstrated that the course run by academics was as well received by students as were the courses run by trainers. There is a real need for training a 'critical mass' of teachers who are able to facilitate this type of learning.

Just as there is a need for continued practice in teamwork, there is a need to address how learning from the workplace can be drawn on within the rest of a degree programme. The STEP students felt that their increased confidence, their communicative abilities and their understanding of what was required for job application forms were the main outcomes of their participation. These are important but there was no evidence of students making connections with degree study or of them being given the opportunity to do this. Hence, the placement remains an isolated experience without opportunities for deliberate transfer between contexts.

Both STEP and the BP Team Development programmes are continuing to build on what has been successful and what has been learned. They are likely to have widespread and lasting impact only in those universities that are working consistently to change the culture of teaching and learning and that have structures, strategies and a curriculum that can make use of, and build on, the expertise and benefits that the programmes offer. What is important is that major employers are prepared to fund initiatives in higher education that go beyond a relationship premised on recruitment needs, that enable a broader-based partnership and that demonstrate a commitment to enabling higher education to meet the new kinds of demands made upon it.

# 7

# Employers' Perspectives on Skills and their Development

Despite the plethora of studies on employers' demands for generic skills, the overall message remains unclear. As the Dearing Report (1997) commented: 'Nor do we find a consensus from employers of where the main deficiencies in skills lie.' The aim of this aspect of the study was therefore to shed more light on employers' perspectives on the need for generic skills, and their development, in graduate trainees.

Semi-structured, in-depth interviews were held with managers of graduate recruitment and training in 24 major companies. These focused on three areas:

- recruitment processes
- the nature of training programmes
- the learning culture of the organization.

Interviews were recorded and transcribed and returned to the respondents for verification. The analysis of interview data followed the design of the instrument and the chapter is thus organized around these three elements. However, because company culture is so pervasive, it is dealt with first; its influence sustains particular sets of values and standards and its norms of behaviour shape how people learn at work. The way company culture impinges on decisions about recruitment is next considered before outlining company training programmes.

## Enculturation

Most organizations in the study have been forced to change during the past decade, with a consequential shift from endemic mission statements towards policies that encourage employee initiative and self-reliance. Regardless of the degree of change, the culture shock for graduates involved in the transition from higher education to employment is considerable (Graham and McKenzie 1995). Graduate trainees have to adapt and learn how to work in the new environment, how to 'fit in' and how to contribute. Companies were therefore asked to describe their culture and the strategies used to socialize graduates into the company. Questions were also asked about conditions and practices that were thought to contribute towards a workplace learning culture.

## Company culture and the learning/working environment

Organizational structure and policy are important components of a company's culture and the impact of change on this culture was mentioned by over half the companies. For example, change resulted from company merger, where each organization's way of working did not necessarily result in synergy, or as a result of delayering – removing layers of supervision to a 'flatter' organization. Such changes influenced the working environment dramatically, for example, bringing about a shift in relationship between management and staff. The nature of 'delegated empowerment' and 'partnership' is described by Harvey *et al.* (1997); it can be limited, constrained and even counterproductive. In one company, a larger stake in the company and partnership was described positively:

> The relationship between the company and the individual has changed and evolved quite dramatically within the last 15 years. We've gone from a very paternalistic approach to staff welfare to more of a partnership between the individual and the organization. Fifteen years ago we were renowned for some of our welfare benefits . . . a lot of these benefits disappeared, but other benefits have improved, like profit sharing.

Another company was positive about the change from a hierarchical cascade type of culture, where decisions, ideas and procedural guidelines were imposed from the top. This rigid 'vertical' culture (senior managers – department managers – supervisors – employees) was changed towards a 'horizontal' one, as a training manager described it: 'The old bureaucracy was self-defeating and, slowly but surely, the detailed guidelines have disappeared. There's now more feeling of creativity, like an empowering that staff now have.' The new culture was described as more open, where trust and respect were valued, and where IT quickened the process of change:

> A lot of changes are through the introduction of IT; everybody has a PC – we've got e-mail. We used to be very formal (in letter writing) – e-mail changes all that – you wouldn't dream of being so formal. So, it breaks down barriers and makes for better working relationships . . . We're actively encouraging people to do their own thing now, hardly any secretaries, and most people do a lot of their own admin.

The changes meant that top management created a more flexible organization and trusted employees to learn about wider and different roles. It was seen to be more equal-footed too, the buildings were re-vamped so that: 'all managers will be out in the main forum, you wouldn't know who were the managers and who were not'. One consequence of empowering the staff was 'a general feeling that anyone can teach anyone else . . . I taught one of the managers to do Excel graphs'. In this company, a reconceptualization of company structure created a different learning culture and demanded a reappraisal of training in generic skills, particularly in collaborative skills.

Many other companies, not necessarily in the throes of dramatic change, described how empowerment altered the contexts of jobs and the relationship between management and employees. A more open supportive atmosphere, group decision making and initiative by individuals is characteristic of a system based on a 'bottom–up' approach. In one company, the emphasis of training and acquiring generic skills utilizes employees' knowledge and encourages on-the-job learning and group collaboration:

> The thing that has beset so much of the word 'development', including higher education, is the arrogant notion that it all has to be top–down – it all has to be brought about by institutional intervention – that students learn nothing unless they're taught those things, etc. It seems to me that is a less and less appropriate approach . . . If I had to choose between the top–down and bottom–up approach; between building key skills in a formal way through institutional trainers, or empowering individuals to think much more constructively about learning, reflect upon their experiences and their achievements, and plan for their future learning – if I had to choose between those two, then I would go for bottom–up and empowerment.

The policy of this company is clearly towards lessening central control and providing support for continuous learning; in the process respecting the diverse experiences and prior achievements of its workforce. A similar overarching policy of developing collaborative skills and insistence on con-tinuous improvement, such as 'looking for better ways of doing things', is made easier for training managers when the influence of a country-culture is strong. The human resources manager in a company influenced by Japanese culture explained how the company credo permeated activities:

> The company has three formal guiding principles, which are 'harmony, sincerity and pioneering spirit'. Some people think that's a load of old rubbish but it's not actually, because the Japanese idea of harmony, and the group is more important than the individual, [means] you have to get a consensus decision made. You see that every day. The sincerity element comes through as well, and then pioneering spirit is about technology and moving the business forward and being innovative . . .

These three basic concepts – about respecting the opinions of others and cooperating, being open and honest and sincere, and having a purposeful approach to one's work through individual initiative – are expressed in other companies in less poetic terms. The language of intent may be informal,

*Table 7.1* Summary of contrasting descriptors, taken from interviews, describing top–down and bottom–up philosophies

| Top–down | Bottom–up |
|---|---|
| Formal, leading by example | Personal commitment and reflection |
| Paternalistic intervention | Partnership |
| Competency framework imposed by trainers | Competences as part of personal development plan |
| Being taught | Teaching each other and self-learning |
| Teaching through course structures | Learning in different ways/learning preferences/self-management |
| Dependent | Empowered |
| Formal appraisal | Self-appraisal, discussion and cooperation open, honest, sincere, respecting others, innovative, trusting/open |

often expressed as a vague 'psychological contract'. The words used to describe the culture in directive hierarchical management and collaboratively run institutions are shown in Table 7.1. For convenience they have been labelled as 'top–down' and 'bottom–up', but the reality of organizational practice often reflects a mix of attitudes and behaviours. For example, empowerment can take a range of forms, from self-management to controlled and limited decision making.

Functioning in the 'bottom–up' environment means that even young trainees feel able to be innovative, have their views listened to within a team, on occasion take risks and to a large extent be responsible for their own learning. Companies with a 'top–down' philosophy, or 'telling people what to do philosophy', provide a vivid contrast.

For example, in one company the competency framework structured the way graduates were socialized into the workforce and developed skills:

> . . . it states specifically the behaviours which the company expects of its people. The down side to it, it's only one vision of the world, it's the company vision and people *are* different! . . . We have a lot of sessions with senior management, where the objectives of the company are communicated to staff. That will then result in individuals repeating the process for their own teams. So, there's leading by example, there's a lot of hierarchical cascade-type events that happen, that will end up with each individual, at every level, having objectives that are all aligned with the company business plan . . . if you're involved in an activity that isn't included within this range of activities, then you're not doing the right thing.

In another company a similar 'top–down' learning culture is achieved through placement, graduates working alongside senior management.

Messages about the culture are passed on implicitly, 'by osmosis' as one person said, rather than via formal avenues:

> ... they sit with an experienced manager in the office. They literally sit there ... They learn on the job. You get a feel. You look around. You realize those people that are doing well. Why are they doing well? It's quite a specific culture. It's a very strong meritocracy ... about being very good, and achieving ... if you ask the trainees now (after 2 and a half months) they'd say, 'Yes ... I know about the culture.' So, it isn't anything we formalize, it's something more that they learn from observing.

Learning from observing and apprenticeship in the form of practical training, can be taken to an extreme when the professional or 'lead' body's philosophy dominates, prescribing training course content. In engineering companies, in particular, specialist training is 'geared towards meeting professional body requirements', accreditation from, for example, the Institution of Electrical Engineers or Institution of Civil Engineers. In one company:

> ... the needs that drive training and determine the content of programmes is the lead body ... We are a company in which the lead body is a dominant factor in determining the type of learning that goes on ... the training courses are only 10 per cent of their training. The rest of it is on-the-job training ...

Few would deny that practical work experience can lead to better understanding than passive reception of theoretical knowledge. However, one consequence of a restrictive 'top–down' philosophy of a professional (lead) body is its minimal attention to generic skills training. Training within this culture is acknowledged as insufficient for future managers, and as providing less organizational flexibility:

> ... we are aware that that's a problem. We have in place a variety of management development activities for middle and senior managers to make sure they're broadly educated. Where I think we've got some more work to do is the step before that. How do you get into it in the first place if you're functional? How do you go from functional to managerial.

Many admit that the concept of 'learning culture' is difficult to express. It is made even more difficult in large organizations within which discreet cultures flourish, maintaining individual identities in spite of hierarchical pressures to conform. With different placements early on in training, graduates are likely to get different messages, particularly when one role for line managers and mentors is to make employees aware of the workplace culture: 'If he sees you doing something which may not be in the culture-fit he will guide you and say, "look, in this company you do things this way".' Similarly, in another organization the mentor is expected to 'act as coach, tutor, intellectual stimulator to expand the individual, to socialize the graduate'. The policy demands a great deal of the mentor, when socialization emphasizes 'striving to make feedback part of the culture of our organization'. This is particularly so when the culture is developing 'soft skills', including 'listening, empathizing, diplomacy, sharing, cooperating, forging reciprocal relationships and confronting constructively'.

It is clear that most companies thought that socialization into the company culture was important and a necessary ingredient for competitive success; 66 per cent of the sample stated that induction was the main strategy used to introduce graduates to their culture and ways of working. For example: 'they're introduced to the company's vision and values, and the way we expect people to behave, and that's with openness and integrity and to respect each other'.

Induction programmes were described as opportunities to: 'be "indoctrinated" into the ways of the company, to meet directors and senior managers who talk to them about the company and its philosophy'. Surprisingly, induction was chosen as the means to give explicit messages about company culture, even though it was frequently admitted that induction was far from being effective for imparting such important understandings. As one manager indicated: '. . . we give them some idea, but I think to be fair, it's something they learn on the job'.

## Teamworking skills as a reflection of company culture

The language used to describe the way teams operate is often vague, yet team functioning is an important indicator of and contributor to a company's culture. Stasz *et al.* (1996) point out: 'teamwork is not a "skill" but a description of how work is organised'. Research indicates that, to be maximally effective, the culture in practice is not to have teamwork as 'bolt-on' training, but rather embedded team functioning in all training activities. Jones (1996) offers practical advice when she points out that the team skills of communication, problem solving and decision making are very general and vague and: 'do not inform people exactly *how* to perform those skills or what they actually need to *do* to develop them'. To be effective, underlying functional skills are required, (she includes the ability to initiate, consult, request advice, give alternative ideas, weigh up different viewpoints . . . ), which in turn require interpersonal skills (she includes listening, openness, non-abrasiveness, tolerance, self-reflection . . . ) to develop an effective team person.

Some companies have endeavoured to be more precise and have broken down the broad team skills to provide detailed lists of functional and interpersonal skills. These are not necessarily given as word-lists but as sentences that describe the behaviours necessary to become effective at 'working with others'. For example, activities designed to develop teamworking in one company are intended to be used alongside the company competences:

Develop your own ability by:

- Listening to what each team member, including yourself, contributes to the team. Include both the work they do and any extra things (e.g. humour, focus, attention to detail) they bring.
- Analysing your own contribution to the team. Where and how could you contribute more? Ask others for feedback and ideas.

Develop the ability of those who work for you by:

- Giving positive feedback to people who support others and work cooperatively within the team.
- Discussing problems that threaten harmony in the team openly with the appropriate team members. Work with them to find a solution.

In another company, teamworking skills are built directly into the competency framework. Each competence has written descriptors, for example: 'A manager asks someone who has been successful to share the method with others' and these are provided to illustrate 'How could I do it?' However, such detailed suggestions and guidance of what to do to develop team skills was not common. (Eraut *et al.* 1998, give examples of informal ways people learn from others in the workplace and how company culture affects the quality of learning support.)

There is more to team effectiveness than the development of functional skills; underpinning collaborative interpersonal skills are so-called 'soft skills', which include attitudes towards others and oneself. To make for effective team cooperation, attitudes of respect, trust, empathy and liking others were stated as important. One manager said the set included: '. . . wanting to be part of a team, wanting the team to succeed and really promoting, not just the individual perspective, but the success of the team itself. It's really about valuing other people's input.'

Although the intent to encourage collaborative team culture and team learning skills may be part of the culture, the process may still be daunting if, during training programmes, graduates are not encouraged, or given the opportunity, to perform as genuine team members. In reality, the notion of 'valuing others' and 'contributing' may be made easier if trainees are made to feel equal. For example, wearing distinctive uniforms in the Armed Forces was stated as undoubtedly contributing towards an ethos of camaraderie but not, as was explained, to producing 'sausages out of a factory'. There is a learning culture, not: 'the tabloid view of the military which encompasses people who are not questioning, and do as they are told . . . this is a very anachronistic view . . . we want humility, tolerance and patience . . . and people who have an enquiring mind'. In non-military organizations, dress code creates a particular ethos of equality:

The egalitarian ethos is taken further in this company where individuals, regardless of status wear the same style clothes . . . managing director, manufacturing staff; I think the acid test for us is if you go into any work group, that it is not immediately apparent a) what the hierarchy is and b) where is the graduate? Who is the technician? That's actually quite important in terms of this notion of liberating peoples' full contribution.

This instance of single status clothing was only one element that promoted a team culture. As Wickens (1987) has pointed out, teamworking and commitment is: 'not dependent on people working in groups . . . [and] cannot be achieved by introducing a "flavour of the month technique" . . . it's something which develops because management genuinely believes in it and acts accordingly'. In the above example, newcomers were empowered to solve problems, given responsibility and encouraged to discuss with those in hierarchical positions.

One enabling device used by another company infused ideas about *how* groups functioned. TV footage of actual business meetings were shown, as a form of modelling: '. . . clips of what's happening within the business, in terms of ways of working . . . day-to-day life . . . showing how they [managers] work with colleagues'.

Another company felt that the true work culture could be understood only through immersion in *real* meetings, as early as possible, to realize the way teams function effectively. It provided a strong supportive team culture, in which new graduates were enabled to make significant contributions. An additional benefit for newcomers was to get acquainted with particular expertise of individuals, to build an effective 'network of relationships to get things done':

> . . . graduates are given exposure to various structural meetings during the course of a project . . . These are extremely sophisticated and are very complicated . . . looking at some of the commercial, technical and financial aspects of how the project's developing, and not least with customers. So, what we do is expose young graduates to that at a fairly early stage . . . so they begin to see the way in which people operate . . . And it's not unusual for new graduates who have specialist knowledge to be asked particular questions, but in a very supportive way . . . it's about growing people's confidence and competence to be able to operate in a productive way, with customers and with suppliers and with their peers.

Effective team functioning, through appropriate practical workplace procedures, was perceived as a powerful means of providing a continuous learning culture. It was also seen as a way genuinely to empower and motivate, particularly those graduates who could make full use of their recently acquired knowledge. Companies obviously do not operate exclusively in groups or as individuals, for differences in balance reflect the nature of the business as well as the policy of the company.

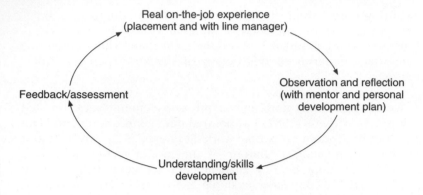

*Figure 7.1*　Kolb's learning cycle

## Self-learning as an indicator of company culture

Companies provide many opportunities for learning from experience or learning by doing. Three companies specifically mentioned how Kolb's (1984) applied theory of experiential learning (Figure 7.1) influenced their training programme.

This process approach is described in one company where, on placement, there is a learning agreement between the trainee and the company; objectives are identified so that performance can be measured against expected standards:

> The significant thing is the individual's performance in the workplace . . . an approach which values practical first-hand experience and values most highly experiential learning and the demonstration of practical competence . . . What provision is there to reflect? We have what is described as a personal development file . . . and we encourage every trainee, to use it, to reflect upon their achievements, their experiences and to review their learning for the future. The notion of records of achievement and individual development plans is the way in which we turn the rhetoric of lifelong learning into practical reality. So, review and reflection, capturing evidence, is something which is built into that initial [induction] week, and which is then continued in their training.

The workplace culture is seen to be vital for continuous improvement, and there were many variations on the theme of 'working coaches' to illustrate how trainees were helped to make sense of theory and encouraged to question and to interact. One form of guided practice is provided by peer assistance – more experienced working coaches who share their expertise. Some companies acknowledge that the skill 'helping others' requires training

(Eraut *et al.* 1998), not only in explaining and giving feedback, but in perceiving when help is needed.

Other companies have created an effective learning environment by extending this idea; trainees themselves are trained to help other trainees learn. For example, 'coaching and development' in one company is a key competence, which involves personal reflection and helping others:

> 'Coaching and developing' is the ability to analyse one's own perform-ance, to identify what mistakes one has made and to do something about it . . . working for self improvement . . . But it also incorporates other people and how you develop them . . . we are looking for evidence of learning, not only of an individual skill, but also learning from interfacing with others.

Brown (1994) draws attention to successful practice in Japanese training, where the commitment to learning and continuous improvement is deeply embedded in cultural value, and where the idea of 'working coaches' is seen as most compatible with the learning company. This form of support is given in one company, already mentioned, which produces a guide to help graduates understand what competences like 'leadership' look like in prac-tice. For example: 'volunteering to act as a support tutor on training courses where feedback to participants will be required, and maintaining a record of the feedback you provide to individuals, including the ratio of praise to criticism'.

To assist self-learning, trainees are sometimes told about different learning styles. Only one company produced the means (questionnaire, scoring sheet, descriptions) for graduates to determine their learning style, the degree to which they were an 'activist', a reflector', 'theorist' or 'pragmatist' (see the similar approach to teamwork training in Chapter 6 on the BP Team Develop-ment programme). Choosing a preferred way of learning was intended to help self-learning and a library of books, CD-ROMs, video and audio tapes provided considerable support for this. Concomitant with this provision was the message that graduates were 'in charge of their own careers'.

Mention has already been made of the influence of lead bodies on the culture of an organization. Individual learning, often completed in com-pany time, to gain higher qualifications and chartered status, is common in engineering and finance. The practice was described as providing motiva-tion for the individual and the company benefits from a highly educated workforce. However, an environment that encourages study for qualifica-tions and status, regardless of how generous the time allocation, does not necessarily cultivate loyalty and commitment to the company:

> . . . [improving qualifications] that's practically automatic. If you're in Finance, you'll do a finance qualification, which is very transferable. It's particularly good for the company if somebody is qualified, CIMA for instance, and it gives them the enthusiasm to stay, but they're more poachable. So, it's a real gamble [for the company] but I think it pays off.

It would appear that this problem is endemic to training in industry in the UK and it is important to address it, for it has repercussions on recruitment, training programmes and working practices.

## Recruitment

There is every indication that companies value their recruitment programme and that recruitment is taken seriously. Advertising is through directories, newspapers and, more recently, the Internet, but less so than previously through recruitment fairs. Brochures deliver the company message, often linked with glossy and imaginatively designed graphics with visual appeal. Some provide case studies of trainees to help candidates make decisions about whether company rewards are commensurate with the responsibilities described. The uniqueness of the company, its 'contract', training and promotion opportunities appear to be described honestly, for brochures and interview statements support each other. A few include a self-score questionnaire, based on life in the organization, and candidates can interpret whether they would be suitable.

What qualities are employers looking for in potential employees? The Dearing Report (1997) has clearly signalled the need for a highly educated and highly trained workforce. For one company, this message is translated into requirements for their ideal candidate:

> . . . not just the academic level, second class degree honours, but also what accompanies that, in terms of development, work experience, any positions of responsibility that the student might have held, added to their personal set of skills . . . and also fluency in another language.

Competition between companies is fierce for such 'intelligent, but rounded people'; the selection process has to cope with enormous numbers of applicants, from which only a handful can be offered employment. The 1997 intake from six companies illustrates this point:

* 70 from 5000
* 150 from 3000
* 80 from 8000
* 700 from 12,000
* 40 from 3500
* 10 from 800.

Despite using a different vocabulary, companies' initial requirements for graduates were similar:

* commercial awareness/experience ('what they've got out of work experience');
* enthusiasm/drive/proactivity/initiative/challenging;
* working with people/interpersonal skills/team players/'fitting-in';
* leadership qualities;

- communication capabilities;
- degree/technological awareness/thinking and problem-solving skills.

The criteria for recruitment reflect those competences that are used for company-wide appraisal. Different companies naturally emphasize some criteria more than others. For example, whereas for many any degree is acceptable, some recruitment policies, for example in engineering, law and actuarial work, have specific academic requirements. In these instances the focus changes: '. . . quite a lot of emphasis is on technical functional skills, a good financial person, marketing person, or a good engineer or good researcher'.

Competency frameworks, used for screening, are ambiguous when broad terms like 'communication' and 'teamwork' are used (Stasz *et al.* 1996). These terms are weak and need to be contextualized if selection is to be more than a bureaucratic procedure. In one company, descriptors (for example, for 'intellect') relate to specific job demands:

- applying logic to solving problems;
- sifting and sorting complex information;
- grasping new concepts quickly;
- producing innovative solutions.

Careful identification of competences is much more likely to provide what is needed. However, there is a dilemma that needs addressing: what if the selection of graduates with desirable generic skills (for example of being 'assertive', 'a risk-taker', 'innovative') was found on arrival not to 'fit' the culture of the organization:

> We do definitely want those type of people. We call them Mavericks. Once these people were in, we were suppressing their ideas, we were suppressing their creativity and we were throwing our cultural norms on to them. They were either frustrated, so they left the business, or they became very much corporate led . . . we do want these people who can ask questions and be creative and be the risk takers, and our environment is becoming more tolerant towards taking these people on.

Many companies indicated that they really did not want company clones and, perhaps unexpectedly, the Armed Forces train personnel to: 'question what they are doing, but this has to be sensibly within the bounds of military discipline'.

A further recruitment problem is that criteria may be effective for immediate requirements but may not necessarily reflect longer term needs:

> There are concerns that if we have people, for instance with too heavy a reliance on team working, they cannot lead, and find managing very difficult in complex situations . . . if you're seriously looking to tomorrow's top managers, they exhibit different types of competences, because they're high performing . . . So we need to track back when we're recruiting. What are people's analytical skills? How can they conceptualize? How do they make judgements?

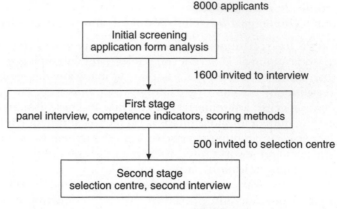

8000 applicants

Initial screening
application form analysis

1600 invited to interview

First stage
panel interview, competence indicators, scoring methods

500 invited to selection centre

Second stage
selection centre, second interview

80 selected

| | |
|---|---|
| Initial screening: | Paper sift, generally in-house (selection holistic – no single hurdles) |
| First stage: | 45-minute interview using a set of competence indicators (for example, teamwork, organizing, leadership, business focus) and a scoring sheet (reference made to application form) |
| Second stage: | At Selection Centres, carefully constructed activities test, among other things, numerical, verbal and abstract reasoning abilities. Candidates are asked to give a presentation, take part in a group exercise (4–8 per group) and individual exercises in problem solving. Assessors record evidence of, for example, 'organizing and planning' and 'influencing' skills. Judgement is made on a number of defined positive and negative indicators, for example: |

Plans and modifies approach with
people to achieve desired outcomes

Uses the same approach to
different people

Assessors rate candidates' performance using a matrix (skills against exercises); this provides a final score at the end of the second stage. Discussion of the matrix scores and results from a second interview lead to selection.

*Figure 7.2*   General pattern of selection for graduate entry (numbers are actual figures from one company for 1997)

The evidence shows that many employers are well aware of the need to have long-term goals, balance 'safe' recruitment for immediate jobs with innovators for future strategic managers and revise their selection criteria annually. At whatever risk level a company operates, recruitment patterns indicate that the selection process is rigorous, can be lengthy and can provide many opportunities for candidates to show their capabilities. The process is in general characterized by the sequence shown in Figure 7.2. Variations to this general pattern include:

- Companies' selection procedures are totally in-house. The rationale is: '. . . about relevance of the exercise . . . if you out-source it, you're then

reliant on their interpretation of what you want. The second issue concerns the people who are involved in our assessment centre, they have to ultimately manage and train these individuals'.
- Reducing the labour intensive paper sift by handling applications through a web-site: 'they can apply on-line . . . no need for an application form, and we acknowledge it immediately electronically'. First-stage screening can be done electronically too. Candidates' CVs are scanned into a database, electronically matched against criteria and letters generated to successful and unsuccessful candidates.
- Some companies use psychometric testing, in addition to interviews.
- The nature of the tests at centres can be of a general nature (for example, the well known 'Zin Obelisk' problem, used to elicit skills of teamworking). Alternatively, tests are specific; a candidate applying to marketing: 'would have market research information to analyse and interpret'.
- Fast-track recruitment as, for example, found in some branches of the Civil Service, is particularly demanding: 'There is no prerecruitment sift; all candidates are invited to sit the qualifying test which is a series of cognitive tests (verbal organization, verbal reasoning, data interpretation).' Selected candidates are then invited to a centre for assessment against defined criteria, including cognitive ability, group functioning and personal qualities. Challenges include an in-tray decision-making exercise, letter-writing and summarizing technical writing for a non-technical person. In addition, there are three separate interviews. There is focus on a candidate's ability to argue: 'to think quickly and laterally, have a view on certain issues, and be prepared not to be swayed, but to volunteer the other point of view'.
- Encouragement of work placements, typically three months in real working environments, providing opportunities to identify potential future employees and for students to assess the company.
- Targeting recruitment, through links with higher education, can be advantageous (an industrial year or industrial placement on sandwich courses, or work experience during vacations). In one company, advantages of sponsorship programmes are considerable, where: 'the degree is totally specified by the company . . . in terms of a standard framework and performance criteria . . . all the things that you would expect to see in an NVQ. That was our starting point for specifying what someone completing that degree would know, understand and be able to do. It is a programme designed by us.'

## Training

As the previous section indicated, there is severe competition for graduate jobs. Employers select those who are academically able and who also have personal characteristics and experiences to become future top managers. These graduates, in general, were selected directly into a company's 'initial

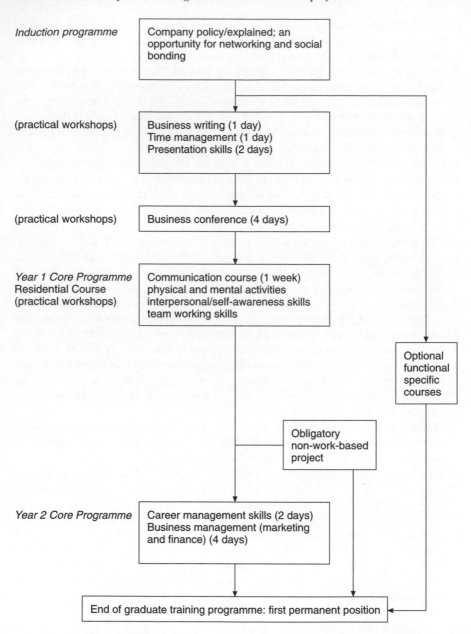

*Note:* The Year 1 and Year 2 core programmes are integrated into on-the-job experience, with real job responsibiltities.

*Figure 7.3*  An outline of training provision by the case study

graduate training scheme'. The scheme could be a mix of in-house training sessions and time spent with outside agencies. If the latter, there was every indication of close partnership, companies indicating the skills training required, within the learning culture and philosophy of the company. Programmes were minimally of six months duration, generally lasted for two years and were structured around placements or work experiences. The importance of the latter was stressed as '*real* jobs from day one'.

All training programmes were a blend of training and learning strategies. It is not possible to describe all the schemes but one case study is provided (Appendix G). Essentially, the two-year programme has optional courses on skill development, which are taken concurrently with the core programme, and an obligatory non-work-based project in the second year (Figure 7.3). There are a number of variations to this particular training programme and five elements of practice are evident:

*Induction practices*

Most companies organize some form of induction. There is no common pattern across the sample to describe the event, either in terms of when it occurs or of its duration or purpose. For some companies the induction starts on the first day the trainee arrives, others one or two months after work experience(s). The event can last a single day or can extend to ten weeks. The location can be at the company site, at an outdoor training centre, in expensive hotels or even in exotic locations in far-flung corners of the world.

The rationale for spending time and money on induction varies considerably. Induction can be the major introduction to the business, often through a director's welcome, where: 'we talk about our values, and our inspirations as a company'. The format is usually a lecture:

> . . . the presentations are angled so that the graduates feel part of the company, not part of a particular department . . . it's about broadening their understanding of the culture and their individual responsibilities for learning and improving themselves . . . in terms of lifelong learning and how we are going to create a learning organization.

It was admitted that the concept is: 'relatively easy to talk about, [but] much more difficult to do'. One approach was to be explicit about management values in the workplace, that is, to tell graduates that their knowledge was valued and to encourage those who were: 'not comfortable in just doing the same things we've done for years'. The workplace was signalled as a place for potential 'change agents' to thrive.

Rhetoric about management theory, learning and empowerment at induction, especially in lectures, was often described by managers as ineffective. To give experience of company philosophy in action, one company sends their graduates on placement for two weeks: 'to see how the store works . . . to introduce them to the world of work and to gain a real overview of the company'. Another company provided business simulation games, opportunities to interact with staff or discuss with recently appointed graduates. These opportunities were thought to make it easier to learn about 'how to learn and function within this company'.

Another company made teamworking on a technical project a major function, with opportunities to meet the hierarchy formally and informally. There were two objectives: one was the obvious 'getting contact lists together' but, more important than networking, the rationale signalled an important message about empowerment, as a right of an individual to information:

> ... networking would be with each other in the graduate group ... working on a 'design and make' project, and with the wider company, because senior people are invited to join for lunches throughout the induction week ... So, they're building up the embedded knowledge that, in doing your task for the company you have the right to the information you need, from whoever else works here ... to help you with your work.

One company initially provided work experiences, followed by induction, with opportunities to network. Graduates who had not met before were involved in activities demanding cross-divisional team activities. During the week's intensive training graduates could talk to each other about their recent experiences. Different perspectives of the company philosophy became known through peer interaction rather than rhetoric:

> The induction week is where ... all the graduates that we're taking in that year come together for a week ... The rationale is very much about sharing perspectives by meeting other people ... and it's about getting those people to network. Networking is really the key to the business ... getting people to work together ...

This company's philosophy of team endeavour and sharing perspectives was developed through collaborative group tasks at an outdoor management centre. After each group exercise they were encouraged to reflect on business issues, about leadership styles and team players. Another company, with the same philosophy about 'cooperative working and learning from each other' also used an outdoor pursuits centre for induction, but the residential course was held at the beginning of training. Also, whereas the latter course emphasized learning to cooperate through physical activities, the means by which the former's training was developed was through actual business activities.

*Placement and the narrow or broad experience*
Initial training often involves job placement in different teams, departments or divisions. In one company, depending on the functional area, placement was job-specific, a narrow experience or of a general nature. In either orientation 'all jobs the graduates do are *real* jobs':

If they move into Finance, they'll always be working within a finance area . . . If they're in Marketing or Sales they rarely move around . . . Within the technical personnel and operations areas, they move across functions. So they could spend six months as a line manager in a factory . . . then six to twelve months on an engineering project or at head office. They could spend six months working in marketing or working in sales or working in one of our logistics depots where we distribute the product to the customers. They have a much more varied scheme.

The rationale behind the broad scheme is to give graduates:

. . . a feel about what the company's about, and help them develop a range of skills from across the business . . . we've watched them move from job to job . . . and we can identify those who adapt quickly and are flexible in their roles . . . Further, by moving around the different functions, they have different opportunities to develop different competences.

Placement was thought to provide experiential learning, developing skills outlined in the competency framework and reflecting work culture.

*The influence of NVQs*
Only three companies incorporated NVQs into their training programme, despite these qualifications being specifically designed for this kind of context. In one company, the rationale for using NVQs was essentially to experience the working environment, the physical demands of the production line, the effects of shift work and repetitive tasks, and awareness of the importance of team collaboration. Placement was based around an NVQ framework and learning objectives were met through observation, work measurement, oral questioning and written evidence. For example, performance criteria in a unit on 'working in an industrial environment' included:

- parts conform to specification;
- own work samples checked correctly;
- quality deviations identified and correct procedures followed.

In this company approximately 80 per cent of the graduates are taken on as a result of a three-month placement. However, it was insufficient time for some to recover from the shock that learning generic skills might include achieving an NVQ Level 2 in production line assembly. The following comment confirms the findings in Chapter 6, that some undergraduates are not keen on NVQ or generic skill qualifications in the context of degree study:

. . . with some graduates . . . the notion of developing skills that are assessed at Level 2 really doesn't sit very comfortably alongside their view of themselves as graduates. So the experience comes as a bit of a shock, but it is entirely consistent with the notion that all of us, in whatever we do, should be working to clear and unequivocal standards.

In another company, the training programme is innovatory, based upon shortening NVQ units, making them specific to the company's requirements and simplifying the evidence-gathering process. Line managers act as mentors with a dual role: '. . . not only would they be setting the targets (for an individual) but they would also be observing to see whether those targets had been met, and giving advice and guidance on the best way to meet them'.

The rationale for the programme is that there is an undoubted need for vocational training and that graduates have to experience the training themselves to be in a position to promote NVQ qualifications in others when they, in turn, become managers.

### The influence of professional lead bodies

Professional regulatory bodies often provide the motivation for lifelong learning within a company. In one engineering company, graduates are recruited with an insistence that they become chartered. Lead bodies dictate requirements in technical and generic skills, and approve the training:

> . . . civil engineering in particular has a very specific list of both technical and professional skills required . . . We have an accredited scheme for civil, mechanical and electrical engineers. Within that, each person has to achieve similar objectives, albeit by different means.

Because of the lead body's influence, the training department operates rather differently from others in the sample. It does not exist to deliver the actual training but to ensure the smooth running of the training scheme, 90 per cent of which is on-the-job, practical application of knowledge on technical matters, that is, structural design, environment, ventilation and the like, on law and contracts, and on safety. Because the scope is very broad, training in managerial core skills is limited, with an emphasis on graduates actively promoting their own training.

The rationale for the training programme in this company is a mix of professional directives for continuous development and business sense:

> . . . the training plan always has to be rooted within the business plan. Our overall aim is to produce chartered engineers, giving them the right skills to gain that qualification, and hence be more valuable to the group. We can charge more to clients for their services . . .

### Developing the whole person: community projects and outdoor pursuits

It is clear that some companies have a broader perspective of management training than others and include such activities as 'outdoor adventure training'. Such activities take individuals out of their normal environment and challenge their ways of thinking and behaviour in unfamiliar settings (as, for example, within the BP training for teamwork decribed in Chapter 6). Common features include an austere environment, working in small groups to achieve physically demanding challenges (like abseiling or building constructions over obstacles) and intense problem-solving activities. The Armed Forces rely on physically and intellectually demanding courses to develop teamwork and potential leaders. In one unit with a 95 per cent graduate intake, austere initial training was perceived: 'as creating amongst them the esprit that they will need, together as a group, when the going gets harder ... the ethos is crucial to us'. Organizations' outdoor pursuit approaches bear a strong resemblance to the practice advocated by Tuson (1994).

However, the outcomes of such programmes, in terms of transfer of skills on return to work, are by no means clear (Hattie *et al.* 1997). Critics see outdoor training as an expensive way to have fun, with little substantive evidence of its effect on management development; some companies in our study have decided to discontinue training outdoors.

No training programme is inherently good *per se*. What makes it good is the quality of instruction and adequate feedback. Feedback is reported as the most powerful single moderator that improves achievement as well as affective outcomes. Companies that offer optional community programmes insist on feedback. In one company, graduates are encouraged to take part in community-based projects through The Prince's Trust Volunteers Scheme. The scheme supports the company's core development training by providing opportunities to develop teamworking and management skills. Feedback is provided by the Trust leader and line manager, but there is a strong emphasis on self-assessment.

There is almost no evaluation data for such community programmes. One company went beyond anecdotal evidence and observed graduates back in the workplace. Evaluation showed: 'there had been a shift in people's behaviours ... [and] ... their team working and communication skills were being practiced'.

## What is being developed in graduate training?

Regardless of a company's philosophy, the range of generic skills being developed in the large majority was remarkably similar. Also, a willingness to learn or an aptitude to acquire a language may be seen as more important than having a qualification. For convenience, the competences described by different training managers are grouped under four headings (Table 7.2). The advantages of using a competency framework as the basis for training were stated as 'setting a standard against which to measure performance and development' and 'they are observable, and understood by everyone, supervisors and employees'. In the context of the framework, there was a strong emphasis on developing 'attitudes towards self-management' and a recognition that the ability to be 'flexible' in collaborative work, and 'to reflect', were vital.

The disadvantage of such rigidly defined role specifications was mentioned by one company, which particularly fostered empowerment of the

*Table 7.2*  Components of competency frameworks used in training

1a. Knowledge: subject, content, technical knowledge, technical 'know-how'

1b. Intellect: applies logic and creativity to problems, analyses complex information, grasps new concepts quickly, willingness to learn, produces innovative solutions, conceptualization, makes judgements

2. Personal effectiveness: expects to succeed as a problem solver, learns from error, takes responsibilities for own actions, persuades others, self-confident, self-aware, manages own career, self-disciplined, capacity for change, self-motivated, relates to others, 'fits-in' well

3. Interpersonal/interactive skills: communicates effectively, persuades others, team-effective person, negotiator, leadership, networking, presentation skills, proactive orientation

4a. Business acumen: understanding of customer requirements, seeing how all parts of the business fit together, seeing wider company perspective, increasing productivity, reading the situation

4b. Management style: being an effective leader, encouraging positive teamwork, motivating others, influencing, delegating appropriately

---

workforce and cooperative learning. It was pointed out that 'competences have to operate over a range of jobs, with an assumption that they are all of equal importance'. Employees therefore have to consider the worth of each one in particular roles and their prescriptive nature can be restricting:

> In contrast to this notion of clear and unequivocal standards in all that we do . . . we encourage every employee to make their maximum contribution to the business. We used to have 1500 separate job descriptions. We don't have them any more. What we want to do is liberate the potential of people, to encourage them to make their maximum contribution to business. But not in some airy-fairy ad hoc way, just hoping that they're doing the right thing . . . Every individual in the organization [has a] main role, with a rag-bag of competences, contributions at a whole range of different levels . . . it doesn't mean that all of one's contribution is only at one level, and therefore you won't actually have to add on some much lower level skills . . . It happens because of the nature of work, once you move away from predetermined and rigidly defined role specifications.

Empowerment requires a certain type of learning culture to flourish. If each individual has a varied range of standards and they are at different levels, success requires a commitment to take a major responsibility for one's own learning. It also requires a person working as part of a team to reflect and to be willing to record evidence of learning and achievement. Little of this would be possible unless a system existed to give feedback in

*Table 7.3* Examples of descriptive behaviours used in monitoring generic skills

| Personal effectiveness (self-confidence) | | | | |
|---|---|---|---|---|
| 0 .................................................. 4 | | | | |
| Has a tendency to deny mistakes and/or fails to learn from them | | | Takes the leading role in initiating action and making decisions | |
| *Intellect (analytical and diagnostic skills)* | | | | |
| 1 or 2 | 3 or 4 | 5 or 6 | 7 or 8 | 9 or 10 |
| Usually unable to perceive problems | Has difficulty in analysing simple problems | Can handle simple problems | Quickly perceives problems | Excellent logical and methodical approach to problems |

constructive ways about threshold standards – for jobs to be performed satisfactorily – for growth and flexibility.

Mentors have the difficult task of encouraging graduates to reflect and to keep personal files of records of achievement. Their role is ill-defined and, in many companies, there is a complete lack of effective training for them.

## Evaluation of training

The major issues raised by companies on evaluation were those concerned with the reasons behind the procedures. The role of line managers is in general quite separate from that of mentoring. It involves:

- formal assessment of work against defined competences
- review, which ensures quality provision and in turn determines progress.

There are quite clear motivational objectives embedded in the appraisal system. Thus the competency list is perceived as a vital underpinning for training programmes.

Considerable effort is made to monitor the development of both technical and generic skills; sometimes elaborate frameworks cater for 'fair' appraisal. The reasons for performance appraisal, and how it is conducted, vary widely (Redman *et al.* 1993). Table 7.3 provides examples of criteria, as descriptive behaviours, used in two different companies. They enable a degree of objectivity in providing feedback to participants on the competences and for quality standard measurement.

A vital part of the training of appraisal managers is to make it clear that they: 'need to be aware of our thought processes and how they can affect our responses, how we are interpreting events'. The problem of translation is more of concern when the philosophy of the company is 'top–down', with appraisal weighted towards defined company standards. The subjective nature of observation appears to be best tackled in those companies where self-appraisal systems operate or where individual development plans are constructed by negotiation.

## Discussion

Transition between higher education and employment is important for employee and employer. It is vital for both to make a good start and it is known (Evans and Heinz 1995) that transition is aided when clear messages are given about the opportunities that exist in the workplace. In this study there is every indication that companies do this, with clarity and openness. What is needed, in addition to glossy advertising literature, is information about what the workplace is really like. Very few companies give application and acceptance figures as indicators of the fierce competition, or details of appropriate generic skills required by employees. Only one company thought fit to visit first year undergraduates to impart such knowledge; the intention being to increase the quality of student application, not only to the company concerned but generally.

It is also interesting that companies with very different activities and concerns recruit graduates using selection criteria that are very similar. Further, recruitment is often designed to meet immediate rather than long-term needs, which has serious consequences for selection for future top management positions. It is clear that companies need to identify specific selection criteria for both long- and short-term goals, defined in such a way as to avoid ambiguous labels such as 'communication' and 'intellect'.

Changes in company structure and policy have resulted in changes in the working environment, creating different learning cultures and a reappraisal of generic skill training. Enculturation into company norms influences the way trainees develop generic skills. However, there is no proven approach to shaping new graduate trainees into particular ways of working; the data indicates the variety of learning environments in which they have to 'fit in' and then learn how to contribute.

Job placement in initial training was either job-specific, offering a narrow experience, or of a general nature. Whatever the orientation, it was important for them to be seen by the graduates as 'real'. Further, courses by themselves were considered ineffective unless training attempted to directly model the actual work the graduates were going to do. An appropriate learning culture also needed to be in existence, to which the trainee could return with new skills and not be faced with obstacles. One way of accomplishing this was to adopt competency frameworks to create the learning culture, drive the training schemes and provide the means for continuing learning.

Realistically, any learning culture has to balance an individual's development whilst recognizing company needs, but to support an individual through personal development programmes often created something special;

this was described as: 'a natural want – a need to know more'. The awareness of this crucial affective component in self-regulated learning is discussed in Boekaerts (1996). Those companies that capitalized on this
awareness in trainees promoted self-learning within company development
plans; they provided the means, libraries and resources to learn in different
ways.

Training programmes vary considerably, with different emphases on teaching
and learning. Some operate a formal systematic training, with an emphasis
on formal teaching; others guide, support and empower their workforce
and encourage the individual thinker. The majority subscribed to the latter.
The move towards continuous workplace learning, often of an informal
nature, is in part a means of coping with change to ensure competitive
success. Underlying the training framework in those companies with a
developing learning culture is the notion of self-development and a responsibility for one's own career. Encouraging individuals to be responsible for
their own careers might appear irresponsible on the part of the company.
However, in reality, freedom of choice can be restricted and the consequences of the choices made by the graduates supported by management.

Most training programmes appeared not to take into account the trainee
competences that had been identified at assessment centres and there was
little evidence of tailoring programmes for new trainees. Also, in most companies graduates are not formally assessed on what they have learned during training. Lack of evaluation was seen as a perennial weakness and, at
best, evaluation took the form of reflections on the course. In general,
managers assumed that training had been effective. Research by Mulder
(1998) emphasizes the need for companies to recognize the effectiveness
of training programmes. What is required is information on the quality
of the course itself and its impact on the trainee's performance on return
to the workplace. However, in this context, many companies reported that,
although they were aware that line managers and/or mentors had to be
trained to assess desired generic skills competently, training for them was
lacking.

# 8

# The Graduate Experience of Work

This chapter focuses on the realities of the first two years of work. Previous studies have shown that among the typical problems encountered by graduates in this period are culture shock, frustration created by ambition outrunning experience and misallocation of roles and responsibilities. The previous chapter raised additional issues about the role of organizational culture in shaping employees' conceptions, the compromises involved in balancing individual development with the company's needs and the assumptions held by employers about the extent and usability of a graduate's generic skills. Our major concerns here, therefore, were to enhance our understandings of graduates' early socialization or enculturation into organizations by ascertaining what factors mediated the melding of individual knowledge and skills, the demands of the work context and the training opportunities to produce workers who were both more motivated and highly skilled.

A balanced sample of 24 male and female graduates in their first year of employment was selected randomly from a mixed range of employers in both the public and private sectors. The organizations varied in size and type and included the police, museum service, food, aircraft and software manufacturers, solicitors, accountants and engineering consultants. The initial interviews, which were conducted within two to three months of taking up their post, took place in the work setting and were approximately 1 hour in length. Ten of these graduates were followed up one year later to identify any developments in their roles, responsibilities and skill use.

The content analyses of the interviews revealed a rich mixture of common and unique perceptions and, in order to adequately retain these, we first set out the common elements below, before portraying individual realities through the eyes of four graduates chosen because of their contrasting experiences. The common elements are outlined in the following paragraphs.

 The same terminology meant something very different in practice. The clearest example of mismatch was 'communication skills', which included chatting, interviewing, using the telephone and dictaphone, and different writing skills. Higher order skills were also mentioned, such as dealing with clients and colleagues 'at different levels', people management and negotiation. The latter was perceived by some as a communication skill, others as a team-building skill. Hence 'communiction' included a wide range of activities.

In terms of our model of generic skills, the main skills used were thought to be those associated with 'management of information', particularly communication; these were mentioned by every interviewee. As might be expected in young employees, skills of 'management of others' were least frequently mentioned. The use of skills of 'management of self' and 'management of task' varied according to the demands of the job. In general, although a common vocabulary was used to describe skills used, the variety of tasks undertaken and unique contexts meant that, at a detailed level, what was being practised was quite different.

Some thought that they had acquired skills at university as part of disciplinary knowledge that were directly relevant to their work, for example, studying English enabled them 'to read and write critically'. Others thought that the subject matter was of secondary importance and that the value of a degree was training in 'being methodical', 'to learn more effectively and to get higher order mental skills'; in particular, 'organization of self' was mentioned. Proponents of this view, from vocational and non-vocational courses, thought the university experience was about developing self and questioned whether the purpose of the degree was vocational. One said 'it wasn't its job to do that'. Those who had had work experience as part of their degree appreciated the direct relevance to their employment.

A number of factors were said to be important in determining opportunities for the development of skills, either on-the-job experiences or through formal training. The culture of the organization was at times described as rigidly hierarchical. Training was restricted to following procedures as to how a particular task might be executed. In other cases the degree of autonomy was great, decision making was left to the discretion of the graduate and there were many more opportunities to develop skills through arranging one's own courses.

The working environment was also mentioned as a determining factor.
The size and nature of the work group varied enormously. A few worked alone, hardly moving from their offices, and at most dealt with senior colleagues. Others had many more opportunities to develop skills of negotiation, managing others and communication, working as part of management teams or dealing with the public, adapting every day to different situations and the unexpected.

The personalities of the individuals, their attitudes and beliefs naturally
affected the way they thought their skills were developing. For example, three thought that skills were innate, yet at the same time agreed with the rest that generic skills were for them improved with on-the-job experience, particularly about learning how they should behave in their own organization.

There was a wide variation in belief about transfer of skills; the value of skill development was seen very much as relating to preparation for using specific skills in a specific context.

It was clear from these interviews that the graduates' job demands and their work environments gave rise to very different practices. These practices, together with their personalities, shaped their perceptions of the skills they were using and developing.

Although there are common elements, each graduate tells a different story – narratives grounded in context. These stories all demonstrate contrasting experiences, experiences that are portrayed here by the stories of Corinne, Nicole, Tanya and David, chosen because they illustrate diversity in their roles and the different ways in which they were expected to acquire and use core skills in their day-to-day activities.

The framework for describing each story comprises six categories – the context, main skills used, origin of skills, development of skills, organizational pressures and perceived importance of subject knowledge. These categories derive from analyses of the whole sample, and exemplify the main issues and concerns felt.

# Corinne

Whilst at university, Corinne read history of art and also worked on a voluntary basis for two years in a local art gallery. This experience enabled her to be accepted, after graduation, for a Diploma in Art Gallery and Museum studies. Gaining employment was difficult and, after doing various temporary jobs in London museums and galleries, she was accepted as assistant curator for fine art in a city museum. Corinne described herself as self-reliant, diplomatic and responsive to others.

## *The context*

Corinne was the only person in the department. Initially her job was 'essentially to document the collection, which hasn't ever been done before'. She described how she had to go into the art store, sort out everything and start making computerized records: 'of things that have been stuffed under cupboards all round the museum in a very haphazard way!' She also had to attempt to find relevant paper work, to ensure that: 'we do legally own it and then get those records on the computer'. Besides researching the collection, part of her role was to communicate with the public, answer queries, organize tours and curate exhibitions on a small scale. Corinne was extremely busy: 'everyone is so pressured', working to a large extent independently, with hierarchical support conspicuous by its absence. She said that: 'everyone is so isolated here'.

One year on she was still struggling with the task of classifying the art collection on her own. She was happy in her job, still very busy, using the same skills as previously. Her role in dealing with the public was increasing.

## Main skills

In the first interview Corinne emphasized the use of the following three sets of skills:

- Organization skills – setting own goals and organization of self; organizing others, for example, to hang pictures in a display; basic administration skills.
- Communication skills:
  (i) writing detailed letters and learning to address different audiences, on both technical and general issues;
  (ii) dealing with others, having patience and being diplomatic.
- Research skills – in documentation and recording, putting forward an argument. In the second interview, Corinne was more specific in describing the skills she was using. She cited 'problem solving', both in physical and mental terms, as the most important 'organizational skill':

> Physically hanging the exhibition, fitting a very large exhibition into a limited space, actually fitting 8 foot by 8 foot works on the walls, how physically to do that without anything breaking, and not injuring myself in the process . . . We had to work out how we were going to get those pieces from the lorry into the museum, so there's a lot of issues around actually hanging an exhibition.

> . . . I had a phone call the other day from the people at the local fire station who have a painting which we think may be ours and they think may not be, and that's a problem that I have to solve, . . . and ascertain whose painting it was . . .

Within 'communication' skills, Corinne discussed her increasing role of dealing with the public:

> . . . [They] tend to come to the front desk and say, 'Can I speak to the curator and can she show me X.' They should book if they want an appointment; I could be in the middle of moving a picture, or something that is demanding a lot of concentration, and you have to go down and speak to them . . . people want quick answers to things and hope that I can provide it.

> Last week I had to go and collect a lot of costumes for the exhibition and it involved going into people's homes and explaining about the exhibition, explaining what we wanted. We got quite a lot of clothes, and had to, in some cases, say 'No' and explain why. . . . So that involved a lot of communication, and social work!

Although Corinne described teamworking skills within a communication framework, particularly 'putting an argument across', her description was not in cooperative terms; rather it was acting as an individual with other individuals. She talked about 'getting on with colleagues professionally rather than socially, and having to be diplomatic':

> There are lots of small teams functioning on different problems, and you're put on a team as and when it relates to you. I'm on a team relating to Gallery One which is the refurbishment and fund-raising for the art gallery, and I'm on the exhibition team . . . we have to thrash issues out for the Gallery One team . . . we need to find a lot of funding, and I've had to think about what might be needed in the new gallery, how I want the gallery to look, what works of art I might put in there, how we might physically change the shape of the gallery, so I'm having to think about issues that relate specifically to my collection and are my responsibility, and how best they can be displayed in the new space . . . [The main skill is] putting an argument across.

## Skill origins

Corinne attributed her organizational skills primarily to her university days (deadlines for essays and organizing herself for study purposes) and communication skills (giving presentations and dealing with people) coming from university and her work experience in an art gallery. She felt that her research skills originated at university.

## Development of skills

In the first interview Corinne emphasized how difficult it was to: 'deal with people to get things done, because there are not set rules in this place . . . and being aware not to tread on people's toes'. Over the year, she thought she had mostly developed her communication skills and had also learned to work as a team member, albeit with only one other. She felt she was no longer totally independent:

> I've learnt a lot about teamwork, pulling together to pull off a project. For example, in the exhibition we're just having, there have been two of us who have hung the exhibition in a week, on a very tight schedule . . . I've learnt a lot on the technical side of hanging exhibitions, . . . particularly large and difficult pieces, or perhaps how to handle certain tools which I wouldn't have used before. I've learned a lot about diplomacy, how to operate within a council-managed organization, how to conduct myself . . . I'm a bit more world-wise.

In addition, Corinne felt she was getting better at dealing with the public: 'I'm getting more and more enquiries from the public for example, and dealing with those (letters)' and also training gallery guides.

## Contextual expectations and pressures

It is clear that there was little organizational culture to shape Corinne's perceptions of management and staff relationships, or ways of developing group effectiveness. Her remit dictated an expectation for self-reliance, as these two early interviews indicate:

> . . . you have to be able to stand on your own two feet and it is a very isolating experience, my office. It's just me, . . . other offices are dotted all over the museum, so I can feel very isolated. Because I make an effort to have a cup of coffee with someone I actually speak to some-one in the day. No one is looking over my shoulder, telling me what I should be doing. So I have to organise my day myself, set my own goals and make sure that I reach them.

> In other places there are certain systems in place, of how to do things and how to get things done, but here it is very much down to the individual . . . I find it frustrating, as I don't think it is very healthy for people to be stuck on their own. There is a curator here I have never even met, God knows what he does; he's in the bowels of the museum.

Similarly, the lack of organizational culture failed to provide initiatives for a learning environment; no training courses were provided, even in the use of computer software, and her line manager's influence was strictly limited: 'I think that is just the nature of my line manager, he is not very forth-coming with information.' During her second interview she explained how training relied on her own initiative:

> As an environment it's quite tricky because everyone is so pressured, so things tend to happen and information exchanged off the cuff, over a cup of coffee. (There is) recognition that I need training . . . I need to get out and see good curatorial practice . . . for example I'm going to London on Tuesday – I requested that I went, and there was no problem for them to say 'yes and we'll pay for it'.

## Importance of subject knowledge

Considering the importance of employers' perceptions of 'knowledge and intellect' as an important core skill, the graduates were asked to reflect on the use of substantive knowledge learned at university. Corinne thought her subject knowledge was vital to her job:

> The whole point of my job is to document the collection. In some instances there's no records of anything, so when I put the information on the computer, I have dates, a painting I have to chase, an artist, where that artist lived and worked, what is happening in the painting. So even at a very basic level, identifying something about each painting is a daily occurrence because that's what I'm doing . . . I was taken on to this post for being an Art Historian and having that knowledge.

In addition, Corinne thought that her computer skills, and knowledge of specific software that she had learnt on job-experience, enabled her to do her job effectively. She thought she was probably appointed with that expertise as a governing factor.

# Nicole

Nicole is a production manager working for a large food manufacturer. She started an HND course at university and then transferred to an engineering degree in materials science. She described her course as 'very industrial based'. The company in which she had worked during her vacations provided her with work experience and offered her a sponsorship contract. As part of the degree course she also did her sandwich year in the company. She obtained a first class degree and started full-time industrial life as a production manager. After one year she moved to another company. Nicole had 'a passion for the job' and described herself as having a desire to succeed, integrity, perseverance and determination.

## *The context*

The first company provided Nicole with good managerial experiences and 'really good mentoring'. Considerable changes were made in the company and one outcome was a 'process improvement group' to look at factory production. Nicole was in charge. The ethos was one of resentment from her older colleagues and continual struggle to overcome barriers to changes she suggested:

> They asked me to set up this department and then start to work on long-term process improvement . . . but there were frustrations . . . resistance to change, something in the environment I was working in – it was immense . . . The excitement of what could have been achieved was amazing, but it made those barriers to change all the harder to get over . . . The support that I needed wasn't there, and that was something to do with my age and experience . . . there was a little bit of resentment in that I was aware of what was going on, behind closed doors . . . and I was challenging something that somebody's done for a very long time, procedures that have been followed for a very long

time, and trying to prove that something isn't working, but we don't exactly know why, but let's try it this way . . . trying to get people to change habits was the biggest thing, especially coming from someone like myself.

In the second company, a food retailer, she was again a production manager and thrived in the new context: 'Basically in the factories we have production lines . . . fresh ingredients coming in at one end, the pallets of boxed food going out of the other and I manage one of these production lines . . . on an eight-hour shift basis.'

The culture in this company was very different from her first experience. The new context actually gave her the opportunities to succeed. It was a very large company and 'very finance driven'. Her young age was never considered a disadvantage, there was a strong team spirit and she frequently mentioned: 'that definitive drive from everyone, although achieved in different ways':

> . . . there are a lot of people like myself, graduated, with a bit of experience, trying lots of new things . . . It's a culture thing I think . . . our seniors are very clued up on where they need to go . . . the direction is there, so it doesn't matter whether you're 65 or 15, and how long you've been with the organization, there are very clear directions of where and why we're going somewhere. So that gives everyone a cohesion and motivation . . . and the drive is the same at every site.

The company culture makes explicit to the workforce what 'drive for results' means, as a basis for improving performance:

> (One) conversation I'd had with a manager was about being up to my nose in water, and he said 'don't worry, when it gets above your head we won't give you a snorkel, but we'll tell you where it is'. That's their philosophy. That's what the business is about.

## Main skills

In the first interview, Nicole felt the following skills were important:

- Organization of time and self.
- Communication skills:
  (i)  dealing with different 'levels' of people;
  (ii) leadership and helping others to learn.
- Teamwork skills:
  (i)  negotiating;
  (ii) learning to compromise to get maximum efficiency.

Working in the second company, Nicole felt the most important skill she had developed was managing people:

> When I first came to this company, one of the things that worried them was how I would relate to people management and the numbers of people ... The role they put me into on my first assignment, 62 people reporting directly to me ... a huge variety of people with different needs and different abilities. The company said to me from the start 'we're throwing you in where we know you're weakest' and that's the way they operate, 'and if you swim and you don't sink then we know you're going to be an asset'.

Nicole also mentioned learning a great deal about the technical side of the business and the constant improvements to the equipment and the large scale of the operation. Her increased understanding of the process improvements gave her more confidence in developing leadership and team skills. She described developing teamworking skills with peers and immediate management where: 'because of a lot of openness ... the relationships were quite close'. Also, on the shop floor she had more expertise at distinguishing those workers who required supervision and those who could work independently, and yet still be responsible for facilitating their needs.

Problem solving was an important part of her work. She was required to take calculated risks and make effective decisions:

> There is an encouragement to take risks. If we've got a potential contamination in the factory – the word potential being the key here – what do we do in that situation? You're here in the factory on your own, it's 9.00 at night and you've only got yourself to look upon to make that decision ... if you make the wrong decision consequences result ... business financial implications, and yet, on the other hand, making a decision to safeguard the consumer ...

Nicole indicated that risk-taking and problem-solving skills were used frequently; one example was in weekly production scheduling:

> At the beginning of the week our Head Office says, 'This is what we expect this factory to produce this week.' There's a number of things before that product can be manufactured – raw materials, for instance, need to be on site, and we need to have the plant up and running. One of the biggest problems ... is making a production change, because we've finished part of an order, or overrunning on part of an order ... Running over and making up a certain order means that we run the risk of actually scrapping that product, because there is no customer for it. And that's a problem that comes up quite regularly. It involves a lot of fast talking and phone calling to relevant people to say 'Can we run this production? Can you get rid of it if we do?'

## Skill origins

Nicole was critical of a module on 'communication studies' during her HND year. It did not cater for those who had presentation and public speaking skills, as Nicole had from school days, and was theory based. It was not applied or tailored to the individual as she explained: 'You see, I know how to do it, but how do I get the result that I want? How do I make people interested, it was that sort of thing that I was interested in . . . not just the ability to speak in public.'

During her degree – an industry-based university course – she found the high standards demanded of report writing and of presentations to be valuable, as were the team tasks, for example, design projects in engineering developed cooperative skills. Her placement year gave her experience in communicating with others, at different 'levels', and learning management skills. Of particular importance was learning to cope with resistance to change when working as a team member and what she considered 'a lack of professionalism' of some peers.

## Development of skills

Nicole's enthusiasm and drive, with a clear determination to succeed in all areas, was prominent during interview. She recognized that 'people management' was not her strength in the first company and thought that that was her major development in the second company: 'One of the biggest things that I've learnt as part of my role is people management . . .' A second skill that she had developed was associated with one of the company's appraisal criteria called 'Drive for results'. She described learning about problem diagnosis: 'I burn to sort problems out . . . and don't always analyse which problems can just be lived with and which problems are going to make the difference. I don't always channel my energy into the ones that really matter . . .'

## Contextual expectations and pressures

Nicole mentioned the strong team cohesion and bonding created by the common company philosophy. She felt the ambitions and drive of the company matched her own career ambitions: 'the buzz that I got from the people was really what sold the company to me'. She also explained that the means of achieving the company's goals was through a highly structured set of personal expectations, the competency framework, based on a set of key performance indicators:

> The key performance indicators are my accountabilities as a manager. These are the targets that I need to achieve, ranging from quality measures . . . such that the quality of the food is of a certain standard, and cost in terms of production outputs, transport, yields . . . and we have the people side. We're expected to demonstrate that we've developed certain people on our line . . . and all these things are measurable and they say 'this is what you did achieve and this is what you

should have done'.... We are very hot on performance measurement of the factory, and also the personal behaviour key competences; we have a set of thirteen of them.

The set includes such competences as 'developing others', 'respect for others', 'intellectual curiosity', 'team leadership' and 'problem solving', each with detailed descriptors. For example, the 'Drive for results' competence includes:

- has a bias for action and getting things done;
- aggressively pursues business objectives;
- takes calculated risks;
- tests self against a high standard of excellence.

Appraisal is regular and:

What the company does is to look at strengths and weaknesses and give you assistance in making you better . . . for example, you might feel that you've not actually been in an environment to demonstrate a particular skill, so our senior management gives us the opportunity. There is also a set of training packages and we can actually go on courses.

The competency framework spells out in detail both the short- ('The expectations for myself are laid out on a daily basis') and long-term expectations of the company ('I have certain accountabilities, which are laid out at the start of each year').

## Importance of subject knowledge

Nicole was quite clear that her specialism in materials engineering was very important, as was her course in 'financial management in industry, . . . because you can talk in a language that everyone can understand'. However, she stressed that it was not only learning about one particular field that mattered, but also:

the *way* you get things done, as well as actually doing the tasks . . . the speed at which you achieve things, the way you affect people when you do something . . . and learning how to achieve results, how to perform the best for yourself . . . especially when working under pressure.

She thought that her engineering training had taught her 'to question things a lot . . . to be inquisitive . . . to question what we class as being normal', a sound basis for succeeding in the key performance of 'analytical thinking':

There's an analytical side to everything . . . you might choose to suddenly think 'why is it that this particular quality parameter is always in the yellow' and you might decide that you really want to analyse that, whereas you might be happy to live with it in the yellow . . .

# Tanya

Tanya has wanted to be a police woman since her school days, but decided she wanted a 'fall back, in case it didn't work out', so read law. She obtained a first class degree and was accepted on the police force's accelerated promotion scheme, a programme with limited places for graduates. She was particularly keen on having a: 'good career with good prospects', and would expect to take her police sergeant's examination within two years. Eventually, Tanya hopes for a managerial, non-operational position; she rejects the idea, held by many, that experience is vital for such posts and that more than two years is needed to do an inspector's job effectively. She thinks that the police force is recruiting graduate managers, not police officers. Tanya described herself as an effective listener, professional in what she does, reliable and good at taking the initiative and making decisions.

## *The context*

Initially, being a graduate gave Tanya no concessions; her eight-hour shift was the same as others. In ward community policing she described the police cars as being the first to respond to an incident: 'unless you are out and something happens'. The follow-up work would happen at the station and her job entailed: 'getting all the statements, interviewing offenders or suspects, telephoning . . . you get a crime and you work through it, start to finish'. She worked on her own for much of the time but: 'obviously dealing with people every day was really the main part of the job'. The workload was allocated by the sergeant but occasionally she would use her initiative:

> I had some information last week from an informant of mine that someone was in possession of something. So I ended up arresting them. That was mine because I wanted the job . . . and in an area that is rife with car crime, then I might be part of plain-clothes surveillance . . .

In addition, Tanya was given periods of tutorship and training courses, including fitness training. Part of the culture was:

> . . . the public sort of perception of the police force – like canteen culture – and everyone swears and it is just rude jokes all the time. It is like that most of the time . . . one of the things that was getting me down a bit was that I couldn't have an intellectual conversation with anyone . . . so you have to have a certain sensibility for others . . . and accept their ways . . . and be able to talk to them.

In essence, part of the culture was one of coping with variety: 'The real beauty of the job is that it is different every day . . . confrontation one day, mental work the next, physical confrontation the next and demanding work of different kinds the next day.'

However, the other part of the culture was coping with working in a male-dominated environment:

> Since I joined three people have said to me that the problems I have to face are (a) that I am female and (b) that I am intelligent. People know that and feel threatened by it. That is not what I would say myself, but there is some truth in it. . . . I think you have got to be able to get on with people and show respect for people and if you do that, you get the same back. . . . it is essential to get on with colleagues.

## Main skills

In the first interview Tanya felt that the most important set of skills was communication:

> There is no way you could operate in this job if you didn't have good, solid communication skills – the ability to adapt. People would be surprised . . . but there is an absolutely wide range of people that we deal with . . . But there is a way of saying things in every instance. There are times when you have to be sympathetic, or encouraging, or you have got to be in control and hard . . . a lot of that (communication skill) is really attitude, i.e. your own perceptions of how you should treat people. . . . Good communication skills will lead to a good rapport with somebody, and that makes all the difference.

Another communication skill she thought was an awareness of 'audience':

> . . . the ability to present things in a logical manner, so it is understandable to different people. . . . I think you have got to be clear obviously, authoritative as well . . . dealing with the victims for instance . . . unless you show them that you are knowledgeable and that you are in control, through your communication skills, then they don't want to know you, they [want to] get somebody older. An example is the attempted murder that I dealt with recently. That was an incident where communication was very important. Because obviously the victim in that case was absolutely distraught . . . yet I had to speak to her, sorting things out for her, and at the same time collect evidence.

Organization skills and decision making were important to the work, in and out of the station:

> Organization is a skill – the difference between being organized and disorganized is incredible . . . because you are dealing with such a heavy workload, you need to be completely organized, and set targets for the day . . . and work methodically . . . but you have to prioritize . . . [and work] on those that are worth the time. For example, if someone's car is broken into at 2 a.m. in the morning and there are no witnesses, unless there are good fingerprints, the likelihood is you are never going to find out who did it.

Tanya indicated that, for most of the time, she worked on her own, but on occasion worked with colleagues. Although there was a camaraderie in helping each other, and she mentioned 'a team sort of supporting', it appeared to be sporadic and not an essential part of the structure of operating.

In the second interview she elaborated on her problem-solving skill, to include her 'digging around' and weighing evidence:

> We have a lot of robberies here where peoples' 'giros' are stolen, so although from the outset you are impartial and open-minded, we do get some where there are untrue allegations. So I had one of those last week, where a bit of digging around led to withdrawal of the allegation, because it just hadn't been stolen from the person.

## Skill origins

Tanya thought that the application of her university legal knowledge was important, because: 'legal knowledge gives you confidence. If you know the theory it makes the practice that much easier.' However, she pointed out that:

> ... despite everybody's thoughts, a law degree is not a police law degree ... at university the criminal law and police law side are tiny, so it's the law that I've learnt through 15 weeks at training school in this job ... or I've basically learnt it myself.

In addition, she felt that it was essential to be well organized and work methodically, both: 'are products of university, because I was like that in my degree work, planning things properly and not doing an essay the night before'.

## Development of skills

Tanya mentioned that: 'the learning curve is massive!' and thought that during the year she had developed teamworking skills and communication particularly. For example, she thought that there were more examples of genuine cooperation in day-to-day work:

> Teamwork – I think that's been facilitated by those that I work with ... people are very open and wanting to help you ... as a good example, because the next shift came in at about quarter to ten, you can foresee that a lot of people are going to be working on (because of the serious nature of the case). Because the whole section came together, people did various jobs, so we all had to stay on for a bit, but not a whole eight or nine hours.

She had also developed communication skills: 'you learn to deal with a variety of different people ... interviewing, taking exhibits, dealing with important enquiries, there's so much going on . . .' Problem solving had developed because she used the skill every day. She thought that another word for problem solving was 'investigation, which I would say we do all the time', and elaborated on the skill: 'You're collating and analysing information all the time, because you're getting a number of sources, say witnesses, and it's up to you to sift through that and sort out which is as close to the truth as you can hope to get.'

In addition to skills, Tanya had also developed knowledge: 'knowledge is obviously procedural, and as for legal knowledge I've also learned an awful lot there'.

## Contextual expectations and pressures

Tanya's job is a full one, and she has learnt to cope with the variety of tasks that she has to perform: 'people expect you to be everything don't they? It is very challenging from that point of view, you never know what someone is going to come up with next!'

Occasionally she makes mistake, and gives an example of attending a domestic violence case: '. . . and in error ended up warning both of them, which is an option we can do, but really the offender should have been arrested . . . so you learn from that'. So she has the ability to turn a critical incident or an error into a learning situation. She also manages change, because: 'our remit and boundaries change all the time'.

Besides the pressure of dealing with the unexpected, there is a pressure of making correct judgements. Tanya stressed that she did reflect on events and decisions were not taken lightly; she was conscious of how her decision making might effect people's lives: 'For instance, taking away someone's liberties is a big decision . . . and it is very important that I ask advice from colleagues – there is no way I would know how to deal with every situation . . . it's endless!'

She indicated that she did not feel autonomous, even though on occasion she had to use her initiative and make decisions quickly, often on her own:

> For instance, if you've gone through a red light, I can give you a fixed penalty so you'd have three licence points and a fine. I could take no action against you, I could verbally warn you, formally caution you, so in that sense we are autonomous in the decisions we're making because it is not stipulated which one of those options you have to go for . . .

However, she did indicate that: 'There is an awful lot of responsibility in this job, and you are making decisions all the time', but normally she worked and acted within laid-down procedures.

## *Importance of subject knowledge*

Tanya's thought that her law degree was of limited value: 'The studying element of it was valuable in that it teaches you how to study effectively ... content-wise we didn't deal much with criminal or police law ... basically it was a qualification to get on the scheme I'm on.'

# David

David works in a medium-sized accountant's office. He studied accounting and finance at university: 'not because I wanted to become an accountant, but because the course would equip me for management ... I want to become a manager and eventually start my own business'. He thought the course would provide him with appropriate 'entrepreneurial skills' because the extra modules offered included marketing, law and an independent study on market research. David described himself as ambitious, amicable, mature and professional; he thought he was well organized and thorough.

## *The context*

David worked in a highly structured environment:

> Within the job we're very structured, because you do different things depending on your grade; we've got a very regimented grading system. ... In the first year you are very much an assistant, you do as you are told, and you're put on courses, and you learn a lot about auditing and accountancy ... It's only in the second year that you take on any responsibility, low-risk lines, and report directly to a senior.

Part of the job is preparing accounts in the office, but most time is spent visiting clients as part of a team, with a senior in charge: '... so I can always draw on the people above me who've got more knowledge'.

David moved to another office and in his second interview was more senior:

> Having staff under me and coaching them ... and it's mainly auditing now ... viewing sets of accounts to check that they give a true and fair picture ... There's loads of legislation which the government wishes companies to comply with ... they have to prove that they are capable of running – and that's what we do, we go in and check it all.

## *Main skills*

David believed that his communication skills were particularly important, talking with more junior peers in the office, explaining to them, talking to seniors and supervisors and speaking with clients:

... because we go to clients and you've got a whole range of people to talk to ... someone on the shop floor ... and then a finance director or a managing director ... so you have to try to express your ideas in a terminology that they understand.

Although David stressed that: 'one cannot upset a client', part of his job he saw as a form of verbal interrogation: '... talking to someone face to face, and getting an answer ... being seen as a trusting fellow, and getting others to tell him what they may wish to hide!' In so doing he thought he used higher order skills, of analysis and synthesis, to get the whole story from data provided by clients. He thought it was a form of problem solving:

People believe that auditing is a case of sitting down with a set of numbers and agreeing about the source of information. That doesn't really prove anything, so the way our firm look at things is, certain numbers will paint a story, and what we try and do is make sure that that picture actually makes sense.

Sometimes when there was a discrepancy in the client's data, David indicated that: 'we substantiate what they're saying by going back. . . . the set of numbers has to support what's actually happening'. For example:

Problem solving – I had a case where an element of legislation had changed, we spotted – the client hadn't – so we had a problem. We talked it through with the client, explained why they had gone wrong, explained to the juniors the problem and then fixed the problem so that everyone was happy.

## Skill origins

David thought that his university training was too academic and not vocationally orientated. The most useful part of his degree was the Independent Studies research project and the marketing module:

... every week we'd prepare a presentation ... in front of 30 people ... and watching them – how they are responding to what you're saying – you can soon see if they are turning off! ... that's very useful in this job because we're talking to people all the time.

He thought that he had developed some higher level thinking, like analytical skills, at university but his criticism was that: 'it doesn't prepare you for the job ... it was on paper ... not for a real-life situation in an office with a client'.

He felt he was an organized person by nature, and was certainly so at university.

## Development of skills

During the second interview, David felt that he had learnt a great deal of knowledge, and its application:

> There's just so much of it – there are so many things feeding you information and you've got all your studies, which are filling you up with information about accounting . . . [and] you understand the principles behind the law – I could never reel off a particular section of law – but you would look it up.

He maintained that communication skills were still the most important in his job, but that now he had improved his organization skills, organizing time in particular. He felt that the job did not entail risk taking: 'we don't take risks, we manage our risk . . .' but that it did involve more and more ability to respond to change: '. . . we've got constant change in the firm, constant change in procedures that we use – as a result of government changes, with massive implications to our clients and subsequently to us'.

Teamwork and use of cooperative skills was still limited. People worked individually and asked for help as needed: 'The way we work in teams is very much, if you've got a problem, you talk about it within the team. It doesn't matter who's listening . . . no one feels superior, it's just what you happen to know at the time.'

## Contextual expectations and pressures

David mentioned the need, now that he was more senior, to see the whole picture: 'you have to make sure all stories tie in and are true'. This was a priority in his job:

> What's important I'd say is 'the whole picture' – is something that you get more and more as you move up the firm, . . . you understand a bit more, and also organizing your time so that the further you get, you have more fingers in pies, you've got more clients on the go at any one time – time is very important.

The pressure was organizing oneself to get things done 'on time' and accurately, but at the same time being aware of the 'whole picture'. An important part of the whole picture was keeping abreast with new knowledge: 'knowledge is the key factor'. Individual risk and responsibility was lessened because a highly developed tight structure for procedures was in place. Opportunity to be autonomous was strictly limited, and: 'one can always draw on the people above me who've got more knowledge'.

David also thought that his new role of instructing juniors created a pressure, and he would: 'have to get used to people asking me questions which I am supposed to know the answers, which is quite daunting'.

## Importance of subject knowledge

David talked about substantive knowledge as auditing and accounting practice, about application. The firm's expectation was that trainees would continually learn through professional examinations and, afterwards, everyone was expected to keep up to date. The lead body demands it and underpins the culture of such organizations. The firm offered generous time allocation for study at home and organized on-going professional courses. Courses in general were about substantive knowledge of the profession, but there were skills courses on offer too:

> The firm is generous in giving us time, but you could do with a little bit extra . . . and we stay away (from the office) when you're studying. Then there's the Firm's Practice, which is how a firm wishes you to do things, and how we manage our risk. We have ongoing training. Every year we go to training centres, which prepares lots of material, keeps us abreast of what's going on within the profession and within legislation.

## Discussion

All four graduates appeared to be working extremely hard in their first few years of employment. Nevertheless, they appeared to be highly motivated and talked with enthusiasm about their experiences, the characteristics of which are adumbrated below.

All four graduates emphasized that their degree gave them specific subject knowledge; for example art history, finance and marketing. They acknowledged, in addition, the generic skills they had acquired, particularly forms of communication, time management and organizational skills. One problem in getting a true picture of graduates' knowledge, is that they are often unaware of skills they previously acquired and are currently utilizing in their job (Nicholson and Arnold 1989). In this study, David, who thought his university education was 'a complete waste of time', agreed later that university courses had provided him with 'a way of thinking'.

A common vocabulary was used by the trainees to describe the generic skills being used but they meant different things in different work contexts. For example, 'communication' including chatting, interviewing, using the telephone and dictaphone and different writing skills, but also higher order skills such as dealing with clients and colleagues 'at different levels', people management and negotiation. The latter was perceived by some as a communication skill, by others as a team-building skill. Similarly, there is considerable variation in what skills are being used under such global descriptors as 'teamworking' and 'problem solving', because they are related to specific job requirements.

One obvious implication for this variation is in selecting potential candidates, where there is a need for specific context-dependent factors to ensure effective screening procedures. However, it is evident that labels such as 'communication', 'working with others' and 'problem solving' have currency value in the workplace, regardless of the range of interpretations. It is the complexity of the workplace that, as Stasz *et al.* (1996) state: 'defy simplistic categorization of skills and straightforward matching of skill requirements to jobs'. Yet such categorization is essential for developing university courses to enable students to be better prepared for the world of work.

There was also a consensus among the four that effective communication skills and interacting with others resulted from workplace experience, but the major skill for the trainees to learn was to 'fit in'. This meant adapting to cultural expectations and organizational pressures and learning the 'language of the job'. They agreed overwhelmingly that learning on-the-job was vital. The context and culture of the organization shaped their experiences, to discover 'the way things are done', for example, how to deal effectively with people, working in a team and learning appropriate procedures. Nicole's experience of working in two company cultures is particularly interesting here. She describes working initially for a company where her management of people was never allowed to develop fully, because of the attitude of the employees to her age and sex. In the second company culture she thrived.

The contexts and organizational pressures in different companies clearly affected the skills the graduates used. They were remarkably different. For example, whereas Corinne and Tanya and David worked essentially on their own, Nicole worked as part of a management team, collectively, to achieve common goals. Corinne was independent, managed her own department and had almost no help from others, whereas Tanya and David could and did ask for advice from their peers, especially about correct procedures.

Company expectations and pressures were also very different. Corinne had deadlines for exhibitions but day-to-day organizing of meeting the public and classifying the art collection was through self-directed initiatives. At the other extreme was the pressure under which Nicole worked, to tightly structured schedules, with clear directives to achieve the company slogan 'drive for results'.

Finally, training opportunities for the four graduates varied considerably. There was no training programme for Corinne; for Nicole, the company provided a series of training programmes that were completed within her first 3 years with the business; Tanya received an introductory 15-week course but little training after that; and for David training was taken very seriously indeed.

Overall it would appear that the vision of a learning organization as envisioned by Beckhard and Pritchard (1992) is hardly in operation. According to them, an organization should operate with members understanding the need to learn and include a reward system that encourages learning, information systems that support the balance between learning and doing, and training programmes that support this balance. Only David's experiences of training falls anywhere near this ideal.

# 9

# The Challenges of Implementing Generic Skills

## Higher education

When this study was conceived in 1995 the higher education policy landscape was characterized by philosophical conflict. Adherents to an ideology of academic competence railed against that of operational competence, which, it was claimed, incorporated increased state control of curriculum, unthinking prescription of transferable skills and a focus only on those human attributes that were seen to improve economic performance. This landscape continued to change throughout this study, during which time the ideology of operational competence took firm control, not least through the influence of the Dearing Committee of Inquiry, which supported the role of higher education in the new economic order and advocated closer links with employers and the development of what were called key skills.

Indicative of this movement are recent speeches by the Secretary of State for Education and Employment calling for a minimum period of work experience for each student, a requirement that every student undertake a module giving them insight into the world of work and announcing new sector-specific graduate apprenticeships integrating higher level study with work-based learning. Similar sentiments have recently been expressed by CVCP, CBI and CIHE (CVCP 1998), in their update of their 1996 joint declaration. They claim, with reference to skills, that 'in most institutions a consensus is developing that it is part of their job to enable students to develop the personal and intellectual attributes that will help them succeed at work and in life generally'.

Although the Dearing Report (1997) was influential in setting future policy direction, it did nothing to clarify the conceptual confusion surrounding the notions of key or, as we have called them, generic, skills; indeed, it exacerbated them. It amply illustrates the lack of any theoretical or conceptual base to their consideration of these skills by forcing very different categories of skill into the same 'key' box, whilst at the same time limiting their number to those which seem most able to be assessed.

It is therefore not surprising, in the light of the above, that the notion of key and generic skills has attracted criticism. Hyland (1998), for example, has recently asserted that key (generic) skills have all the necessary ingredients of first rate educational slogans: 'They fully satisfy the motherhood-and-apple-pie test by advocating practices to which no one could possibly object, and they are so vague and nebulous that they can be made to include just about anything.' He concludes that the pursuit of such skills: 'is nothing more than a chimera hunt, a disastrous and costly exercise in futility'.

What such criticism highlights is the crucial necessity of a justifiable conceptual and theoretical base for the analysis and identification of generic skills in any study that aims to gain enhanced understandings of skill acquisition in higher education and employment. This, then, was our first priority. Our model of generic skills was, in part, empirically derived and was designed to be an adaptive, flexible instrument, capable of being used for different purposes, in different contexts, by different people. The four broad management skills – of self, others, information and task – provided that flexibility as evidenced by its effective use with, and by, groups of university teachers, students, graduate employees, their line managers, employers and trainers, both in data collection and in subsequent staff development initiatives.

A model of generic skills is of limited use in the higher education context unless these skills can be clearly differentiated from disciplinary core skills and knowledge. This was achieved through an analysis of theories of learning and skills development, together with current theorizing in curriculum and epistemology. Its purpose was to identify the patterns of course provision identified in Chapter 4. Although generalizations cannot be claimed from these data, they illustrate practice that presents some comfort for both sides of the ideological divide.

A major feature of the data presented in Chapter 4 is the variety and complexity of conceptualization and practice with regard to skills development, the extent of its embeddedness within disciplinary study and the relationship of the skills to the workplace. Generic skills were visible in all degree courses, although sometimes as the core skills of the discipline, for example, communication skills in law, problem solving in engineering, IT skills in computer science and various forms of analysis in all disciplines. In more vocationally oriented courses, skill and knowledge acquisition is more professionalized, not least because the curriculum is shaped by external lead bodies, which accredit and monitor course provision. In these circumstances, university teachers see their role more as preparing the architects, pharmacists and engineers of tomorrow, rather than as preparing graduates with general intellectual and personal skills for society. In these courses, skills development is also likely to be more contextualized, either through direct work experience or through authentic simulations of real world contexts.

There was evidence of great care being taken in these contexts to maintain academic rigour and, in many departments, there was little evidence of

Barnett's (1994) distinction between discourse within and outside academe. Some argued that they are as much about the external world as the academic, especially where there are strong vocational links. This is reflected in pharmacy, for example, where the discourse of practice of a hospital pharmacist and academic discourse about patient care in an intensive unit, is the same. Behind the decision making of a trainee or new graduate in the hospital environment is an underpinning of theory and disciplinary knowledge, which was, at one time, the province of university discourse.

Despite the care to maintain rigour in skills courses there was a common reluctance to assess generic skills. In general, teachers professed that they were more used to assessing products than processes and held a common perception that to assess skills objectively was very difficult. In some courses, formative assessment was a part of the programme but was not carried forward into the summative grade. Most departments were tolerant of an element of skills assessment for level one modules, but only if this did not count toward the final degree. In some instances, institutional and departmental policies lacked flexibility and new assessment procedures were difficult, if not impossible, to accommodate. In one institution, on the other hand, no student could obtain a degree without passing specific generic skills modules. These same institutional and departmental discrepancies were also apparent in policies regarding student feedback.

These findings are of particular interest not only because of what is known about the role of assessment in effective learning and teaching but also because they are in direct conflict with student perceptions. Assessment of skills requires teachers to be explicit about skills development and students to devote attention to it and take it seriously. Students were very clear in their views that assessment played a central role in course recruitment and subsequent motivation. When skills remain embedded and implicit within disciplinary study, and are not assessed, students are least likely either to recognize skills or to be eloquent, or even interested, in their description.

Another factor affecting student recognition of, and motivation towards, skills is whether courses are integrated or 'bolt-on'. The latter courses are often criticized and may not be taken seriously by students because they are not seen to be relevant to disciplinary study. From the modules observed, one way of ensuring student recognition of generic skills is to teach them out of the context of disciplinary subject study, but within the disciplinary setting, with teachers of that subject and perhaps using disciplinary examples. What is then important are the ways in which these skills become embedded within disciplinary study in order to support and enhance it. The clamour from employers often suggests that students should be equipped with generic skills only because they are necessary in the world of work. In this sense, generic skills become a preparation for work. This kind of conception is, for many teachers, inappropriate. In the courses observed, an explicit focus on generic skills was almost always intended as providing a foundation that would be central to effective learning throughout higher education. First year students were introduced to generic skills so that they could use, practise and develop them in new contexts, and in particular within disciplinary study. Generic skills modules are considered an investment by those who teach them. This investment may have the additional pay-off of providing graduates who are well equipped to deal with the requirements of work, but the rationale is provided from within higher education and the major purpose is to enhance students' experiences of higher education.

Bolt-on courses developed and funded by employers may have a somewhat different rationale. Here, there is an inherent danger that the use of activities that have been successful in employer training environments, without knowledge of the students, their context, or their curriculum, will not transfer easily to higher education. The evidence from the BP programme relevant to this is that it succeeds best when reinforced within the processes used for disciplinary study, as evidenced in the law department evaluation. Here there was evidence of a considerable pay-off from putting time and effort into team development. Students who were trained to operate in self-managed teams were enabled to become more responsible for their own long-term learning, they achieved expected standards in terms of disciplinary knowledge and could also be explicit about skills development. The demand on staff time to prepare a learning environment conducive to teamwork, and to manage the associated changes in monitoring and assessment, was great. In the long run, however, these efforts should improve the learning environment and reduce contact time.

The successful continuation of such courses, run by academic staff rather than by external facilitators, will require a critical mass of teachers who have the ability or training to facilitate this type of learning. It will also require the full support of their peers, the lack of which hampered both the BP and Shell initiatives in this study.

Another factor that hampered implementation of the Shell scheme, and one particularly relevant to contemporary political prescriptions on work experience, was the difficulty in finding work placements. Problems lie ahead if workplace experience is to become more prevalent, and in particular more widely available to non-vocational students. Enterprise reports (for example, Biggs *et al.* 1994) have already noted such difficulties, especially over long-term negotiating of placements. Further, in the Shell scheme, local employers wished to 'vet' students for placements in order to check for their acceptability and to ensure that only the 'best' students were taken. It thus seems likely that workplace experience will be easier to achieve in departments where a vocational or professional training forms some part of the degree. For example, schoolteachers take considerable responsibility for the professional development of trainee teachers. For some teachers this is a time-consuming burden but for many the benefit of new ideas and practices brought in by students is welcomed. It may require the long-term building of relationships to make this kind of partnership successful, but it is accepted as one aspect of a teacher's role.

The issue of the quality of placements is also one that may need further consideration. STEP students are taken into small companies in order to achieve a specific, short-term project, but here there is some evidence of a lack of commitment by employers to developing learning. Students taken into local SMEs for the duration of a year were not always happy, nor well catered for; some felt used or were given a job that made use of their present skills but did not extend them. Some mature students in this context felt a long placement to be worthless as they had plenty of general work experience already; what they needed was updating at the forefront of knowledge and skills and this was not achieved. Further, Auburn *et al.* (1991) suggested that although some general gains were evident from long placements for psychology undergradutes, many of these might be achieved more rapidly once in employment. Disenchanted students discussed a catch-22 situation in which they are told they have to get work experience in order to get a job, and have to get a job in order to gain work experience; hence a placement, whatever its worth in terms of learning, is at times seen as a means to an end rather than as an experience to be valued. The value of placements, their aims and the nature of learning available within them may therefore need more careful scrutiny.

## Changing practice

The aim of our study was to inform practice, with a view to its improvement. Central to the achievement of improvement in the planning and delivery of curriculum are the teachers themselves, as Fullan (1991), among others, has argued. Richardson *et al.* (1991) also show that genuine changes can come about only when teachers think differently about what is going on in their own classrooms and are provided with practices that match their different ways of thinking. Their argument is straightforward – no lasting curriculum change is possible without a prior change in teachers' behaviours, attitudes and beliefs. This is no easy feat, however. The most effective staff development strategies identified at school level require opportunities for teachers to confront the assumptions and beliefs underpinning their own practices (Fullan and Hargreaves 1992; Bennett *et al.* 1997). However, approaches of this kind tend to be resource hungry and also assume a level of pedagogical knowledge that is unlikely in university teachers, most of whom have experienced little or no training. The effect of this in terms of university teachers' knowledge of teaching and student learning and their abilities to reflect on, and articulate, their beliefs are only too apparent in Chapter 3. These teachers were also surprisingly cautious about implementing change despite the fact that they had been selected for having been involved in such efforts.

Part of this caution, and the lack of any clear relationship between their beliefs and practices, were a consequence of contextual factors and constraints outside of their individual control. Those mentioned included the research assessment exercise (which took the focus away from teaching and course development), teaching quality assessments, institutional and departmental policies regarding curriculum delivery and assessment (such as modularization) and increasing student numbers.

Evidence from research in schools on achieving effective innovation shows that attempts to change individual teachers is likely to fail unless there is support, and a similar willingness among their colleagues, together with appropriate supportive policies within the institution itself. Hannan *et al.* (1999) present the same picture from their analysis of innovators in higher education, where a large number of interviewees commented on resistance by departmental peers. In other words, attitudes, conceptions and practices are mediated by situational or contextual factors, most immediately at the departmental level. Some of the findings from our interviews with teachers leave little grounds for optimism in this respect. Many reported that their attempts to change or innovate were not supported by their colleagues and that there was little evidence of planning for future change at the departmental level. Tradition, particularly with regard to assessment practices, appears to die hard: 'There is a heavy element of tradition here, so that lots of things are going unquestioned. We do it the way we do it because we do it that way . . . kind of circular.' Lack of departmental and institutional support, and indeed active resistance, was also evident in some of the evaluations of the STEP and BP schemes.

Hannan *et al.* (1999) suggests that innovations of any kind encounter their main difficulty at departmental level but argues that this is not restricted either to higher education or to this nation. The international literature on higher education abounds as much as that of industrial practice with discussion of underlying conservatism and he quotes De Woot (1996) to the effect that: 'Change in our universities is slow and difficult because of our culture. Whatever does not come from inside, what is not in our habits or traditions, is too often regarded with distrust or simply ignored.'

Departments, in turn, are willing or unwilling victims of institutional policies with regard to such broader curriculum structures as modularization and assessment, and these in turn impinge on teacher intentions and the manner in which they are able to plan for progression and continuity across course levels. The influence of centralized decision making was clearly apparent in our data and also in that of Hannan *et al.* (1999), where some staff felt that changes were implemented under duress.

Although institutions are often seen to constrain innovation, they are increasingly unable to act autonomously. Several interrelated macro influences bear on institutional policy decisions concerning the teaching and learning of skills. One of the most powerful of these, the Higher Education Funding Council for England (HEFCE) has been instrumental in operationalizing government policies to increase student numbers while at the same time driving down unit costs. This has had a predictable impact on institutions. According to Laurillard (1993) the pressures being brought to bear have nothing to do with traditions and values. Instead, the pressure is for financial input to go down, and some measurable output to go up. There is an appetite for reform from within higher education, but it moves slowly as we all scurry about in response to the increasing external pressures which exercise their own peculiar forms of change. In recognition of this, HEFCE currently funds a range of initiatives designed to enhance students' learning experience and employment prospects. Institutions are being encouraged to develop learning and teaching strategies that may reflect their relationships with employers and encourage the development of what it calls 'employability' skills. It also provides a fund for the development of teaching and learning in subject-based projects that address employability to varying degrees. Similar initiatives have also been approved by the Welsh and Scottish Funding Councils.

At governmental level, the Dearing Committee made the specific recommendation that all institutions should increase the extent to which programmes help students to become familiar with work and help them reflect on that experience. In its response, the government endorsed the view of the Committee and, implicitly, the exhortations of employers that enhanced employability should be one of the objectives of higher education. The government has since supported a range of projects to encourage the spread of key skills and work experience. The Quality Assurance Agency (QAA) is another powerful influence through its teaching quality audit and appraisal procedures as well as its programme of work on establishing and clarifying standards and qualifications. Similarly, professional lead bodies are able to impose demands through their accreditation procedures.

It is apparent that no university teacher is an island but is inescapably moulded and constrained by departmental, institutional and national policies. Therefore, in considering strategies for change each of these levels must be considered.

Achieving institutional change is complex and there is little guidance available on innovation in higher education. There is a dearth of literature on the topic and what is available is, as Hannan *et al.* (1999) reports, concerned either with description of, or proposed strategies for, initiatives or with discussion of the adaptation of new technologies to the needs of an expanded and more diverse higher education system under severe economic constraints. He does, however, conclude that innovation is conditioned by institutional or systemic structures, departmental or disciplinary cultures, individual history and priorities, and that deliberate change at any level has policy, cultural and ideological contexts.

Change efforts can be instigated by individuals, as our data show, but bottom–up initiatives of this kind, although admirable and often groundbreaking, do not provide an effective model for change across an institution, as research on innovation in schools has too often shown. Neither will institutional initiatives succeed simply through centralized exhortation. They require a concerted and integrated approach that recognizes that the first necessary stage is a shift in teacher attitudes towards the innovation. Hord *et al.* (1987), for example, document seven stages of teacher concern that occur through the change process and require appropriate response for effective change to occur.

Selling the teaching of key or generic skills is unlikely to be straight-forward, as Barnett (1994) and others have claimed, because what is at stake for some is the nature and authenticity of a university education, structured around the primacy of substantive knowledge. It is instructive in this respect that some teachers in our sample, although innovating in the delivery of generic skills, justified their change not on providing skills for employment but on achieving improvements in student learning in tradi-tional degree programmes, that is, in the belief that enhanced generic skills improve performance across the range of traditional academic activity.

Change initiatives will also need to be complemented by models of imple-mentation, whereby teachers can come to understand, and judge, the diverse range of teaching approaches that have been successful in skill delivery. It is in this context that the model, and resultant patterns, of course provision generated in this study have proved useful in staff development efforts. Further, the theoretical perspective underpinning the model, together with the findings from associated empirical studies, provide a powerful justifica-tion for direct workplace experiences, or simulations of these, particularly in vocationally oriented degree schemes, not only to achieve domain-specific knowledge and skills but also to ensure their transfer. They also provide direct support to employer demands and to the Dearing recommendation for extension of work placements in order to help students towards success at work, to improve links and to bridge the skills gap, although our con-cerns about the quantity and quality of placements still hold.

Nevertheless, the logic of placements can be overstretched. If knowledge and skills acquisition and use are largely domain- or context-specific, then, for work experience to be optimal, it would have to be located in a setting closely related to that of subsequent employment. In some disciplines, such as medicine, education, social work or engineering, this could be reasonably achieved but what kind of work placement would be optimal for a history, classics or English graduate? The STEP scheme provides an example of a successful placement scheme for just such students, with its emphasis on generic skills. But the characteristics of an optimal placement for such students is still not known. Are all placements of similar value irrespective of their focus, length and degree of student choice?

With regard to innovation initiatives, the proposed Institute for Learning and Teaching in Higher Education (ILTHE) could provide a real stimulus for change efforts. It would therefore be a pity if it prioritizes pedagogical developments in interactive technology, as initial responses suggest, rather than concentrating on more basic, but more important, issues such as understandings of how students learn, of the role of assessment and feed-back on student achievement and motivation and of the necessity for teach-ing for transfer. These would seem to be crucial given our data on the lack of understanding of university teachers on how students learn and the lack of evidence on teaching for transfer. The available literature on transfer implies clearly that effective teaching for transfer requires deliberate planning, delivery and assessment, with objectives made clear to learners and opportunities for practice in varying contexts. Thus the impact of ILTHE would be maximized if these aspects of pedagogy are built into their criteria for membership and if institutions match this by offering appropriate courses in pedagogy, as well as providing incentives for staff membership.

In the absence of verified models of effective implementation, the CVCP, CBI and CIHE paper (CVCP 1998) invites each university and college to reflect on the following four questions:

1. How far does the teaching and learning practice in all courses reflect the general intentions of its 'mission statement' and strategic plan. If the two are not consonant, which needs to be changed?
2. How can academics get appropriate recognition, promotion and reward for good work and innovation in developing skills courses?
3. Are departments encouraged to learn from each other? Does the institution as a whole seek out good practice to adopt? Against whom does it benchmark? Have learning partnerships been established?
4. Could the institution work more closely with local employers and FE colleges to extend the scope for work-related education?

These are sensible questions for any institution to consider but they will not, in themselves, change pedagogical practice. Lacking here is any consideration or guidance on strategies for, or models of, change that take into account the broader institutional influences on actual practice elaborated in this chapter.

# Employment

The import of contextual influences is also reflected in our data from employment settings. One of our major findings with regard to graduate employees is that although there appeared to be agreement among employers about the generic skills they prioritized, the skills actually needed and used, as well as the way they are defined, depended crucially on the characteristics of the work context. Communication skills are prime examples of this, as is shown in Chapter 8, where the demand and nature of such skills varied widely across work contexts and tasks. Here lies the problem of transferability, as some graduate employees, who were known to be able to argue a point of view in an undergraduate tutorial, reported being ineffectual when communicating with clients. The problem lies, in part, in the ambiguity of the label because as Barnett(1994) argues, this is a multi-dimensional skill with a uni-dimensional label. Thus, whatever skills training new graduate employees have had in their higher education, it is likely that they will lack the propensities for the varied, yet contextualized, communication demands of their company.

Although the focus of this discussion has been communication skills it should be noted that the graduate employees pointed to the fact that other generic skills, such as teamworking and problem solving, have little meaning outside of specific work contexts. In other words, global generic descriptors hide enormous variation in actual skill use. These sentiments echo Eraut's (1996) claim that the use of the same terminology does not prove that the skill itself is identical in each sector, or even readily transferable. It seems intrinsically improbable that problem-solving could mean the same when applied to a student completing the first level of higher education as when applied to a senior manager of a company. Stasz *et al.* (1996) also concluded that such general terms as problem solving and communication are too broad and ambiguous to be of much use to employers for either recruitment or training.

Our findings in this area mirror those of American research. Stasz *et al.* (1996), for example, concluded that workplaces are socially constructed and reflect the decisions of people; skills can only be understood from the perspectives of people within a particular context. More specifically, Stasz and her colleagues (1996) showed that generic skills varied with work context. The characteristics of problem solving, teamwork and communication are related to job demands, which in turn depend on the purpose of work, the tasks that constitute the job, the organization of the work and other aspects of the work context.

Studies in Australia present a similar picture. Billett (1996) overviews those that have addressed the degree to which the knowledge required for skilful performance is generic or specific to the particular situation and concludes that situational factors were significant enough to suggest that generic statements of performance were abstracted from, and invalid indicators of, actual performance. Beven (1996) assessed the extent to which some of the national key competences (that is, skills), such as problem solving and using mathematical ideas and technology, were indeed generic. He concluded that although some could be described as generic, the degree of applicability to each site, and the degree of success achievable, varied according to the specific site contexts. He also found, as did Resnick (1987), that generic skills may be impossible to apply if the user lacks domain-specific knowledge; in other words, the completion of workplace tasks is dependent on the capacity of workers to have domain-specific, as well as generic, knowledge and skills.

These findings, in common with ours, fit neatly with theories of situated learning and cognition. It was shown in Chapter 1 that this perspective is critical of approaches in which the activity and context in which learning takes place are regarded as ancillary to learning and distinct from what is learned, because what is learned is thereby separated from how it is learned. This, in turn, defeats the goal of providing usable, robust knowledge (Brown *et al.* 1989). Instead, proponents of situated learning perspectives argue that the activity in which knowledge is developed and deployed is not separable from, or ancillary to, learning – it is an integral part of what is learnt: 'Situations . . . co-produce knowledge through activity.'

Approaches such as cognitive apprenticeship are based on the above theoretical analysis (Collins *et al.* 1989). This technique supports learning by enabling students to acquire, develop and use cognitive tools in authentic work contexts, in a similar way to craft apprentices acquiring and developing the tools and skills of their craft through authentic work at, and membership in, their trade. Through this kind of authentic activity, knowing and doing become interlocked and inseparable. Billett (1994) advances a similar view about how individuals construct knowledge through participation in everyday activities in the workplace, based on the belief that learning is inherent in individuals' everyday thinking and acting and that situations and social partnerships influence the knowledge that is structured. Eraut *et al.* (1998) also investigated, from the perspective of social learning theory, knowledge embedded in the normal activities of the workplace and how it was acquired. They found that the most important sources of learning were what they called the microculture of the workplace, that is, the challenge of the work itself and interactions with other people in the workplace.

These findings certainly provide theoretical support for the current initiatives on graduate apprenticeships and work experience but real concerns must, on the basis of our data, remain regarding their effective implementation, particularly in smaller and medium-sized enterprises.

Our findings on employer training appear to conform, implicitly at least, to a situated view of learning. Although the generic skills sought, and trained for, were somewhat similar – as would be expected from the homogeneity of employer wish-lists of skills – development of these tended to be situated in particular work and task contexts. Several concerns emerged from these data, including the lack of training of line managers whose job it was to monitor performance against often elaborate competency frameworks. Eraut *et al.* (1998) comment on the recent literature on human resource management, which highlights the role of the manager as staff developer, conceived in terms of appraisal and target setting, planned development opportunities, mentoring and coaching. Aspects of this role, such as mentoring and coaching, were rare in their sample of managers and were equally rare in the settings that we studied.

A second concern was the lack of assessment of training outcomes. In most companies there was no formal evaluation of learning outcomes or of changes in job performance. In general, managers simply assumed that training had been effective. Druckman and Bjork (1994) also report from their studies in the US that measures of post-training job performance are often missing or of questionable validity.

Finally, training tended not to capitalize on the incoming strengths of graduates or focus on their weaknesses, appearing to take no account of skills identified at assessment centres. In other words, there was no indication of the development of tailored courses for new trainees. The fact that

the person responsible for recruitment often had no responsibility for training may explain this.

In more general terms, Rajan (quoted by Keep 1997) shows from research in the UK that the kind of broad general training in generic skills
that would underpin employability is simply not being offered by most
employers. Further, an international survey found that British managers
are the most guilty of providing short-term, non-developmental training.
In short, employers' attitudes remain long on intentions and short on
deliverables. Our findings do not conform to this picture, possibly because
our sample was restricted to large national and international companies. It
would appear that the picture in small and medium-sized enterprises can
be very different.

Our results showing that training, induction and work practices were all
influenced by the organizational culture, echo those of Druckman and
Bjork (1994) who reported that they were struck by the key role of the
organizational context in which performance occurs: 'Without an organizational culture that fosters the changes needed to implement those innovations, proposals for change, however credible their source or convincing
the evidence, will have little effect.'

Organizations are, of course, subject to some of the same outside influences experienced by higher education institutions. Here, however, the
influences are more diverse, including world markets and competition as
well as national priorities. We collected no data on these influences but the
increasing move from 'top–down' to 'bottom–up' organizational structures,
for example, seems more related to increased demands for efficiency, as a
result of international market pressures, than to internal considerations.

## An agenda for future action

The study reported here set out to gain better understandings of generic
skills in higher education and employment in what turned out to be a
shifting policy landscape. The implications of our findings for the effective
implementation and utilization of these skills are considered below in the
form of an agenda for future action:

1. The discourse on generic skills, and all its variants, is confused, confus-
   ing and under-conceptualized. Employers and policy makers alike have
   been seduced by the slogans, with scant consideration of their definition,
   characteristics, transferability or utility. Yet the unity of future action on
   skills, whether it be in higher education, employment or partnerships of
   both, as advocated in the Dearing Report (1997), can only follow unity of
   thought and understanding. Future discourse must therefore be grounded
   in the theoretical underpinnings of skills and their relationship to domain-
   specific knowledge and skills, as exemplified in our model.
2. Allied to the above is evidence of the lack of a common language of
   skills between higher education and employers. It seems to be assumed,

by politicians at least, that this will be ameliorated by the improvement of links and collaborations with business, particularly in the provision of work-based learning opportunities. Here, the political rhetoric is high on the 'what' and low on the 'how'. In a recent speech, the Secretary of State for Education and Employment spelt out what must be done to equip students to meet the needs of employers and reach their full potential. They included: a minimum period of work experience for each student, a requirement that every student study a module giving them insight into the world of work and a graduate apprenticeship scheme integrating higher level study with work-based learning. There was nothing on how this might be achieved at an acceptable level of quality.

Nevertheless, although work-based learning is justifiable theoretically, because it is clear that the nature and demand for the same skill can vary considerably according to work and task contexts, careful note needs taking of research on work-based training and placements, including that reported in Chapter 6. More does not mean better. There is considerable variation in the effectiveness and acceptability of these programmes. Recent studies show that the best schemes are jointly planned and incorporate close guidance of experiences and continued joint support by both workplace and university supervisors. In such circumstances, students claim to have developed more generic skills and to have had more satisfying experiences (compare this with Martin 1997). However, they do not happen without careful planning and institutional support.

3. If higher education is to play a full part in raising the level of generic skills then a continuing process of training and professional development will be required. There is little evidence, even from teachers committed to the development of these skills, that their espoused or actual theories of teaching are underpinned by understandings of learning theory or that they intentionally teach for transfer. Although the DfEE is currently providing funding for a host of development and dissemination projects, which have led to the availability of practical strategies for implementation (see, for example, the web site at www.keyskillsnet.org.uk), these studies are largely uncritical and atheoretical. Similarly, there seems little indication that the Institute for Learning and Teaching in Higher Education has any clear strategy or theoretical orientation for generic skills teaching. The absence of central policy initiatives in training is surprising given the perceived importance of skills to economic performance but, in their absence, institutions themselves must take on the role of primary developer and provider.

4. Taking the role of training provider is just one of multiple roles institutions and their departments must play if there is to be effective implementation. The practical strategies provided by the DfEE are useful in this respect because they highlight the need for clear and unambiguous central and departmental policies on the development of generic skills, incorporating systems of monitoring and flexible assessment regulations. For many teachers there will also have to be a shift in beliefs as a necessary

prerequisite of appropriate training, a shift that for some would be more palatable if more closely linked to career prospects.

5. This study has, inevitably, identified issues on which there is the need for further research. The most urgent of these is transfer, on which our data are silent. Nevertheless, given the centrality of transfer in theories of learning, and in the assumptions of employers and policy makers, it is surprisingly under-researched. There is a similar need to elucidate empirically aspects of generic skills. The following list of issues requiring further study is by no means exhaustive:

   • the differential impact of vocational and non-vocational courses on skills transfer and use
   • the extent to which some skills transfer more easily than others
   • the effect on skills development of placements of differing length and format
   • the differential effectiveness on skills development of work placements and simulated work contexts
   • the importance of domain-specific knowledge in skills use and transfer
   • the effectiveness of work-based skills training on job performance.

6. Improving the nature and quality of discourse, of training and of institutional policy making are all essential but all require an ingredient that, to date, has been sadly lacking – the utilization of a defensible theory of learning. We make no excuse for raising this issue again, as indeed we have done throughout the life of this study. Simply put, theories provide the rudder for effective policy implementation. Without this, policy direction is unplanned, random or likely to end on the rocks. We have indicated throughout this text that theories of situated learning provide an appropriate theoretical underpinning for understanding the role, and transfer, of skills in context, for providing the rationale for such policy initiatives as workplace learning and graduate apprenticeships and for informing teaching approaches. Yet consideration of any kind of theory is non-existent in the literature on policy formulation or enactment.

   Coffield (1999) reiterates this point when arguing that government plans to create a new culture of lifelong learning are proceeding without a theory of learning or a recognition that one is required: 'To ask a politician, a civil servant or a professional specializing in education what their theory of learning is and how it helps them improve their practice tends to produce the same kind of embarrassed mumblings which result from a direct question about their sexual orientation.' He concludes that no learning society can be built on such atheoretical foundations. We concur with this. Without a theoretical understanding of how students and graduate employees learn, of how the setting or context mediates what and how they learn, of institutional and organizational change and, crucially, of what is to be learnt, the Dearing Report prescriptions for the role of higher education in economic development, and in lifelong learning, will simply not be realized.

# Appendices

## Appendix A: Details of modules and departments within the four institutions

| Institution | Department | Course/Module | Year | Skill focus |
|---|---|---|---|---|
| 1. | Pharmacy (V) | Pharmaceutical care planning | 3 | Practical application of drug theory/group work |
| | | Intensive care for patients | 3 | Problem solving/communication |
| | | Spectroscopy | 2 | Data analysis/group cooperation/subject knowledge |
| | | Practice of pharmacy | 3 | Authentic simulations of practice/communication |
| | | Computer-assisted learning | 1 | Learning subject knowledge/replace practical work/IT skills |
| | Architecture (V) | Analysing architecture | 2 | Subject knowledge/design theory to apply |
| | | Architectural design | 3 | Communicating/justifying design |
| | English literature (NV) | Introduction to children's literature | 2 | Literary theory and criticism/argument |
| | English language (NV) | Academic writing | 2 | Communication/process of writing |
| | Education (not ITT) (NV) | Education media and methods | 2 | Media/communication/group functioning |

| Institution | Department | Course/Module | Year | Skill Focus |
|---|---|---|---|---|
| 2. | Computer science (V) | Short project (3 weeks) | 1 | Teamwork/life skills/ presentation/self-assessment |
| | | Long project (1 term) | 2 | Teamwork/life skills/ presentation/self-assessment |
| | Mathematical statistics and operational research (V) + (NV) | Workshop series | 1 | Teamwork/ presentations/ management |
| | | Communication course | 2 | Teamwork/ presentations/ interviewing |
| | Engineering (V) | Independent project – university based | 2 | Self-management/ organization/problem solving |
| | | Independent project – school based | 2 | Time management/ self-presentation/ communication |
| | French (NV) | Reportage (newspaper) | | Group work/IT/ presentation |
| | | IT for Arts Students | 2 | Search tools/writing Web pages |
| 3. | Psychology (NV & V) | IT (Word, Excel) | 1 | Basic word processing/ spreadsheet use |
| | | Workplace visits and presentations | 2 | Theory–practice link/ career planning/ presentations |
| | Geography (V) & (NV) | Personal transferable skills A | 1 | Communication/IT/ presentation/lab. skills/group work |
| | | Personal transferable skills B | 2 | Career/CV writing |
| | Computing (V) | Personal/prof. development | 1 | Communication/ presentation/group work |
| | | Sandwich courses, project | 3 | Workplace experience/career planning |
| | Art and design (V) | Fine art | 3 | Application of theory/ self-evaluation |
| | | Design | 3 | Communication/ media/presentation |

| Institution | Department | Course/Module | Year | Skill Focus |
|---|---|---|---|---|
| 4. | Geography (V) & (NV) | Skills for geologists | 2 | Drawing/independent lab. skills/viva exam. (communication, self-presentation) |
| | | Compulsory workshops | | Communication/group work/presentation |
| | Art and design (V) | Placements | 2 | Self-management/self-review/time management |
| | | IT for self-presentation | 1 | Written graphic presentation presentation to employers |
| | Interdepartmental workshops options (70 for 1300 students) (NV) | Course representations | 1 | Presentation/representation |
| | | Career management | 1 | Communication/presentation/CV |
| | Interdepartmental foundation courses (NV) | Numeracy and English language | 1 | Low-level subject-based skills |

Key: V, vocational element in course; NV, non-vocational element in course.

# Appendix B: Teachers – final interview schedule

*Skills/purposes*

**What do you believe are the purposes of an undergraduate degree?**

What do you think students consider the purposes of a degree? Mature/gender differences?

**Definitions**

Is the term 'learning society' one which has any meaning for you? } ... try

Is the term 'lifelong learning' one which has any meaning for you? } something

Do you think you prepare students for this? In the ways taught? In the experiences provided?

Can you provide a definition of 'core skills'?

Are 'core skills' different from 'personal transferable skills'?

Give views on Generic skills framework/knowledge and Skills framework

*Teaching/learning*

**How do students learn?**

How does this relate to the sessions observed?

Do you plan for *how* students learn as well as *what* they learn?

Prompts: active learners/processes/application of skills or knowledge

**Learning strategies**

To what extent do students need to develop awareness of learning strategies?

In what ways do you encourage this? (e.g. self-/peer evaluation)

What does the term 'reflection' mean to you?

How can we promote 'reflective learners' in HE?

**Transfer**

What are the difficulties of transfer (of skills/knowledge) ... to new modules/the workplace, etc.?

Are some students more able than others at doing this? In what ways? Why?

In what ways do you encourage transfer?

Does the term 'metacognition' have any meaning to you?

*Assessment*

**What is the role of assessment in learning?**

Should personal transferable skills be assessed separately from disciplinary knowledge?

Are there differences in the way that each should be assessed? (e.g. process/product dichotomy)

Is it easier to assess some kinds of skill than others? (e.g. performance/thinking dichotomy)

What does it mean to have a skill/to be skilled?

Do you make use of formative as well as summative assessment?

How can quality of *learning* be assessed?

How can assessment be used to enhance learning/to motivate students?

**Feedback**

What kinds of feedback do you give to students?

What is the role/purpose of this in terms of student learning?

*Change*

**Departmental**

To what extent do you act on what students/HEFCE/W/lead bodies say they want?

What guides any decisions to respond to these parties?

What do you think is the future of HE, particularly in your department?

**Personal**

Have you changed your practice in response to publicized needs for change in role of HE?

Are you motivated by/do you accept change?

*Links with employment*

Are skills for a good degree and skills for a good job the same?

To what extent do you feel responsible for preparing students for the workplace?

Whose responsibility is it to prepare students for the selection process for employment?

How much do you know/students know about this selection process?

To what extent should careers advice be drawn into departmental activities?

Will your students be able to talk readily about their skills to prospective employers?

# Appendix C: Student focus group interview schedule

*1. General*
   How are you getting on/coping with this course/module/session?
   Do you have any particular difficulties/concerns?

*2. Purposes/skills*
   What do think was the major purpose/focus of this course? (Skills or knowledge or both?)
   What are the main skills you have been using/developing/practising?
   How do you know: materials or other written briefing; reinforced verbally during session? (if necessary, provide some examples and ask for comment)
   To what extent do you take notice of your course documentation? What does it say about skill development?

*3. Knowledge/experience (transfer)*
   Is what you were doing 'new' to you? Were you using knowledge or skills you had gained elsewhere?
   What kind of knowledge did you need/did you have/use (prior knowledge)?
   What kind of experience?

*4. Learning outcomes/motivation*
   What do you think you have learnt/achieved during this course?
   Does this course help you to think about how your learning is developing?
   In what circumstances do you find learning worthwhile/easy/difficult?
   What kinds of session do you really enjoy/motivate you to do your best? Why?
   In what kinds of session do you feel like giving up? Why?

*5. Assessment/evaluation*
   Is there a clear link between the skills you are developing and the way you are assessed?
   Do you think this assessment is/will be useful to you in terms of understanding your progress?
   What kinds of feedback have you had/will you have from this module?
   What kinds of feedback do you find the most useful? Why?
   How important is your assessment grade/final degree category for you?
   Does this course demand that you think over/reflect on your learning/progress/performance?
   Are you encouraged to assess your own progress/performance?
   Are you provided with ways or means of evaluating/assessing yourself: criteria, schedules, etc.?

*6. Expectations/purposes*
   (Options: why did you choose this option?)
   Is/was this course what you expected? In what ways?
   Does it fit with your expectations of university learning?
   What, to you, is the purpose of a degree: knowledge/skills; future/work; access to . . . high pay?

*7. Employment*
   To what extent in HE do you feel you should be prepared for the workplace?
   Should careers guidance be drawn into departmental activities?
   Do you feel you have been prepared to talk to employers about your skills?
   What could you do to make yourself better prepared?
   How much do you know about the selection process for employment?

# Appendix D: Employers' interview schedule

| | |
|---|---|
| Name of Company: | |
| Nature of business: | |
| No. of employees: | |
| Date of interview: | |

**Recruitment**

1. Can you tell me something about your recruitment process? (any application form available?) What is the rationale behind the process?
   *Probe*: Does the recruitment process involve the use of an assessment centre?
   What type of tests are used?
   In the recruitment process, how important are core skills, in relation to degree subject or class/knowledge?

2. Are core skills assessed on entry? If 'Yes', in what ways?
   *Probe*: Do you use NVQ criteria?

3. Are core skills considered to be as important as the employee's knowledge base?
   *Probe*: What is included in your definition of core skills? (What term is used – key/core/generic: skills/competences?)

**Training**

4. How do you assess what training is needed?
   *Probe*: Any psychometric tests used?

5. During the first years of employment is there a structured training programme?
   *Probe*: What is the rationale behind the training programme?
   What specific skills does the training focus on?
   Is there an individual pathway tailored for the individual, or is it general?
   How specific or how broad is the programme? (one period or continuing)
   What *reasons* are there for in-house training or use of outside/independent training agency?

6. Could any of this training be done better in HE? In your opinion, what could HE provide that it does not provide already?

7. *After* training courses do you evaluate what has been learnt? (or do you assume they have learned on the course!)
   *Probe*: If 'Yes', what methods/means are used? What type of evidence collected?

8. Are all graduates treated the same way? (Degree class/vocational and non-vocational degrees)

**Organization**

9. How do you socialize graduates into your particular ways of working?

    *Probe*: Is there an idea of learning about 'How to function in this organization'?

    Is there any informal/formal contract between employer and employee?

10. Can you describe any aspects of the workplace learning culture within this organization?

    *Probe*: supportive/trust/openness . . . etc.? Is everyone expected to teach others, or only supervisors?

11. Is there a mentoring programme? (personal mentor/line manager? What are their roles?

12. Is there anything that I haven't asked about that you would like to mention?

Show the skills diagram and underline the major skills the organization is training for.

# Appendix E: Format for log record sheets

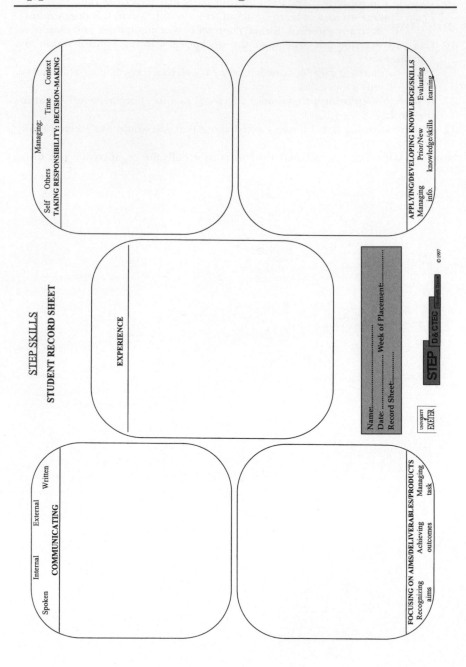

STEP SKILLS
STUDENT RECORD SHEET

EXPERIENCE

Managing: Self Others Time Context
TAKING RESPONSIBILITY: DECISION-MAKING

APPLYING/DEVELOPING KNOWLEDGE/SKILLS
Managing info. Prior/New knowledge/skills Evaluating learning

Spoken Internal External Written
COMMUNICATING

FOCUSING ON AIMS/DELIVERABLES/PRODUCTS
Recognizing aims Achieving outcomes Managing task

Name:....................... Week of Placement:..........
Date:...........
Record Sheet:.............

UNIVERSITY EXETER

STEP D&CTEC

© 1997

# Appendix F: STEP – work experience skills (examples from initial interviews with students and employers)

| | | |
|---|---|---|
| Communicating | Internal | • The hectic schedule of the directors meant that I was often lacking supervision. Naturally my responsibilities increased so I organized regular meetings with my supervisor to inform him of my weekly activities and my ideas (*personal authority/attitude*). |
| | | • I found making working relationships with outgoing and sometimes intimidating staff fascinating (*interpersonal styles*). |
| | | • My contact was off sick and nobody else had heard of me. This was a bit of a surprise but I convinced a youth worker to allow me to shadow his work for the rest of the day (*personal authority/ attitude*). |
| | External | • I have also been out on a number of visits to clients and have been able to answer questions they have asked, along with taking comprehensive notes for further investigation back at the office (*using/developing networks*). |
| | | • An unreliable supplier had been a problem to the company for some time. After one particular event, I called the company to register my complaint. Although I found the manager quite awkward when I asked for a discount, my persistence paid off in the end (*interpersonal styles/personal authority/attitude*). |
| | Spoken | • Sarah's telephone manner was confident and persuasive, she had a positive use of language. Verbal skills are well developed. She was always happy to explain progress and effects of research to all who were interested (*awareness of audience/ personal qualities*). |
| | | • Susan made a series of presentations to employees at all levels of the company, from shop floor to the board of directors. She was able to communicate with her audience and persuade them to accept her recommendations with enthusiasm and commitment (*awareness of audience/personal qualities*). |
| | Written/ visual | • I designed a selection of OHPs. I encountered problems with the content. Some of the information is confidential and cannot be presented. Some of the information is quite technical and would not be understood in the time allowed (eight minutes). I tried to make the presentation |

informative but easily understood by people with little technical knowledge (*awareness of audience/ contextualization*).

- I produced a report for the company, to supplement the drawings and diagrams produced last week. It is constructed in such a way that someone with little technical knowledge could understand, but it also contains all the necessary information for someone with some technical experience to use or build copies of the equipment (operating instructions, suppliers, etc.) (*awareness of audience/contextualization*).

| | | |
|---|---|---|
| Focusing on aims/ deliverables/ products | Managing the task | • I researched, wrote and compiled an information pack. I also began the production process, organizing a photographer, graphic designer and printers. The pack now awaits funding before it can be sent to the printers (*maintaining targets/ contextualization*).<br><br>• My placement uncovered a lot of classic real-world situations. In many cases staff had been taught the best possible ways to utilize the computer equipment at their disposal, the computer systems were useful, but not as useful as they could be (*contextualization*). |
| | Achieving the task | • I have also realized that small companies run to tight schedules and my motivation to produce a result had to come from within; by setting myself targets and using my initiative I was able to produce a solution to a problem (*maintaining targets/contextualization/personal qualities*).<br><br>• I particularly enjoyed writing the case studies that I included in the pack. They were based on fact, but allowed me to be very creative as I tried to pull at the heart strings of the reader (*awareness of audience/extracting information/personal qualities*). |
| | Recognizing company aims | • Mike has shown great insight into how a company is constrained by commercial and market factors as well as internal resource restrictions. He has fully investigated the company's present and future needs and taken all of these considerations into account in his recommendations (*extracting/synthesizing information*).<br><br>• The main task set for me was to decide whether the company should change to a new computer system they had been offered. After reading up on the new and old systems, the manufacturing process and deciding exactly what was required, I amassed a great deal of knowledge about their business and the majority of the technology on site (*extracting/synthesizing information*). |

| | Taking risks | • I recommended a new motor for the fan and I had to buy a hundred of those and that was £60 each motor so that was £6,000. Basically my signature said 'yes' or 'no' (*personal authority*). |
| | | • Basically I had to make a judgement whether it would be worth spending £10,000 a day to test out some new equipment. It did turn out well and the company have become experts in that field (*personal authority*). |
| Taking responsibility through decision making | Managing time | • This week I have been working on the report for the company as well as developing the testing equipment further. I have improved the probe clamp design and test rig. These modifications will make the equipment more user-friendly. I have had to manage my time carefully so that the project doesn't fall behind schedule while I work on the report (*maintaining targets*). |
| | | • There are 50 staff in four departments. My attempts to meet them all and learn about all of their work proved over optimistic. My solution was to target key workers, the team leaders and the director and deputy director (*alternative solutions/maintaining targets*). |
| | Managing self | • I have gained in the form of developing my personal skills and also in the enjoyment of meeting what I consider to be a tough challenge. This is not a place for the shy or timid. All the workers have strong and intimidating personalities. This project required me to work with all of them and I quickly learnt to be assertive and make my presence felt (*interpersonal styles/personal attitude/authority*). |
| | | • I feel that the main outcome has been the development of my self-confidence. This skill has developed as a result of realizing what I am capable of. A consequence of this is that I now feel far more comfortable discussing ideas in teams, communicating my ideas in discussions and tackling difficult problems (*personal authority*). |
| | Managing others | • My project coordinator, the director and the fund-raising head had conflicting ideas of what was demanded of me. Therefore, I proposed a meeting of minds – the Project Management Group (*personal authority*). |
| | | • The most difficult part of the project has been dealing with the politics surrounding it. There has been enthusiasm by everybody for changes to be made, but all have had their own ideas on how to solve the problem. It has been a challenge to integrate these ideas and meet the actual requirement (*interpersonal styles*). |

|  |  | • I have acquired skills in teamwork and communicating ideas to other team members and enhanced my problem-solving and analytical abilities. |
| --- | --- | --- |
| Applying and developing knowledge/ skills | Managing information | • Mike's ability to solve problems quickly and thoroughly stems from his way of combining knowledge, resource and company culture to produce solutions which will be readily accepted by others working with him (*contextualization*). |
|  |  | • The direction of this project depended almost entirely on initial fact finding. He has demonstrated above average organizational skills (*extracting information*). |
|  | Making use of prior knowledge/ skills | • As I am an engineering student it has been a great benefit to be placed in an engineering environment and to put theory into practice. |
|  |  | • The project has also reinforced some of the aspects of my university course – this will be very useful in future years when project work plays a major role (*future/career*). |
|  |  | • Responsibility has been high, especially in areas where I am most knowledgeable (Internet web sites) (*personal authority*). |
|  | Developing new knowledge/ skills | • With lots of projects covering many varied aspects of multimedia, I had to apply my current knowledge in new ways and also learn lots of new software, skills and techniques. This led to an improved technical and interpersonal ability (*personal attitude/extracting information*). |
|  |  | • The problem was writing about things of which I had little knowledge. My approach then was to go back to the worker in question and discuss what I had written (*extracting/synthesizing information*). |
|  |  | • He grasps new concepts very quickly and communicates well at all levels. We would recommend him to any future employer (*extracting/ synthesizing information*). |
|  | Evaluating own learning | • I now have a better idea of what I am good at, what I enjoy doing, and what careers options might suit me. I have also learnt a lot about people, and forming working relationships. I believe that the effect will be to give me a lot more direction in the future (*personal attitude/future/career*). |
|  |  | • I surprised myself when I had the confidence to just go up to people in the organization. I believe that I showed a positive attitude that I hope to build on in the future (*personal attitude/future/career*). |
|  |  | • My computing and communication skills have definitely improved and I am now more assertive (*personal attitude/future/career*). |

# Appendix G: A case study of one company's 2-year graduate training programme

This case study describes one company's programme, of both management core skills and technical skills training, integrated with on-the-job experience. A summary of the programme is given in Figure 7.3 (p. 134).

From the very first day, the graduate has a real job with real responsibility. The programme emphasizes flexibility. Flexibility from the company standpoint is providing exposure to different subcultures within the organization, albeit within one function, such as retail management or finance. Through this varied management experience, the training policy also encourages graduates to be responsible for their own progress, so both the pace of development and career direction can be adjusted by the individual. The training manager emphasized the support provided within the programme but also the individuals' responsibility to recognize their own needs and develop their own learning portfolio, so that:

> When they finish the training we can point them to the two or three jobs that we think are suitable for that individual. . . . we don't want to be too prescriptive, for they are really good people, they should be able to make decisions themselves, but we recognize there is support needed too.

## Year 1: Core programme (developing the core skills of management)

*Induction*
When the selected graduates arrive their immediate training needs are not assessed. As the training manager explained:

> . . . we have a fair idea of the sorts of core skills we think they *all* need to develop, and we develop those in the first couple of years. . . . When they join, the graduates take part in the company induction, where we discuss our values, the company's social responsibilities and ambitions – they get a sense of what the company's about.

The way the company socializes the graduates into thinking about the company's expectations is to ask the graduates to discuss in groups, 'What do you think is expected of you by the company?' and 'What are your expectations?' After the group discussions, the debate that follows is particularly interesting:

> . . . because it is essentially about the psychological contract between the individual and the company, and words like 'initiative', 'flexible' and 'loyalty' are used. The Board Director of Personnel officially welcomes the graduates and delivers an informal session on the values and future direction of the company. Emphasis is on the importance of taking responsibility for personal development and to expect change – a changing culture is important for the company and the graduates should not expect things to stay the same.

Besides teaching skills, the induction, and the core programme as a whole, also: 'creates a tremendous informal network for these graduates; there's a strong social bonding between them all'.

In summary, the function of the induction is:

- to find out about the philosophy of the company and the work culture;
- to meet senior managers;
- to network.

After induction, all graduates attend a core training programme to develop their personal and managerial skills.

*Presentation skills: two-day course*
The presentation skills workshop focuses on style and presentation techniques. It includes using overhead projection and computer software to enable more sophisticated displays to be produced:

> The graduates are expected to deliver two or three presentations which are videoed. Graduates are asked to present something in the business with which they are familiar. It's good for the other graduates to get an insight into different areas of the business.

*Time management: one-day course*
One function of the course is to introduce graduates to a culture very different from their undergraduate days. The graduate manager explained it this way:

> At university they're very used to working by themselves, for themselves, achieving their own goals. In business, it's very much about whatever you do has an impact on your colleagues, your boss and so on. And I think they find that quite hard to adjust to. It's something we really have to drive home.

Another vital aspect of training in time management is to sort priorities and deal with emergencies when one is already fully preoccupied:

> . . . One thing we always say to the graduates on the course is that you're never going to manage all of the time. You can't have 100 per cent of your time organized by yourself that day. We suggest they allow for some time during the day which isn't planned for, to allow for the immediate things that crop up in business. . . . This can be very different for somebody working in retail, where the stock hasn't arrived in the store, or the till has gone down . . . to somebody working in IT.

The approach used to train graduates in time management involves the use of in-tray exercises, in essence 'situated' knowledge within company business. Graduates have to cope with real issues:

> We talk about time management techniques and we introduce them to different diary management . . . we emphasize the importance of understanding the department priorities, . . . where do they fit in and how can they achieve their performance contract. We get them to think about, 'What are my priorities?' 'What does my typical day look like?', 'Where is my time spent?' The key message is 'Focus your energy on important tasks'.

*Business writing: one-day course*
One function of the writing course is to challenge the graduates' preconceived ideas about the form of writing used in their undergraduate studies. They are encouraged to think that each and every letter, regardless of the content, is representing the company, and that it is important for the letters to be short and concise. More

importantly, it was explained: 'We try to encourage them to write as they would speak and they find that quite challenging.'

A large part of the course focuses on report writing, as this is seen as a big problem for newly recruited graduates: 'They tend to write at length, and in such archaic language. We constantly emphasize that line managers, and upwards, have very limited time – if managers get something that's short and snappy, that they can read in five minutes, they'll be more encouraged to deal with it'.

*Business conference: four-day course*

The focus of learning is on presentation skills and teamworking:

> We have a four-day graduate conference which focuses on investigating an issue in the business. For example, 'What is the business strategy at the moment?' and 'What role do our people have in achieving business goals?' Graduates work in teams, interview senior people, and the result of their work is presented to a panel of senior managers. It's very intense for the graduates, but really rewarding.

Although there is no direct assessment: 'at the end of the conference we ask participants to write themselves a learning contract. "What are the key things they've learnt from the conference?" We expect them to go back to the line manager and to their mentor to discuss the main learning points, and how they can transfer back to the work place.'

*Residential course (communication): one-week course*

After six months in the company, graduates attend a week-long residential course focusing on interpersonal and self-awareness skills. They reflect on their individual strengths and areas for improvement and consider how others perceive them. It is essential that they are honest and give open feedback, and they are encouraged to do so.

During the week there are both indoor and outdoor activities, designed to build teamworking skills. The tasks are designed to cater for different learning styles, to accommodate those who are very practical 'outdoor pursuit' types and those who are more reflective and analytical:

> . . . by using those (different) sorts of exercises, we highlight how people are different and how you need to bring on people's strengths. Because what can happen when you're doing the outward bound stuff is the extroverts really enjoy it and they go straight over to those who are quite shy. And they say 'let's just get on and do it.' And then the coin flips when the teams are doing more analytical exercises. There's a good feedback session at the end of that whole day and a lot of learning happens.

Part of the learning is to challenge the general preconceived ideas about learning types and behaviour, for example that leaders are necessarily extroverts. The rationale behind discussing different learning preferences to the group was to make explicit the theory of Kolb's learning cycle and its application to the work place.

> We try not to pigeon-hole people because I think there's a tendency to say 'well you are a . . . therefore', so we just say it does help [if] you talk [this theory] language amongst each other . . . There is an emphasis on reiterating the company's policy – to recruit high calibre people, who have lots of drive, lots of

energy, who want to get on – but acknowledging that different types are equally able.

Both indoor and outdoor tasks are of a general nature and the context is not that of the company business. The reason for this is because: 'there's such a huge diversity in what the graduates do . . . the benefits of the cross-functional representation out-weighs each business having their own graduate programme'.

The week finishes with each person reflecting on the value of the course in relation to their work: '. . . they focus on what they've actually developed from the course, as a person, and what they therefore need to build on, back in the workplace. We ask them to sign a contract with their line manager when they return.'

*Year two: Core programme*
During the second year, graduates attend two more courses and take part in non-work-based projects.

*Business management: four-day course*
This series of workshops focuses on marketing principles and understanding finance and is split over a period of two to three weeks, so that some time is spent back on the job:

> It is about understanding the business . . . we're about adding shareholder value and it's very important that graduates understand the philosophy, and can relate what they're doing back to the business. More recently we have developed a project where the graduates investigate a real issue in the business. As a team we ask them to review one aspect of the market, . . . and later present their findings to management.

*Careers forum: two-day course*
The final part of the graduate training programme, at the very end of their two years, focuses on self-development – their career management tools. The importance of this part of the programme is to make graduates realize that their career prospects in the company depend on their own effort – they need to realize that they cannot succeed if they rely on the type of structured programmes that they experienced as undergraduates. Further, they need to realize the importance of the appraisal system in providing feedback:

> It can be a very hard thing for them to get to grips with: 'Oh, what do you mean it's up to me? Aren't you going to pick me up and put me over here? Doesn't it work like that?' And we're saying 'No, it's very much up to you to manage your career. If you want to get to the top, we'll support you, and here's how we support you, but you're going to have to drive that.' So, we've decided that the careers forum . . . is the means for them to make that happen.

*Learning through non-work-based projects*
In the second year there is an obligatory activity – essentially an opportunity for individuals to develop, amongst other attributes, organizational and management skills – outside the training environment. There are about 12 non-work-based projects from which a choice can be made; for example, some graduates organize a week-long residential for underprivileged, disadvantaged young people.

The company believes that the context of community work co-exists well with the more traditional courses. It offers huge potential for individual learning and, signific-antly, a benefit of learning organizational and managerial skills out of business:

It provides the opportunity for graduates to 'have a go' in a safe environment. It's okay for them to make mistakes. It's not going to have the same consequences they might have had if they did that in the business. They can then say to their boss: 'Look what I've done, here's the skills I've developed. I think that would help me now in this position or to have more responsibility.'

There is a potential tension between the value of this experience for the individual and the problems a line manager has to face when releasing a graduate for prolonged periods of time. Also, individuals find it is a large commitment of time especially when, in the second year, graduates are beginning to get to grips with their jobs and are wanting to add some value in their placement.

**Optional courses (concurrent with the core programme)**
Optional courses are diverse and focused on company needs, in both core skill development and technical aspects. They include, for example, courses on negotiation skills, creativity, assertiveness, people management and leadership. In keeping with the philosophy described, the company is not prescriptive. The onus is very much on individuals deciding how to broaden their horizons, rather than the company providing what might be considered appropriate courses.

*Rationale for training*
The overall rationale behind the training programme is to develop in graduates those competences that are known to be qualities displayed by top management – it is a matching process, developed through carefully structured training and learning activities:

The graduates we've recruited have the potential for senior management and we have discussed the skills and knowledge they are going to need for them to get to the top. The developmental model is based very closely on our senior management criteria framework. From this we have identified the most appropriate developmental opportunities, and are constantly reviewing their effectiveness.

Part of the rationale of the company training programme is that there is a need to develop the whole person, in addition to developing an individual with company needs in mind. The balance is crucial:

The balance between the two is that we want them to display the right transferable skills no matter where they work in the company. In addition, we know everybody's not alike, so what we need to do is encourage them to develop their own skills, in whatever format that takes, which ultimately gives them the broad generic criteria we're looking for.

The company is supportive in that it encourages individuals to reflect on their career aspirations and to interrogate senior people. The questions graduates are encouraged to ask are, for example: 'You're a marketing manager, you're only 35, how did you do it?', 'You're somebody in IT, but you worked for 12 years in personnel, why did you make that move?', 'How did you make that move?' The training manager gave this example:

The company message is very much 'to know what your transferable skills are'. For example, I have a very strong logistics knowledge, or marketing knowledge, plus I have developed my leadership skills, my business awareness. I can transfer that from retail into IT.

Learning preferences are made explicit to the graduates and, to some extent, the company offers them training in different formats, opportunities that are quite specifically tailored to the individual's development:

> The majority of development opportunities are 'course led', but not everyone will select a course. Somebody else who, perhaps, may have a different preference, may do some sort of project or report, or do some work shadowing. We'll also offer a whole host of recommended reading.

The roles of mentor and line manager are clearly different; both are vital in the individual's training and personal development:

> The mentor is a senior manager, and usually within the same function as the individual . . . Their role is to offer advice on issues outside of the day-to-day workplace, for example, in career moves. The line manager should be the coach . . . as well as playing a vital role in appraisal.

### Appraisal

The appraisal system is two-fold. There is a performance management system and a development review:

> The graduates come in, work in a specific function, but in different parts of the business, giving breadth of experience as well as depth of their functional expertise. The graduate joins a department on their first placement and they're given specific targets that have objectives, which can be reviewed at the end of that period. Their manager will discuss their performance rating and they get a clear idea of how they're getting on. We recognize we're giving graduates quite a challenging job, and they need the skills to achieve competences in various criteria. Each graduate has a development review every six months and will discuss with their line manager: 'What sort of activities can I get involved in?', 'What sort of project work can I do?', 'What development programmes can I go on?'

The graduates are encouraged to produce their own learning log, that is, a personal portfolio of learning opportunities. As they move from placement to placement around the business, they can record what they think they are achieving, as evidence of a role well performed or, conversely, record an awareness of lack of exposure to particular performance criteria and what needs to be done to rectify the deficit. The logs provide the means to:

> . . . encourage them to be responsible for their own development through these learning portfolios. They can move around the business, so at the end of the two-year scheme they've got a clear idea of how they're getting on generally against their targets, their work performance, but also what their development needs are. So they are able to build better when they go through the programme. That should also act as the foundation for them when they leave the graduate programme.

### Evaluation

In this company, the training manager did not evaluate what the graduates may have learnt during the training programme, and explained:

> We are planning to. We haven't historically had a clear process for achieving this. Whilst on the graduate programme graduates move around the business.

Before each move is decided, we ask them what their development needs are, what their strengths are and, throughout their two years, we're beginning to build up a picture of that individual.

At the end of the two years' training, it is that picture of the graduate that enables the training manager to suggest avenues for development and suitable jobs but, within that framework of support, it is up to the individuals to make decisions for themselves.

# References

Adair, J. (1986) *Effective Teambuilding*. London: Gower.

Althusser, L. (1996) Ideology and ideological state apparatuses, in B. Cosin (ed.) *School and Society*. London: Routledge & Kegan Paul.

Anderson, J.R. (1983) *The Architecture of Cognition*. Cambridge, MA: Harvard University Press.

Anderson, A. and Marshall, V. (1996) *Core versus Occupation-specific Skills*. London: DfEE.

Anderson, J.R., Reder, L.M. and Simon, A. (1996) Situated learning and education. *Educational Researcher*, 25(4): 5–11.

Angeles, P.A. (1981) *Dictionary of Philosophy*. New York: Barnes & Noble.

Arnold, J. and Mackenzie Davey, K. (1992) Self-ratings and supervisor ratings of graduate employees' competences during early career. *Journal of Occupational and Organisational Psychology*, 65: 235–50.

Assiter, A. (1995) *Transferable Skills in Higher Education*. London: Kogan Page.

Association of Graduate Recruiters (AGR) (1995) *Skills for Graduates in the 21st Century*. Cambridge: AGR.

Auburn, T., Arnold, J. and Ley, A. (1991) Work experience programmes and psychology: undergraduates career development. CNAA Project Report, University of Plymouth.

Australian Business/Higher Education Round Table (1991) Aiming Higher. Commissioned Report No 1. Round Table, Victoria.

Australian Business/Higher Education Round Table (1992) Educating for Excellence. Commissioned Report No 2. Round Table, Victoria.

Australian Business/Higher Education Round Table (1993) Graduating to the Workplace. Commissioned Report No 3. Round Table, Victoria.

Barlow, G. (1989) Deficiencies and the perpetuation of power: latent functions in management appraisal. *Journal of Management Studies*, 26: 499–517.

Barnett, R. (1990) *The Idea of Higher Education*. Buckingham: Open University Press.

Barnett, R. (1994) *The Limits of Competence: Knowledge, Higher Education and Society*. Buckingham: Open University Press/SRHE.

Barnett, R. (1997) *Higher Education: A Critical Business*. Buckingham: Open University Press/SRHE.

Barrow, R. (1987) Skill talk. *Journal of Philosophy of Education*, 21(2): 187–95.

Beaty, L., Gibbs, G. and Morgan, A. (1997) Learning orientations and study contracts, in F. Marton, D. Hounsell and N. Entwistle (eds) *The Experience of Learning*, 2nd edn. Edinburgh: Scottish Academic Press.

Becher, T. (1989) *Tribes and Territories*. Milton Keynes: Open University Press.

Beckhard, R. and Pritchard, W. (1992) *Changing the Essence*. New York: Jossey-Bass.

Bennett, N. and Dunne, E. (1992) *Managing Classroom Groups*. London: Simon & Schuster.

Bennett, N., Wood, E. and Rogers, S. (1997) *Teaching Through Play: Teachers' Thinking and Teachers' Practice*. Buckingham: Open University Press.

Beven, F. (1996) Implications for training of context-dependent knowledge, in J. Stevenson (ed.) *Learning in the Workplace: Tourism and Hospitality*. Nathan, Queensland: Centre for skill formation, research and development.

Beven, F. and Duggan, L. (1995) A conceptualisation of generic skills and context-dependent knowledge and a methodology for examining practice, in J. Stevenson (ed.) *Learning in the Workplace: Tourism and Hospitality*. Centre for Skill Research and Development, Griffith University, Australia.

Biggs, J. (1996) Enhancing teaching through constructive alignment. *Higher Education*, 32: 347–64.

Biggs, C., Brighton, R., Minnitt, P., Pow, R. and Wicksteed, W. (1994) *Thematic Evaluation of EHEI*. Research Series No. 30. Sheffield: Employment Department.

Billet, S. (1994) Situated learning – a workplace experience. *Australian Journal of Adult and Community Education*, 34: 112–30.

Billet, S. (1996) Knowledge, learning and work. Paper presented at ANTARAC Conference, Melbourne, April.

Blagg, N., Ballinger, M. and Lewis, R. (1993) *Development of Transferable Skills in Learners*. London: Employment Department and N. Blagg Associates.

Boekaerts, M. (1996) Self-regulated learning at the junction of cognition and motivation. *European Psychologist*, 1: 1–20.

Bridges, D. (1993) Transferable skills: a philosophical perspective. *Studies in Higher Education*, 18(1): 43–51.

Bromme, R. and Tillema, H. (1995) Fusing experience and theory: the structure of professional knowledge. *Learning and Instruction*, 5: 261–7.

Brown, A. (1994) *Review of the Characteristics of Effective Learning Programmes for the Development of Occupational Competence*. Guildford: Department of Education Studies, University of Surrey.

Brown, J.S., Collins, A. and Duguid, P. (1989) Situated cognition and the culture of learning. *Educational Researcher*, 18: 32–42.

CBI (1989) *Towards a Skills Revolution*. London: CBI.

Cheetham, G. and Chivers, G. (1996) Towards a holistic model of professional competence. *Journal of European Industrial Training*, 20(5): 20–30.

Clark, C. and Peterson, P. (1986) Teachers thought processes, in M.C. Wittrock (ed.) *Handbook of Research on Teaching*. New York: Macmillan.

Claxton, G. (1996) Integrating learning theory and the learning teacher, in G. Claxton, T. Atkinson, M. Osborn and M. Wallace (eds) *Liberating the Learner*. London: Routledge.

Coffield, F. (1997) A tale of three little pigs: building the learning society with straw, in F. Coffield (ed.) *A National Strategy for Lifelong Learning*. Newcastle upon Tyne: University of Newcastle.

Coffield, F. (1999) Breaking the consensus: lifelong learning as social control. Inaugural lecture, University of Newcastle.

Collins, A., Brown, J.S. and Newman, S.E. (1989) Cognitive apprenticeship: teaching the crafts of reading, writing and mathematics, in L.B. Reswick (ed.) *Knowing,*

*Learning & Instruction: Essays in honour of Robert Glaser.* Hillsdale, NJ: Lawrence Erlbaum Associates.

Committee of Vice-Chancellors and Principals (CVCP), Confederation of British Industry (CBI) and Council for Industry and Higher Education (CIHE) (1996) *Helping Students Towards Success at Work: A Declaration of Intent.* London: Council for Industry and Higher Education.

Committee of Vice-Chancellors and Principles (CVCP), Confederation of British Industry (CBI) and Council for Industry and Higher Education (CIHE) (1998) *Helping Students Towards Success at Work: An Intent Being Fulfilled.* London: Council for Industry and Higher Education.

Dall'Alba, C. (1990) Foreshadowing conceptions of teaching. *Research and Development in Higher Education*, 13: 293–7.

Dearing Report (1997) *Higher Education in the Learning Society.* London: HMSO.

Department of Employment (1993) *Development of Transferable Skills in Learners.* Sheffield: Employment Department Methods Strategy Unit, Report 18.

Dewey, J. (1946) *Problems of Men.* New York: Philosophical Library.

De Woot, P. (1996) Managing change at university. *CRE-Action*, 109: 19–28.

Drexler, A.B., Sibbett, D. and Forrester, R.H. (1988). The team performance model, in W. Reddy and K. Jamison (eds) *Team Building: Blueprints for productivity and satisfaction.* Alexandria, VA: NTL Institute for Applied Behavioural Science, and San Diego, CA: University Associates.

Druckman, D. and Bjork, R.A. (1994) *Learning, Remembering, Believing: Enhancing Haman Performance.* Washington, DC: National Academy of Sciences.

Drummond, I., Nixon, I. and Wiltshier, J. (1997) *Transferable Skills in Higher Education: the Problems of Implementing Good Practice.* Draft project paper. Universities of Hull and Newcastle.

Dunne, E. (1995) *Personal transferable skills.* Final Report. Exeter: University of Exeter.

Dunne, E. (1997) *The development of competences in STEP (Shell Technology and Enterprise Programme).* Evaluation Report. Exeter: University of Exeter.

Dunne, E., Bennett, N. and Austin, L. (1991) The impact of training on the quality of social interaction in cooperative groups. Paper presented at the conference of the European Association for Research on Learning and Instruction. Turku: University of Finland.

Edwards, K. (1994) The changing demands on graduates. *CVCP News*, 2(5): 2–8.

Enterprise in Higher Education (1989) *Key Features of the Enterprise in Higher Education Proposals 1988–1989.* London: Enterprise in Higher Education Training Department Group.

Entwistle, N. (1984) *The Experience of Learning.* Edinburgh: Scottish Academic Press.

Eraut, M. (1996) The new discourse of vocational education and training: a framework for clarifying assumptions, challenging the rhetoric and planning useful, theoretically informed research. ECER 96, Conference at Seville, September.

Eraut, M. (1997) Perspectives on defining 'The Learning Society'. *Journal of Educational Policy*, 12(6): 511–58.

Eraut, M., Alderton, J., Cole, G. and Senker, P. (1998) *Development of Knowledge and Skills in Employment*, Research Report, No. 5. Brighton: University of Sussex, Institute of Education.

Evans, K. and Heinz, W. (1995) Flexibility, learning and risk: work, training and early careers in England and Germany. *Education and Training*, 37(5): 3–11.

Fenstermacher, G.D. (1996) The knower and the known: the nature of knowledge in research on teaching. *Review of Research in Education*, 20: 3–56.

Finn, B. (1991) *Young Peoples' Participation in Post-compulsory Education and Training.* Melbourne: Australian Education Council Review Committee.

Fletcher, S. (1991) *NVQs, Standards and Competence.* London: Kogan Page.

Fox, D. (1983) Personal theories of teaching. *Studies in Higher Education,* 8(2): 151–63.

Fullan, M. (1991) *The New Meaning of Educational Change.* London: Cassell.

Fullan, M. and Hargreaves, A. (1992) *Teacher Development and Change.* London: Falmer Press.

Further Education Unit (FEU) (1979) *A Basis for Choice.* London: FEU.

Gibbons, M., Limoges, C., Nowotny, H., Schwartzman, S., Scott, P. and Trow, M. (1994) *The New Productions of Knowledge: The Dynamics of Science and Research in Contemporary Societies.* London: Sage.

Gibbs, G. (1995) *Assessing Student Centred Courses.* Oxford: Centre for Staff Development.

Gow, L. and Kember, D. (1993) Conceptions of teaching and their relationships to student learning. *British Journal of Educational Psychology,* 63: 20–33.

Graham, C. and McKenzie, A. (1995). Delivering the promise: the transition from higher education to work. *Education and Training,* 37(1): 4–11.

Great Britain Department of Education and Science (1987) *Higher Education: Meeting the Challenge.* London: HMSO.

Great Britain Department of Education and Science (1991) *Higher Education: A New Framework.* London: HMSO.

Green, A. (1994) A psychological approach to identifying transferable skills and transfer skills, in D. Bridges (ed.) *Transferable Skills in Higher Education.* Norwich: University of East Anglia.

Green, D. (1994) What is quality in higher education? Concepts, policy and practice, in D. Green (ed.) *What is Quality in Higher Education.* Buckingham: Open University Press/SRHE.

Green, S. (1990) Analysis of transferable personal skills requested by employers in graduate recruitment advertisements in June 1989. Internal report, University of Sheffield.

Greenan, K., Humphreys, P. and McIlveen, H. (1997) Developing transferable personal skills: part of the graduate toolkit. *Education and Training,* 39(2): 71–8.

Greeno, J.G., Smith, D.R. and Moore, J.L. (1993) Transfer of situated learning, in D. Detterman and R. Sternberg (eds) *Transfer On Trial: Intelligence, Cognition and Instruction.* Norwood, NJ: Ablex.

Griffin, A. (1997) Knowledge under attack: consumption, diversity and the need for values, in R. Barnett and A. Griffin (eds) *The End of Knowledge in Higher Education.* London: Cassell.

Gubbay, J. (1994) A critique of conventional justification for transferable skills, in D. Bridges (ed.) *Transferable Skills in Higher Education.* Norwich: University of East Anglia/ERTEC.

Handy, C.B. (1985) *Understanding Organisations,* 3rd edn. Harmondsworth: Penguin.

Hannan, A., English, S. and Silver, H. (1999) Why innovate? Some preliminary findings from a research project on innovations in teaching and learning in higher education. *Studies in Higher Education,* 24(3): 279–89.

Harvey, L. and Knight, P. (1996) *Transforming Higher Education.* Buckingham: Open University Press/SRHE.

Harvey, L., Burrows, A. and Green, D. (1992) *Criteria of Quality.* Birmingham: QHE.

Harvey, L., Geall, V. and Moon, S. (1998) *Work Experience: Expanding Opportunities for Undergraduates.* Birmingham: The University of Central England, Centre for Research into Quality.

Harvey, L., Moon, S. and Geall, V. (1997) *Graduates' Work: Organisational Change and Students' Attributes.* Birmingham: The University of Central England, Centre for Research into Quality.

Hattie, J., Biggs, J. and Purdie, N. (1996) Effects of learning skills interventions on student learning: a meta-analysis. *Review of Educational Research,* 66(2): 99–136.

Hattie, J., Marsh, H. and Neill, J. (1997) Adventure education and outdoor bound: out-of-class experiences that make a lasting difference. *Review of Educational Research,* 67(1): 43–87.

Healy, T. (1996) Lifelong learning for all: international experience and comparisons, in F. Coffield (ed.) *A National Strategy for Lifelong Learning.* Newcastle upon Tyne: University of Newcastle upon Tyne.

HEQC (1994) *Choosing to Change: Extending Access, Choice and Mobility in Higher Education: The Report of the HEQC CAT Development Project* (Robertson Report). London: HEQC.

HEQC (1996) *Guidelines on Quality Assurance in Higher Education.* London: HEQC.

HEQC (1997) *Assessment in Higher Education and the Role of Graduateness.* London: HEQC.

Holman, D. (1995) The experience of skill development in first year undergraduates: a comparison of three courses. *Assessment and Evaluation in Higher Education,* 20(3): 261–72.

Holmes, L. (1994) Competence, qualifications and transferability: beyond the limits of functional analysis, in D. Bridges (ed.) *Transferable Skills in Higher Education.* Norwich: University of East Anglia.

Hord, S., Rutherford, W., Hurling-Austin, L. and Hall, G. (1987) *Taking Charge of Change.* Austin, TX: University of Texas at Austin.

Hounsell, D. (1984) Students' conceptions of essay writing. Unpublished doctoral thesis, University of Lancaster.

Hyland, T. (1998) *Competence, Education and NVQs.* London: Cassell.

Industry in Education (1995) *Towards Employability: Addressing the Gap Between Young People's Qualities and Employers' Recruitment Needs.* London: Industry in Education.

Jackson, P.W. (1986) *The Practice of Teaching.* New York: Teachers' College Press.

Jacques, D. (1991) *Learning in Groups,* 2nd edn. London: Kogan Page.

Jessup, G. (1991) *Outcomes: NVQs and the Emerging Model of Education and Training.* London: Falmer Press.

Jessup, G. (1997) Establishing a learning society. Paper presented at ESRC Learning Society Conference, Bristol, January.

Johnson, D. (1991) Stress among graduates working in the SME sector. *Journal of Managerial Psychology,* 6(5): 17–21.

Jones, S. (1996) *Developing a Learning Culture: Empowering People to Deliver Quality, Innovation and Long-term Success.* London: McGraw-Hill.

Keep, E. (1997) There is no such thing as society. Some problems with an individual approach to creating a learning society. Paper presented at ESRC Learning Society Conference, Bristol, January.

Kemp, I. and Foster, K. (1995) From ivory towers to factory floors. *Education and Training,* 37(2): 26–32.

Kolb, D.A. (1984) *Experiential Learning: Experience as the Source of Learning and Development.* Englewood Cliffs, NJ: Prentice Hall.

Laurillard, D. (1993) *Rethinking University Teaching: A Framework for the Effective Use of Educational Technology*. London: Routledge.

Lave, J. and Wenger, E. (1991) *Situated Learning: Legitimate Peripheral Participation*. Cambridge: Cambridge University Press.

Lawson, T. (1992) Core skills 16–19, in T. Whiteside, A. Sulton and T. Everton (eds) *16–19: Changes in Education and Training*. London: David Fulton.

Layton, D. (1991) Science education and praxis. *Studies in Science Education*, 19: 43–79.

Maclure, S. (1987) The political context of higher education, in T. Becher (ed.) *British Higher Education*. London: Allen & Unwin.

Maclure, S. (1991) *Missing Links: The Challenge to Further Education*. London: Policy Studies Institute.

Marshall, R. and Tucker, M. (1992) *Thinking for a Living: Education and the Wealth of Nations*. New York: Basic Books.

Martin, E. (1997) The effectiveness of different models of work-based university education. Melbourne: Curriculum and Academic Development Unit, Royal Melbourne Institute of Technology.

Marton, F. and Säljö, R. (1976) On qualitative differences in learning: I – outcome and process. *British Journal of Educational Psychology*, 46: 4–11.

Marton, F., Dall'Alba, G. and Beaty, E. (1993) Conceptions of learning. *International Journal of Education Research*, 13: 175–83.

Marton, F., Hounsell, D. and Entwistle, N. (eds) (1997) *The Experience of Learning*, 2nd edn. Edinburgh: Scottish Academic Press.

Mayer, E. (1992) *Employment related key competences for post compulsory education and training: A discussion paper*. Melbourne: The Mayer Committee, Australian Education Council.

Mulder, M. (1998) Comparing quality profiles of training organisations: a multi-level approach. Paper delivered at ECER, Ljubljana, Slovenia, September.

Murphy, R. (1999) Current projects in the Centre for Developing and Evaluating Lifelong Learning. Internal report, University of Nottingham.

Newman, J.H. (1853) *The Idea of a University*. Oxford: Oxford University Press.

Ng, J., Lloyd, P., Kober, R. and Robinson, P. (1997) Building generic skills: a first year perspective. Paper presented at the 5th Annual improving student learning symposium, Glasgow, September.

Nicholson, N. and Arnold, J. (1989) Graduate entry and adjustment to corporate life. *Personnel Review*, 18(3): 23–35.

Ohlsson, S. (1994) Declarative and procedural knowledge, in T. Husen and T. Postlethwaite (eds) *The International Encyclopaedia of Education*, 2nd edn. Oxford: Elsevier/Pergamon.

Otala, L. (1993) Trends in lifelong learning in Europe. Paper presented at a TEXT Conference on the theme of Accreditation of In-company Training. Dublin, April.

Otter, S. (1992) *Learning Outcomes in Higher Education*. Leicester: Unit for the Development of Adult Continuing Education.

Perkins, D. (1995) *Outsmarting IQ*. New York: Free Press.

Perkins, D. and Salomon, G. (1994) Transfer of learning, in T. Husen and T. Postlethwaite (eds) *The International Encyclopaedia of Education*, 2nd edn. Oxford: Elsevier/Pergamon.

Pintrich, P.R., Marx, R.W. and Boyle, R.A. (1993) Beyond cold conceptual change: the role of motivational beliefs and classroom contextual factors in the process of conceptual change. *Review of Educational Research*, 63: 167–200.

Prince, S. and Dunne, E. (1988) Group development: the integration of skills into law. *The Law Teacher*, 32(1): 64–78.

Prosser, M., Trigwell, K. and Taylor, P. (1994) A phenomenographic study of academics' conceptions of science learning and teaching. *Learning and Instruction*, 4: 217–31.

QHE (1993) Update 6. *The Newsletter of the Quality in Higher Education Project.* Birmingham: University of Central England.

QHE (1994) Update 7. *The Newsletter of the Quality in Higher Education Project.* Birmingham: University of Central England.

Ramsden, P. (1987) Improving teaching and learning in higher education: the case for a relational perspective. *Studies in Higher Education*, 12(3): 275–86.

Ramsden, P. (1991) A performance indicator of teaching quality in education: the course experience questionnaire. *Studies in Higher Education*, 16(2): 129–50.

Ramsden, P. (1992) *Learning to Teach in Higher Education.* London: Routledge.

Ratcliffe, J.L. *et al.* (1995) *Realizing the Potential: Improving Post-Secondary Teaching, Learning and Assessment.* Pennsylvania: National Center on Post-Secondary Teaching, Learning and Assessment.

Redman, T., Snape, E. and McElwee, G. (1993) Appraising employee performance: a vital organisational activity? *Education and Training*, 35(2): 3–9.

Resnick, L. (1987) *Education and Learning to Think.* Washington, DC: National Academy Press.

Resnick, L. and Collins, A. (1994) *Cognition and Learning*, in T. Husen and T. Postlethwaite (eds) *The International Encyclopaedia of Education*, 2nd edn. Oxford: Elsevier/Pergamon.

Richardson, V., Anders, P., Tidwell, D. and Lloyd, C. (1991) The relationship between teachers' beliefs and practices in reading comprehension instruction. *American Educational Research Journal*, 28: 559–86.

Robbins, Lord (1963) *Higher Education* (Report of the Committee under the Chairmanship of Lord Robbins), Cm 2154. London: HMSO.

Royal Institute of British Architects (RIBA) (1992) *Strategic Study of the Profession.* London: Royal Institute of British Architects.

Ryan, G., Toohey, S. and Hughes, C. (1996) The purpose, value and structure of the practicum in higher education: a literature review. *Higher Education*, 31: 355–7.

Ryle, G. (1949) *The Concept of Mind.* Harmondsworth: Penguin.

Säljö, R. (1979) Learning about learning. *Higher Education*, 8(4): 443–51.

Salomon, G. and Perkins, D. (1989) Rocky roads to transfer: re-thinking mechanisms of a neglected phenomenon. *Educational Psychologist*, 24(2): 113–42.

Samuelowicz, K. and Bain, J.D. (1992) Conceptions of teaching held by academic teachers. *Higher Education*, 24: 93–111.

Schein, E. (1964) How to break in the college graduate. *Harvard Business Review*, 42 (Nov/Dec): 68–76.

Schoenfield, A.H (1985) *Mathematical Problem Solving.* New York: Academic Press.

Schön, D (1987) *Educating the Reflective Practitioner.* San Francisco: Jossey-Bass.

Schwab, J. (1964) The structure of the disciplines: meanings and significances, in G. Ford and L. Purgo (eds) *The Structure of Knowledge and the Curriculum.* Chicago: Rand McNally.

Scott, P. (1997) The crisis of knowledge and the massification of higher education, in R. Barnett and A. Griffin (eds) *The End of Knowledge in Higher Education.* London: Cassell.

Seagraves, L., Kemp, I.J. and Osborne, M.J. (1996) Are academic outcomes of higher

# Author Index

education provision relevant to and deliverable in the workplace setting? *Higher Education*, 32: 157–76.

Secretary's Commission on Achieving Necessary Skills (SCANS) (1991) *What Work Requires of Schools*. Washington, DC: US Department of Labor.

Silver, H. and Brennan, J. (1988) *A Liberal Vocationalism*. London: Methuen.

Slee, P. (1989) A consensus framework for higher education, in C. Ball and H. Eggins (eds) *Higher Education in the 1990s: New Dimensions*. Milton Keynes: Open University Press/SRHE.

Smith, D., Wolstencroft, T. and Southern, J. (1989) Personal transferable skills and the job demands on graduates. *Journal of European Industrial Training*, 13(8): 25–31.

Spurling, A. (1993) Employing science and engineering graduates: the first few years. *Education and Training*, 35: 9–14.

Stalker, K. (1996) *The antinomies of choice in community care*. Bristol: Learning Society seminar.

Stasz, C., Ramsey, K., Eden, R., Melamid, E. and Kaganoff, T. (1996) *Workplace Skills in Practice: Case Studies of Technical Work*. RAND, Santa Monica, CA: National Center for Research in Vocational Education, University of California at Berkeley.

Stephenson, J. and Weil, S. (eds) (1992) *Quality in Learning*. London: Kogan Page.

Svensson, L. (1977) On qualitative differences in learning III – study skill and learning. *British Journal of Education Psychology*, 47: 233–43.

Tate, A. and Thompson, J.E. (1994) The application of enterprise skills in the workplace, in S. Haselgrove (ed.) *The Student Experience*. Buckingham: Open University Press/SRHE.

Training Agency (1988) Development of assessable standards for national certification: Guidance note 3 – the definition of competence and performance criteria. Sheffield: Training Agency.

Training Agency (1989) Development of assessable standards for national certification: Guidance note 2 – deriving standards by reference to functions. Sheffield: Training Agency.

Tribe, J. (1996) Core skills: a critical examination. *Educational Review*, 48: 13–27.

Trigwell, K. and Prosser, M. (1996) Congruence between intention and strategy in university science teachers' approaches to teaching. *Higher Education*, 29: 443–58.

Tuson, M. (1994) *Outdoor Training for Employee Effectiveness* (Developing skills series). London: Institute of Personnel Management.

University Grants Committee (1984) *A Strategy for Higher Education into the 1990s: The University Grants Committee's Advice*. London: HMSO.

Vygotsky, L.S. (1962) *Thought and Language*. Cambridge, MA: MIT Press.

Wagner, L. (1996) Lifelong learning and the relationship between higher and further education, in F. Coffield (ed.) *Higher Education and Lifelong Learning*. Newcastle upon Tyne: University of Newcastle upon Tyne.

Wickens, P. (1987) *The Road to Nissan: Flexibility, Quality, Teamwork*. Basingstoke: Macmillan.

Winter, R. (1994) Work based learning and quality assurance in higher education, assessment and evaluation. *Higher Education*, 19: 247–57.

Wolf, A., Fotheringhame, J. and Grey, A. (1990) *Learning in Context: Patterns of Skills Transfer and Training Implications*. Training Agency: Sheffield.

Woollard, A. (1995) Core skills and the idea of the graduate. *Higher Education Quarterly*, 49: 316–25.

Zemsky, R. (1997) Turning point. *Policy Perspectives*, 7: 2.

# Subject Index

# The Society for Research into Higher Education

The Society for Research into Higher Education (SRHE) exists to stimulate and coordinate research into all aspects of higher education. It aims to improve the quality of higher education through the encouragement of debate and publication on issues of policy, on the organization and management of higher education institutions, and on the curriculum, teaching and learning methods.

The Society is entirely independent and receives no subsidies, although individual events often receive sponsorship from business or industry. The society is financed through corporate and individual subscriptions and has members from many parts of the world.

Under the imprint *SRHE & Open University Press*, the Society is a specialist publisher of research, having over 80 titles in print. In addition to *SRHE News*, the Society's newsletter, the Society publishes three journals: *Studies in Higher Education* (three issues a year), *Higher Education Quarterly* and *Research into Higher Education Abstracts* (three issues a year).

The Society runs frequent conferences, consultations, seminars and other events. The annual conference in December is organized at and with a higher education institution. There are a growing number of networks which focus on particular areas of interest, including:

Access
Assessment
Consultants
Curriculum Development
Eastern European
Educational Development Research
FE/HE
Funding
Graduate Employment

Learning Environment
Legal Education
Managing Innovation
New Technology for Learning
Postgraduate Issues
Quantitative Studies
Student Development
Vocational Qualifications

## Benefits to members

### Individual

- The opportunity to participate in the Society's networks
- Reduced rates for the annual conferences

- Free copies of *Research into Higher Education Abstracts*
- Reduced rates for *Studies in Higher Education*
- Reduced rates for *Higher Education Quarterly*
- Free copy of *Register of Members' Research Interests* – includes valuable reference material on research being pursued by the Society's members
- Free copy of occasional in-house publications, e.g. *The Thirtieth Anniversary Seminars Presented by the Vice-Presidents*
- Free copies of *SRHE News* which informs members of the Society's activities and provides a calendar of events, with additional material provided in regular mailings
- A 35 per cent discount on all SRHE/Open University Press books
- Access to HESA statistics for student members
- The opportunity for you to apply for the annual research grants
- Inclusion of your research in the *Register of Members' Research Interests*

## *Corporate*

- Reduced rates for the annual conferences
- The opportunity for members of the Institution to attend SRHE's network events at reduced rates
- Free copies of *Research into Higher Education Abstracts*
- Free copies of *Studies in Higher Education*
- Free copies of *Register of Members' Research Interests* – includes valuable reference material on research being pursued by the Society's members
- Free copy of occasional in-house publications
- Free copies of *SRHE News*
- A 35 per cent discount on all SRHE/Open University Press books
- Access to HESA statistics for research for students of the Institution
- The opportunity for members of the Institution to submit applications for the Society's research grants
- The opportunity to work with the Society and co-host conferences
- The opportunity to include in the *Register of Members' Research Interests* your Institution's research into aspects of higher education

*Membership details*: SRHE, 3 Devonshire Street, London
W1N 2BA, UK. Tel: 0171 637 2766. Fax: 0171 637 2781.
email: srhe@mailbox.ulcc.ac.uk
world wide web: http://www.srhe.ac.uk./srhe/
*Catalogue*: SRHE & Open University Press, Celtic Court,
22 Ballmoor, Buckingham MK18 1XW. Tel: 01280 823388.
Fax: 01280 823233. email: enquiries@openup.co.uk

**THE LIMITS OF COMPETENCE**
KNOWLEDGE, HIGHER EDUCATION AND SOCIETY

**Ronald Barnett**

Competence is a term which is making its entrance in the university. How might it be understood at this level? *The Limits of Competence* takes an uncompromising line, providing a sustained critique of the notion of competence as wholly inadequate for higher education.

Currently, we are seeing the displacement of one limited version of competence by another even more limited interpretation. In the older definition – one of academic competence – notions of disciplines, objectivity and truth have been central. In the new version, competence is given an operational twist and is marked out by know-how, competence and skills. In this operationalism, the key question is not 'What do students understand?' but 'What can students do?'

The book develops an alternative view, suggesting that, for our universities, a third and heretical conception of human being is worth considering. Our curricula might, instead, offer an education for life.

***Contents***
*Introduction – Part 1: Knowledge, higher education and society: The learning society? – A certain way of knowing? – We are all clerks now – Part 2: The new vocabulary: 'Skills' and 'vocationalism' – 'Competence' and 'outcomes' – 'Capability' and 'enterprise' – Part 3: The lost vocabulary: Understanding – Critique – Interdisciplinarity – Wisdom – Part 4: Competence reconsidered: two rival versions of competence – Beyond competence – Retrospect and coda – Bibliography – Index.*

224pp      0 335 19341 2 (Paperback)      0 335 19070 7 (Hardback)

## DEVELOPING LEARNING IN PROFESSIONAL EDUCATION
PARTNERSHIPS FOR PRACTICE

**Imogen Taylor**

> This is a timely addition to the literature which provides a challenge to professional education: both through its portrayal of a highly innovative problem-based course (and the rich detail of students' experience) which shows how a learner-centred approach can impact on participants; and through its location in much wider contexts of teaching and learning in professional education and in debates about the relationship between university education and professional practice.
>
> Professor David Boud

> At a time when attention is being directed increasingly towards lifelong learning, this book offers an extremely timely guide to the development of the learning skills needed to make this a reality. Readable, relevant and full of practical illustraions, it will be widely read by educators in a variety of professional contexts.
>
> Professor Patricia Broadfoot

This book is about professional education and developing the required knowledge and skills to equip students for the pressing needs of professional practice. Student professionals from health care, teaching, business, law and social work must learn how to practise both independently (to respond to a constantly changing environment) and collaboratively (to respond to the complexity of today's society); also they must learn how to work in partnership with the consumers of professional services. Imogen Taylor explores how professional education can develop approaches to teaching and learning which both help learners to be reflexive, self-monitoring practitioners and meet the requirements of professional accrediting bodies. She draws upon her own research into students experiencing professional education based on small group, problem-based learning; on an extensive range of relevant international theory and research; and on her own long experience in professional education, training and practice.

This is an important resource for all those educators and trainers in professional education seeking to improve their own practice.

### Contents
*Part 1: Setting the scene – Introduction – Uneasy partnerships? – Part 2: Beginning learning – Transitions: traditional expectations and non-traditional courses – The personal is professional: using pre-course experience for learning – Part 3: The learning infrastructure – Learning for teamwork – Facilitating independent and interdependent learning – Restraint, resourcefulness and problem-based learning – Assessment: the crux of the matter – Part 4: Promising outcomes – Non-traditional learners: valuing diversity – Perspectives on education as preparation for practice – Partnerships with users of professional services – Appendix: enquiry and action learning (the structure) – References – Index.*

224pp    0 335 19497 4 (Paperback)    0 335 19498 2 (Hardback)